8-50

analysis and decision
in regional policy

London Papers in Regional Science

p Pion Limited, 207 Brondesbury Park, London NW2 5JN

edited by I G Cullen · London papers in regional science 9 · a pion publication

analysis and decision in regional policy

p Pion Limited, 207 Brondesbury Park, London NW2 5JN

Copyright © 1979 by Pion Limited

ISBN 0 85086 070 9

Printed in Great Britain by Page Bros (Norwich) Limited

Contributors

C P A Bartels   *Faculty of Economics, University of Groningen, P O Box 800, Groningen, The Netherlands*

M Batty   *Department of Geography, University of Reading, Whiteknights, Reading RG6 2AB*

Mary Benwell   *Centre for Transport Studies, Cranfield Institute of Technology, Cranfield, Bedford MK43 0AL*

D Bonnar   *22 Kylepark Crescent, Uddingston, Glasgow*

D Gleave   *Centre for Environmental Studies, 62 Chandos Place, London WC2N 4HH*

B C Goodwin   *School of Biological Sciences, University of Sussex, Falmer, Brighton, Sussex BN1 9QG*

Phyllis Kaniss   *World University, 1430 Massachusetts Avenue, Cambridge, Massachusetts 02138*

J Krieger   *Center for European Studies, Harvard University, 5 Bryant Street, Cambridge, Massachusetts 02138*

P Nijkamp   *Faculty of Economics, Free University, Amsterdam*

G Olsson   *Nordiska Institutet för Samhällsplanering, Skeppsholmen, 111 49 Stockholm*

S Openshaw   *Department of Town and Country Planning, University of Newcastle upon Tyne, Newcastle upon Tyne NE1 7RU*

D Palmer   *Centre for Environmental Studies, 62 Chandos Place, London WC2N 4HH*

A D Pearman   *School of Economic Studies, University of Leeds, Leeds LS2 9JT*

P Rietveld   *Faculty of Economics, Free University, Amsterdam*

H ter Welle   *Economic Technological Institute for Friesland, Leeuwarden*

P Whitehead   *Department of Town and Country Planning, University of Newcastle upon Tyne, Newcastle upon Tyne NE1 7RU*

Contents

Introduction

I CULLEN
University College London

Social scientists have recently become fascinated with Kuhn's (1972) notion of the paradigm-shift. As with all discussions in the philosophy of science, his is metatheoretical. In other words, his interest is at least one step removed from the actual practice of scientific research. Similarly, the interest of social scientists in the methods and unstated assumptions which underpin the variety of their research activities involves stepping back from the performance of social investigation for a self-conscious fit of abstraction.

This is generally a commendable punctuation, for scientists have a reputation for pursuing their own particular specialist interests without every questioning the validity of the chase. Some social scientists, however, seem so concerned with their basic methodological infrastructure that the actual business of research begins to take on a mythical status—each successive philosophical treatise making the feasibility of substantive and useful research more and more remote. Those who are naive enough actually to attempt the test of an hypothesis or the writing of history are sure to fall into one, or more probably several, of the pitfalls so deftly delineated by the increasing army of philosophers in the social sciences.

The truth of the matter is that it is generally easier to comment critically upon research activity than it is to improve it through practice. Kuhn would not be surprised at the trend to which I have alluded since it was his considered opinion that the social sciences were currently at the 'preparadigm' stage. In other words, their methodological insecurity was such that research style and practice was dictated as much by fashion as by a firmly accepted and relatively durable body of knowledge and operational principles. In such a situation of volatile uncertainty and inherent insecurity it is hardly surprising to find academics investing as much energy in methodological introversion as in substantive research initiatives. Couple this immaturity of the social sciences with a prolonged downturn in the business and trade cycles, and a headlong rush for the ivory towers becomes almost an inevitability.

How does regional science fit into this gloomy picture? The apparently unavoidable answer seems to be even more gloomy than in the case of, say, economics or sociology. For regional science has never really existed as a coherent academic discipline at all. Its roots are in geography and economics, but more recently it has borrowed liberally from psychology, sociology, history, and political science. Moreover, a specific interest in research method as a subject for study in its own right is commonly shared amongst regional scientists. Thus it occupies an ill-defined outpost of the social scientific empire in which a predisposition towards abstract methodological musing is likely to be at its highest.

Fortunately the outpost is so ill-defined that most of those who write 'regional science' would not call themselves regional scientists. They practice, research, and advance their careers in disciplines less prone to volatile shifts in direction. They therefore bring much of the tradition of their respective disciplines to the study of regional science, including well-tried methods and research styles. We do not, therefore, have to search for neat intellectual coherence amongst the literature of regional science. It is not even reasonable to marvel at the accelerating rate at which apparently revolutionary 'paradigm-shifts' tumble one over another in the publication race. If regional science is a constantly shifting amalgam of prescientific disciplines, it can have no paradigm to shift. And the corollary of this point is that almost anything in regional science viewed by anyone other than the author and his mates is liable to look, at the very least, a bit like a paradigm threat.

Why then should intelligent planners, geographers, economists, and others gather together once a year in London simply to present specialist research to an audience composed largely of people who do not even speak the same language? To be absolutely fair to those who do not attend, it must be admitted that it is an annual event of limited appeal. The majority of planners, geographers, and economists in the United Kingdom never have and never will attend. Yet the conference manages to retain the atmosphere of a pioneering venture rather than that of a moribund club meeting. Each year papers from new and expanding research areas are attracted. Each year specialist workshops subject their efforts to a spectrum of opinion which ranges from the perspective of academic biology at one end to that of practical planning at the other. Each year mainstream sociology and economics vie with one another for a foothold in the shifting superstructure of what the vast majority of sociologists and economists would agree was a nonsubject.

The paradox cannot be explained purely and cynically in terms of the average researchers' allegedly unquenchable thirst for a platform. If that were the only motive, it would lead to the further proliferation of intradisciplinary meetings and conferences rather than the continued health of regional science. It seems much more likely that there exists a genuine and unsatisfied desire for contact across disciplinary boundaries amongst significant minorities in most social and some natural science research areas. The often trite and cynical dismissal of multidisciplinary research was and is, to my mind, premature. It is difficult enough to devise sensible research strategies within individual social science disciplines. It is almost impossible to maintain meaningful contact between members of different disciplines in the pursuance of a given research goal.

Yet what most of the attendants at a regional science meeting share in common is a belief in the importance of trying. Advance in this difficult area is bound to be slow. Simply inventing university departments with pretentiously multidisciplinary labels is a technique which is bound to fail.

A two-day annual meeting, such as the regional science conference, is nothing if not modest when viewed as advance in this area. Yet at least it is an advance that has continued unabated. Now the annual conference is complemented by an expanding programme of parallel and ongoing workshop activities. None of these workshops, no matter how specialist its focus, is organized along strict disciplinary lines.

Whether or not the annual conference—the broadest level of contact—will continue to succeed as it has in the past will depend upon the efforts of individuals. However, the chances are good for any ongoing forum for cross-disciplinary contact in social science. The reason is simply that in the long term nothing else will succeed. The differences between natural and social sciences have been discussed at length, and no doubt will be much discussed in the future. However, one of the differences, which these days tends to be acknowledged by all but a rapidly declining school of behaviourist psychology, concerns one specific method of investigation —the controlled experiment. When the subject matter of study does not possess the faculty of self-awareness, the concept of a controlled experiment is at least a meaningful one, even if its execution is not (yet) a practical possibility. When the subject matter is human, the concept is not even meaningful since the only element in the laboratory possessing any ultimate independence—the mind of the individual—is incapable of control in an experimental situation.

For this reason, any programme of research devised to provide explanations within an arbitrarily demarcated disciplinary framework will ultimately prove sterile. The only method which might yield closed-system explanations as it does for some natural scientists—the controlled experiment—is denied to the social scientist. All other methods involve an intrinsically open-system approach to explanation, and so eventually they must involve crossing disciplinary boundaries. If the economist follows individuals into the marketplace, the trail will ultimately and inevitably lead out to their families, classes, and emotions. And to ignore the way in which any arbitrarily closed system is inevitably transcended in the minds of those who people it is tantamount to admitting defeat in social science.

None of the papers which follow in this volume admit defeat in that each is intended as a contribution to a debate which is multidisciplinary in nature. Moreover the spectrum of suggested methodological approaches is so great that almost every paper represents some sort of new angle on the question of where we should search for a social science paradigm. Only two, however, are strictly in the philosophy of science tradition in that they are metatheoretical, addressing not particular research topics but the principles which underlie the activity of research itself. Olsson takes the techniques and presuppositions of social science and subjects them to a critique which proceeds by means of a dialectic that owes as much to Wittgenstein and Tantric Hinduism (via Jung) as it does to the early writings of Marx. Goodwin, in contrast, compares the problem of

describing the generation of pattern and order in human society with that
faced by the biologist in examining pattern formation in the natural world.
The approach he recommends, which derives ultimately from Chomsky,
has the effect, in one sense at least, of adding biology to the social sciences.

As we might expect, neither of these papers renders the task of the
regional scientist any easier. Each suggests a new dimension to the many
problems faced in devising an operational strategy for any given
methodological or substantive inquiry. The remaining papers in this
collection reflect the uncertainty which this increasing awareness of
difficulty feeds. There was a period in the sixties when many geographers
and economists believed that social relations and practices could be
adequately described by using the languages of mathematics. This period
has now passed, and along with it has gone the apparent coherence of
regional science. It was always an illusion since even wholehearted
acceptance of a common language is never enough to lend coherence to an
extensive body of research unless that research is designed simply to
explore the language itself. The substantive purpose of regional science
was never just that. Its focus was always upon the real world of the space
economy. And the focus of the remaining papers in this volume is
likewise upon this same incomprehensible phenomenon.

As in those heady mathematical days, the papers also fall into two
distinct groups—those that treat individuals as consumers of spatial
patterns and those that treat them as producers. Studies of shopping,
residential choice, and recreation behaviour are favourite topics in the
first group, and there are several examples in this tradition in the second
section of this collection. Studies of entrepreneurial behaviour—optimal
plant location, office decentralization, and the like—used to form the core
of the second group. However, the increasingly mixed nature of the space
economy, and our expanding consciousness of the importance of social
costs and externalities, has meant that regional scientists have started to
invest more and more of their efforts in investigating the spatial impact of
the state. This shift is well represented in this volume, with a total of
five papers addressing either directly or indirectly the way the state has,
does, or should reach decisions which have differential spatial effects.
These constitute the third and final section of the book.

The studies of space consumption in this volume adopt a variety of
approaches, but the connections with regional science of the past are
apparent in several of the papers. What is now left, as represented here,
of the 'mathematical revolution' in spatial analysis is a body of research
which addresses very specific problems in a much more modest way. The
second section of this volume contains examples of this work, clearly in
the tradition of sixties regional science, but carefully avoiding the arrogant
extremism of some of the writings of its forefathers. At the level of
model design, Batty's argument for simple analytical devices, and his
exposition of an efficient Lowry model calibration procedure which

capitalizes upon and highlights the simple structure of the equation system, is an example of the cautious modesty characterizing methodological development in this area. The papers of Bonnar on residential choice analysis and Bartels and ter Welle on migration analysis reflect a reawakened and increasing interest in straightforward and carefully worked statistical description of aggregate spatial behaviour. Gone is the zest for predictive devices at all costs. Analysts have come to realize that our level of understanding and theoretical development is woefully inadequate, and that in such circumstances a little well-informed inductive fishing with well-tried statistical measures is likely to be as productive as anything more grand. Penultimately in this section, the paper of Palmer and Gleave tacitly acknowledges what many are now saying more explicitly but to less effect. The treatment of spatial behaviour has, in the past, often been wholly divorced from that of the aspatial processes upon which it is based. Palmer and Gleave, in examining the process of occupational mobility, quite apart from its spatial context, are providing information upon which spatial analysis may more sensibly be built. Again the emphasis is on description, and again the use of a stochastic approach acknowledges our uncertainty in these research fields. The final contribution, that of Benwell, attacks the issue of space consumption from a totally different angle. In other words, rather than examining aggregate regularities in behaviour via inferential statistics, she adopts the Fishbein theory of cognitive structure and addresses the individual's spatial choices and related attitudes directly.

Ultimately, of course, the attitudes and choices of individuals also lie behind the decisions of the various branches of the state which mould the environment in which others have to choose their jobs and residences. However, as with the study of space consumption, investigation of the production of spatial patterns—in this case by the state—typically engenders a large variety of methodological responses from regional scientists. The papers in this collection are no exception. Those by Pearman and by Nijkamp and Rietfeld attempt to inform public sector decisionmaking in circumstances where the decisionmaker is faced with multiple criteria. Naturally, both opt for a form of mathematical programming solution, though this still leaves them considerable scope for developing alternative operational strategies. The third paper in this section, that of Openshaw and Whitehead, also addresses the normative issue of improving the quality of public sector decisions through the application of programming techniques, but in this case takes as a case study not the general problem of multicriteria decisions but the specific question of the generation and evaluation of structure plans within a British statutory framework. The principles developed are, however, generalisable to other strategic planning contexts. Kaniss, in her contribution, is more concerned with the descriptive analysis of complex decision situations. However, in adopting a systems theoretic framework, her descriptive analysis lends itself to normative application, as is demonstrated through the use of the example of spatial decisions related to the implementation of a nuclear power programme. Finally in this section, Krieger's contribution to the debate on decision analysis becomes normative in a quite different way. In each of the preceding papers the techniques are treated as intrinsically neutral and thus conceptually independent of their specific applications. Krieger implicitly questions this assumption by adopting a structuralist historical methodology with which to explore the British programme of coal mine closures in the sixties. His whole approach to the problem of interpretation is thus intrinsically normative, without being explicitly dedicated to the task of improving particular decisions.

It is not the role of an introduction to legislate. Each of the main sections of this volume ends with a paper which implicitly questions at least some of the assumptions of those that have gone before. Is an essentially positivist statistical approach to spatial behaviour valid, or must regional scientists always consider directly the attitudes and emotions of those whose choices collectively constitute the aggregate patterns which the statistician may describe? Is an approach to regional policies which assumes the neutrality of either analysis or decision-informing techniques acceptable, or must we drop completely the distinction between analysis and evaluation? We must look to the philosophers amongst us for answers to these questions, and, though simple categorical answers will not be found, the papers of both Olsson and Goodwin may well stimulate us to rethink our own personal answers.

What is perhaps more important is that both Olsson and Goodwin will almost certainly be dismayed to find themselves labelled as philosophers in this volume. They are first and foremost practicing researchers who take epistemological issues seriously, rather than philosophers whose experience of and interest in the world of practical research is purely secondary. Moreover, the poignant way in which assumptions are tacitly questioned in the papers of Benwell and Krieger reflects the importance of the theory in practice principle: there is nothing so effective for the establishment of a research model or paradigm than its successful implementation in practice. I am with Kuhn to the extent that I believe social sciences in general and regional science in particular to be very firmly rooted in the preparadigm phase of their development. Moreover, if this means open-mindedness with respect to fundamentals and a tolerance of alternative positions, this strikes me as a very healthy phase in which to be working. The risks, already mentioned, are that in face of enormous complexities, we either give up doing social science in favour of talking about doing it, or disappear into minutely defined specialisms and refuse to talk to anyone who disagrees with us. Perish the thought!

Reference
Kuhn T S, 1972 *The Structure of Scientific Revolutions* (University of Chicago Press, Chicago, Ill.)

The New Social Science: Toward a Mandala of Thought-and-Action

G OLSSON
Nordiska Institutet för Samhällsplanering, Stockholm

In this piece I shall approach the new social science through three mandalas of thought-and-action. The emerging figures will symbolize that coming together of society and individual which lies at the heart of all social sciences and all political theories. Perhaps it is even in life itself.

The word 'mandala' is Sanskrit for 'circle' and 'center'. It signifies a diagram which symbolizes the thoughts-and-actions of Tantric Hinduism and Buddhism much as the cross symbolizes the content of Christianity. It is basically a representation of the universe in which an encircled consecrated area is treated as a receptacle for the gods and a collection point of universal forces. When man (the microcosm) enters the mandala (the macrocosm), the movement is from the one to the many and the universe is that of the garbha-dhātu or the 'womb world'. Alternatively, the movement can be from the many to the one, represented by the vajra-dhātu or the 'thunderbolt world'. The totality, though, is in the interaction of the two worlds just as thunder in the Noah and Thor myths signifies creation out of destruction and destruction out of creation.

The mandala was introduced into Western psychology by C G Jung, who viewed the spontaneous production of a mandala as a step in the individuation process and thereby as an attempt to integrate hitherto unconscious material. Indeed it was Jung's analysis of mandalas that led him to the conclusion that "the unconscious tends to regard spirit and matter not merely as equivalent but as actually identical, and this in flagrant contrast to the intellectual one-sidedness, which would sometimes like to spiritualize matter and at other times materialize spirit" (Jung, 1972, page 29). It is in this same tradition that I now will use the mandala as a symbolic representation of the archetypical of the collective unconscious. I choose this imagery as my framework, because I believe with Jung that "the severe pattern imposed by a circular image of this kind compensates the disorder and confusion of the psychic state—namely, through the construction of a central point to which everything is related, or by a concentric arrangement of the disordered multiplicity and of contradictory and irreconcilable elements" (Jung, 1959, page 388). The mandala, then, is a cosmogonic symbol which represents creation and dissolution, form and emptiness, social wholes and individual parts.

I begin my search in two famous quotes. One comes from the optimistic Marx, who said that "the philosophers have only interpreted the world, the point is to change it" (Marx and Engels, 1970, page 123).

The other is from the pessimistic Wittgenstein, who argued that "the limits of my language mean the limits of my world" (Wittgenstein, 1922, paragraph 5.6).

Marx and Wittgenstein go straight to the center point of my first mandala. It represents *human thought-and-action*, which is what I propose to deal with, not from the outside of what others say it is, but from the inside of what I believe it is myself. More particularly, I want to deal with thought-and-action as the evolving outcome of a set of opposing forces, all of which interact to keep it suspended at the weightless center of a multidimensional universe (figure 1). Thunderbolts of contradictory forces are bombarding the womb world. In the process, the universe is left at a creative peace with itself—which is merely a way of saying that any creative act consists of a breaking of categories, of a merger or transcendence of opposites. The present task is therefore to isolate some of these contradictory forces and then indicate how what is now split comes together again.

Pushing away from home, I no longer situate human thought-and-action within the paradigm of *scientific* or instrumental reasoning, which we in the universities preach and obey. Neither do I place it within the paradigm of *practical* reasoning and teleological understanding, which is advocated in the various books of wisdom. Rather than being in the realm of the either–or, it instead seems to contain crucial elements from both of the intellectual traditions. Put differently, thought-and-action is in the double heritage of Plato and Aristotle, Descartes and Vico, Russell and Hegel, the Multiplication Table and the Book of Job.

To see this view, it should be recalled that the purpose of scientific, causal reasoning is to answer the question "how". How is something or how does something work? The purpose of practical, teleological reasoning, on the other hand, is to address the question "why".

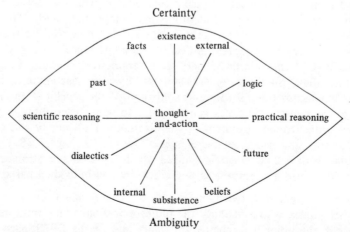

Figure 1.

Why is something done or why does something work?   Using the terminology of phenomenology, it is in the backward tradition of science to ask questions about the 'because motives' of an action.   The practical reasoner, on the other hand, is more interested in the forward looking 'in-order-to motives'.   As a consequence, the pivotal part of scientific reasoning lies in the importance of lawlike statements, of theories and models, while that of practical reasoning is in the concept of intention. A crucial distinction is that whereas good models are time- and place-invariant, intentions are not; laws are in order, intentions in adventure. Put differently, law statements promise that nothing changes, while intentions capture the hope that change is in the making.   This, rather than the work of some Leibnizian monads, is the reason why beginnings never reach their ends, for even though the thoughtful scientist ties us down to the iron laws of the past, the practicing actor lets us free to see the visions of the future.   It follows that, despite all attempts to write difference and differential equations, the scientific enterprise is not concerned with change at all, but rather with the preservation of the status quo.   In a realistic sense, its tradition is more with delimiting the constraints of our actions than with imagining how boundaries can be traversed; it may in fact be more interested in keeping us confined than in letting us free.   In this context it is perhaps more telling than we care to admit that even most Marxists are deeply committed to a positivistic social science; like the Skinnerian behaviorists they tend to treat action mechanistically, and within the framework of historicism.   Despite *The Grundrisse* (Marx, 1973) both schools practice thought and think of action as if the world stemmed from a set origin and went to a final end.

But creative action is not merely a mechanistic repetition of the *past* just as it is not merely an implementation of the *future*.   It is instead from the ever changing now of the present that the Janus-faced actor can watch himself watch.   With one eye, this mythical creature sees the past, its regularities and its scientific lawlike statements.   With that empirical eye we see what still is, namely that which is either true or false.   With the other eye, the actor scans the future thereby seeing what is not yet, namely that which is inherently neither true nor false.   It is in this fashion that we are able to catch—in the same glance—a glimpse of both the determinacy of the past and the indeterminacy of the future.   But the categories by which we make sense of the past and the future are ontological antinomies of each other.   Hence they cannot be reduced one into the other or the other into the one.

It now appears that thought-and-action is not a conjunction of the categories of the past and the future but that it is in its own category of the present of the now.   And since this present is in constant flux, it is like Frege's identity sign (Dummett, 1973), it cannot be defined, only experienced.   But, if thought-and-action is not a conjunction of its constitutive elements as implied by logical atomism, what is it then?

Perhaps it is merely a timeworn way of resolving the paradoxes of past and future, of scientific laws and practical intentions, of assertive promises and hypothetical hopes.

A question, and a suggestion which leads to the next pair of opposites. For, when we speak the scientific languages of the past, then we are speaking about so called *facts*. But, when we talk the practical languages of the future, then we are talking about so called *beliefs*. And it is here that even if my argument thus far may have been difficult to grasp, now it should become increasingly clear. For also here it appears that thought-and-action is situated right in the middle of the two opposites, that it is not merely a mechanistic rerendering of the facts about the past, just as it is not merely a redreaming of the beliefs about the future. Its very essence is instead to make false what now is true, and thereby to change what now is false so that it becomes true. But this temporary new truth will inevitably contain traces of past truths, just as it will anticipate our hopes, beliefs and intentions for the future.

Once here, I may even begin to suspect that perhaps human thought-and-action is inherently self-reflective. Perhaps its motive power comes neither from the Wittgensteinian constraints of facts nor from the Marxian visions of beliefs but rather from the relentless pursuit of itself. Perhaps it speaks to and of itself, just as language does. Perhaps it is in this process of getting locked into itself that thought-language-and-action begins to transcend itself, to move from the confinement of Being into the flight of Becoming.

If this is so, then thought-and-action again appears as a special way of resolving paradoxes, not by fitting opposites together, but by going outside the paradoxical system itself. As people have done for ages, we resolve the paradoxes of thought through action and the predicaments of action through thought. Put differently, we solve our problems by defining them away, by fitting questions to answers rather than answers to questions; the crucial parts of a proof is not in the formulas but in the words in between, for it is there that we change the rules of the game. And so it is, that in the process of grappling with logical paradoxes and moral predicaments, every thought-and-action becomes a spontaneous activity oriented to the future and grounded in the past. And yet, through its very spontaneity, it is locked into itself. Locked into itself, just as all other experiences are locked into themselves.

The next pair of opposites to be entered into the mandala captures the ontological distinction between the classes of *existence* and *subsistence*. The former term refers to objects which lead such an existential life that they can be pointed to, which in turn means that they can be counted. Put differently, existing objects can be reduced to physical things like tables, chairs, bodies, houses, etc. What exists is consequently what can be counted and what can be counted is what we say exists. It is objects of this category that make up our so-called facts. By definition, they are

located in the past and they are the only objects which are admitted into
the strict vocabulary of the positivistic paradigm. They are the stuff
which operationalization tries to bring out. In arguing for their virtue,
we do little but pay homage to the suppressive forces of *Homo significance.*

In contrast, the class of subsistence contains objects of thought. The
difference is that whereas existing objects are in things, objects of thought
are in relations. This means of course that statements of scientific law
themselves belong to the subsistence category, even though what the
statements refer to belongs to the measurable world of quantity and
existence; in an expression like $y = f(x)$, y and x are normally tied to
existing objects, while $=$ and f get their meaning from the realm of
subsistence.

The dialectical relations of existence and subsistence are tremendously
important not the least because we tend to ignore them. Thus it is part
of the prevailing metaphysics of presence that we see only that which
exists. To subsisting phenomena we are often blind, excusing ourselves by
saying that what we cannot see or count, we cannot experience either.
Asking "How much do you love me?" and receiving the answer "1132" is
therefore neither a question nor an answer, but a category mistake
reflective of our own myths of communication, fetishism, and reification.
And so it is that the dialectics of existence and subsistence lies at the
heart also of Marx's work, for what he said about things and relations was
this: "The relations connecting the labor of one individual with that of
the rest appear, not as direct social relations between individuals at work,
but as what they really are, material relations between persons and social
relations between things" (Marx, 1967, page 73). Likewise, Marcel Mauss
in his anthropological studies of the gift, noted that "the bond created by
things is in fact a bond between persons" (Mauss, 1967, page 10). In the
process, existence is transformed into subsistence just as subsistence is
transformed into existence. Where Marx and Mauss come together is
consequently in the profound importance they assign to the activity of
ontological transformations. Likewise, it is worth noting that Sartre's
(1966) *Being and Nothingness* carries the subtitle *An Essay on
Phenomenological Ontology.* Indeed the most important feature of
existentialism is its pluralistic ontology and its conceptualization that
consciousness is both referential and self-transcending.

Already this brief characterization of existence and subsistence suggests
that human thought-and-action is not something merely physical and
observable. Neither, of course, is it something merely mental and
nonobservable. It is instead in both existence and subsistence, one turning
into the other and the other turning into the one. Indeed, I have
increasingly come to think of both thought and action as ontological
transformations prompted by our attempts to grapple with paradoxes and
predicaments. These ontological transformations are not mechanistic,
however, but grounded in the actor's own sense of self-consciousness.

In turn, this self-consciousness is itself reflected both in what comes out of our hands, mouths, and pens and in what goes on in our heads. Hence, it is reflective not merely of things out there or thoughts in here, but of itself. As Hegel saw so clearly, it is exactly this dialectical urge toward self-conscious reevaluation that both liberates and dominates us. Nietzsche said much the same, even thought he termed the driving force 'the will to power'. The studies of authoritarianism and the family by Vico (1948) and much later by Horkheimer (1972) and other critical theorists may in this context be more revealing than we care to admit.

So, once again, I have prepared the suggestion that human thought-and-action is a way of resolving paradoxes, not by having opposites kill each other off, but by allowing them to go beyond stultifying definitions into the level of experience. Like Heidegger and Derrida who speak about words put under the eraser, I conceive of process as a traceable crossing out of what was. And it is in crossing out the boundaries of existence and subsistence that the pronoun 'I' ceases to be a noun and becomes a verb. As a consequence, the individual ceases to be a thing and becomes a person, for things are in static nouns, and persons in the rhythm of dynamic verbs. As Husserl (1970) wrote in his *Logical Investigations*: "When we read this word 'I' without knowing who wrote it, it is perhaps not meaningless, but is at least estranged from its normal meaning". Truth and verification become convertible, for as Vico knew, the only truth is the one we make (Brown, 1974): factum verum; QED; RSVP.

In performing this Hegelian switch of levels, the categories of *external* and *internal* emerge as a new pair of opposites. The two terms come from the distinction Wittgenstein made between the descriptional and the ontological parts of his picture theory. The former states that there is a similarity in external structure between a sentence and what it describes, whereas the latter claims that there is a similarity in internal structure between the particular language and the particular reality within which we operate. Just as the idea of external similarity is inherent in the correspondence theory of truth, so the idea of internal similarity is in the coherence theory of truth. The former focuses on the parts, the latter on the whole.

The logical form of an object is its internal quality. The existence of an atomic state of affairs, on the other hand, is its external quality. The two chairs in my study, for instance, correspond to the external structure of a statement about my chairs, whereas the number two itself—and thereby actually the entire statement—is part of the internal structure of number theory. It was in grappling with similar issues of external truth and internal coherence that Wittgenstein came to conclude that "if I am to know an object, though I need not know its external properties, I must know all its internal properties" (Wittgenstein, 1922, paragraph 2.01231). The talk about the two chairs then quickly becomes talk about numbering, thereby about categorization and thereby at the end talk about itself.

What I happen to say is therefore reflective not only of the external structure of the things I am talking *about*, but also of the internal structure of the language I am talking *in*. And—for the first time in this performance —I thereby recognize explicitly how we are all confined within the same prison house of language.

So, once again, I am led to the recognition that the two opposites can be reconciled only by curling back, by moving away from definition and into experience, from binary codes to mythical serpents biting their own tails. And when this occurs, then the curling back is not on an object other than itself, but on the very self of itself. So, perhaps it cannot really be said more clearly than Wittgenstein (1922) said it himself: "The structures of propositions stand in internal relations to one another" (paragraph 5.2) and "a property is internal if it is unthinkable that its object should not possess it" (paragraph 4.123). On this rendering, internal relations come close to the structure of Jung's collective unconscious. In Freud's words, it is the unconscious wishes which always remain active, for the prominent feature of unconscious processes is that they are indestructible. Kafka seems to have been thinking in the same direction, when he advocated that "the authenticity of life rests upon the correspondence between the inner soul and the nature of the external world" (Heller, 1974, page 46). And for those who grew up in the Sartrean existentialism as I did, the word authenticity may be just another word for the essence of thought-and-action, for what distinguishes authenticity is that it is genuine truth, not merely a truth of bad faith.

The concern with ontological transformations now leads to the pair of opposites called *conventional logic* and *dialectics*. Much has been said about these alternative modes of categorization and I will not repeat it here (Olsson, 1975). It is nevertheless difficult to say anything more profound on the matter than that the main difference is in the different definitions of identity. Thus, whereas conventional logic deals with the categories of the black and white of the either–or, dialectics captures the fleeting rainbow-like categories of the both-this-and-that. And yet, the two principles of identity are really defined in terms of each other such that identity and difference merge as in the crossings of Spencer Brown's (1972) *Laws of Form* and in Derrida's (1976) concept of *Differance*. The same idea is in Frege's feeling that identity cannot be defined except perhaps in the experiential game which only two can play (Keys, 1974; Dummett, 1973). And what, now, is experience? Is it not human thought-and-action caught within the nothingness of itself?

It is when the first mandala approaches this stage of completion that thought-and-action gradually begins to make sense to me. It starts to tickle my intuition not when I reduce it into one category or another, but when I let myself experience it as the prime breaker and the prime healer of categories. Clever cleavage! For to cleave means both to cut apart and to put together. So, there it flashes through again! Thought-and-action suspended within an intricate and multidimensional field of intellectual, cultural, and experiential forces. All of which send fertilizing thunderbolts into the mandala's womb world.

And once here the joint forces of *certainty* and *ambiguity* somehow keep each other in a peaceful state of rest all locked into itself. A state of rest, furthermore, which is destroyed and made invisible by those who work within only one of the two camps. What once seemed fixed and steady consequently begins to dissolve, not into its own opposite, but into the experiential nothingness of itself. And so it is that we may well learn more about the new social science by reading Roland Barthes (1957; 1977) on *Mythologies*, or Jacques Derrida (1974) on *Grammatology*, than by perusing yet another Daniel Bell or Club of Rome report. And why not return for a while to the originals themselves? To sensitive searchers like Vico, Hegel, Marx, Kierkegaard, Nietzsche, Joyce, Duchamp and Wittgenstein. A strange collection, perhaps. But creativity is itself a strange phenomenon, constantly transcending itself into other identities and other ontologies.

The radical lesson I draw from the present mandala is that if we as social scientists want to get on with our job of understanding how individual and society come together, then perhaps the necessary first step is to stop being ashamed of ourselves. Perhaps we must begin to dance as naked as we are. Perhaps we must recognize that even though the emperors try to hide behind the masks of external things, they are really naked; what they show off is not their beautiful clothes but only their internal relations. If Hans Christian Andersen is not sufficient proof, then simply recall Wittgenstein's words that "though I need not know the external properties of an object, I *must* know all its internal properties" (Wittgenstein, 1922, paragraph 2.01231). In bringing the two together, I have been struck by the profundity of E M Cioran's words that, "What I know at sixty, I knew as well at twenty. Forty years of a long, superfluous labor of verification" (Cioran, 1976, page 7)—if I only could learn a little faster! Then, perhaps, there would be more time for roses and poetry, for climbing trees and breaking categories.

Thus far I have sketched a mandala of thought-and-action. From this symbol I shall now work into the even deeper level of the nothingness or *void of action*, which is in the focus of yet another mandala (figure 2).

I enter the mandala where Nietzsche might have entered it. This is the point at which we recognize that *God is dead* and that *man is God*. Rather than blame the outside God when something goes right or wrong, we consequently have no choice but to blame ourselves and our social relations. Rather than perpetuate the belief that God created man in his image, we must accept that man creates God in his image. Indeed the name 'God' is nothing but a symbol for the totality of our own internal relations, of that collective unconscious which is too close to understand.

Marcel Duchamp was on the right track in his grappling with the large
glass. We ignore his thoughts-and-actions at our children's peril.

I use the terminology about man's creation of God as a pointed method
of saying that the *a priori*—the outside hook on which we hang our
thoughts-and-actions—is gone. Gone once and forever. Not only with
Nietzsche and the other modern artists, but with Bohr and Heisenberg as
well. As a consequence, it is not from the facts of the a priori that our
thoughts-and-actions get their power. It is instead from the activity of
self-criticism. I would even suggest that what is involved is a struggle
between the Kantian theory of the a priori and the Hegelian practice of
self-criticism.

But this recognition leaves the Manipulator within us uncomfortable,
for what it implies is that action cannot be cut into. From the Quinean
logical point of view, this is the most awkward of all situations, for it
means that the resolution of *paradoxes* is not sufficient. The idea of
action imprisoned within itself leads instead into the forbidden lands of
logical reasoning, where the ruling principal is that of *self-reference*.
What is there is nothing but the futility of deductive reasoning, for within
the prison walls of reference dwell not master axioms and slave theorems,
but only self-sufficient axioms. It is at this stage, when, once again, I hit
my head against the ceiling of language, that I must repeat Frege's insight
that identity cannot be defined, only experienced. And when we
experience, then we act! So even though action involves paradox, it at
the same time involves self-reference. In Jung's terminology, there is no
linear evolution only circumambulation of the self.

But self-reference is not limited to the one, the single, the individual
self. It is equally much about the cultural and unconscious ego, which is
another term for the collectivity of our *social relations*. And just as
internal and external, subsistence and existence stand to each other, so
social relations stand to each other. Rather than treat human beings
merely as things, we must consequently learn to live with the persons we are.

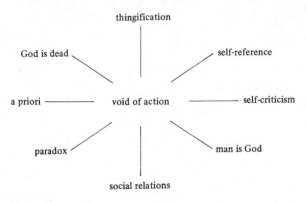

Figure 2.

And when we do, then the many and the one will no longer be separate
and opposed but be as united as they always were. Descartes and Russell
should have known better. But they did not. And perhaps they could
not. For Descartes (1911) in his *Meditations* was at the beginning of an
emerging myth, trying to break categories and thereby create new. And
Russell was at the end of the same religion, trying in the *Principia
Mathematica* (Whitehead and Russell, 1913) to codify it by firming
categories up. All of which raises the question of our current mythology.
What does it contain, that collective imagination which is so internal that
its presence and absence are equally unthinkable? In which institutions
is its power ingrained and who are those heirs of the kings and priests
who perpetuate it without knowing it? Is it in 1984 that our Godot
arrives?

In the two mandalas is not only the structure of human thought-and-
action, but also the direction of the new social science. The charge is to
redress the imbalances which Descartes and the Enlightenment introduced.
And this is the reason why even though all mandalas are supposed to
balance, my constructs do not. Instead they contain that mythical
meaning of direction which says that the Northeast represents *dawn*, the
Southeast *day*, the Southwest *dusk*, and the Northwest *night* (figure 3).
Joyce knew it well, for no one has relived the cultural heritage of our
collective imagination to the same extent; the day of *Ulysses* and the
night of *Finnegans Wake* are connected by a commodius vicus of
recirculation (Joyce, 1934; 1959; see also French, 1976; Seidel, 1976;
Norris, 1976). By remembering Vico on mythology and the new science,
Joyce ontologically transforms Marx's commodities into what they really
are, spiritiualized matter and materialized spirit. In the process he charts
the direction of the emerging social science.

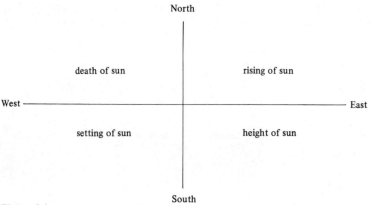

Figure 3.

Myth. Mythology. Perhaps that is not such a bad place to visit. Perhaps it is not such a bad place to be. For mythology is the power which language exercises over thought. The myth of science, grounded in its metaphysics of presence, is perhaps where we accumulate knowledge about facts. But the myth of creation, grounded in its metaphysics of the absence in the present, is perhaps where we find wisdom about relations. And yet I have already noted that the myths which now direct us are so close to our own eyes—are so internal to ourselves and our own ways of living—that we cannot see them. Their absence is indeed as unthinkable as their presence. As a consequence, we cannot see or hear the orders, for they are part of our collective unconscious, of those individuations, which Jung tried to uncover in his mandalas. Beliefs. Subsistence. Internal relations. Self-criticism. Self-reference. Man as God and God as man.

So, here we are again! Curling back. Locked into ourselves. Yet reaching for the outside hook, for that receding horizon which we know is not there.

It is appropriate that this piece has gone in a circle. Or—since I am myself part of the twentieth-century myth of criticism and progress— perhaps it has rather gone in a spiral. Returning to the starting point, albeit on another level. And that starting point was in the two quotes from Marx and Wittgenstein. One spurred us on by prompting that even though we must strive to understand the world, the point is nevertheless to change it. The other held us back by asserting that the limits of my language are the limits of my world.

In performing my mandalas, I have tried to live in the contradictions of the two mottos. I have done so in the surrealistic tradition, for it was Breton—the father of surrealism—who once manifestoed this: " 'Transform the world', Marx said; 'change life', Rimbaud said. These two watchwords are one for us" (Breton, 1972, page 241). One for us the surrealists.

What I have tried to do is to indicate how we might become self-conscious enough to change our own categories of thought-and-action by creating new out of old. To this nonachievable end of seeing what is different in identity I have pursued a set of paradoxes into the recognition of self-reference and the execution of thought-and-action. My argument has been that we must face up to the Nietzschean challenge that God is dead. But most of us refuse to accept the challenge. Instead we continue to turn one concept of god into another. One of these incarnations is clearly the progressive god of Scientific Reasoning. And that creature is just as demanding of sacrifices as all other gods. Indeed it may even look down at this act of reading and writing as nothing but a ritual of obedience.

But a token of obedience is not what this is. It is not, because I have not tried to step into or out of my subject matter. I have tried neither to break into nor escape from the prison house of language, from self-reference and internal relations. I have instead tried to hang right in there by embedding the mandalas of thought-and-action in the thought-and-action of the presentation itself. Perhaps I thereby have achieved a somewhat greater unity between the structure of the phenomena I have been thinking *about* and the structure of the language I have been performing *in*. My ambitious goal has therefore been the same as for James Joyce, Marcel Duchamp, and Samuel Beckett, namely to think-and-act in such a way that it is "not *about* something; *it is that something itself*" (Beckett and others, 1972, page 14). But, what will it look like, the piece of work which will do to the social sciences what James Joyce's *Ulysses* did to the novel and *Finnegans Wake* to James Joyce? And what new conventions of reading will it require? Not so easy! For in a spiraling reference to the quoted passage from Beckett, Joyce himself replied: "Bethicket me for a stump of beech if I have the poultriest notions what the farest he all means" (Joyce, 1959, page 112).

And that is all. Not for good of course. And perhaps not even for truth or fairness. But for the here and now. And until another here and now brings forth in this very piece the traces of what once was and no longer is. In the meantime, may thunderbolts strike the womb world of the social sciences!

References
Barthes R, 1957 *Mythologies* (Editions su Seuil, Paris)
Barthes R, 1977 *Fragments d'un Discours Amoreux* (Editions du Seuil, Paris)
Beckett S and others, 1972 *Our Exagmination Round His Factification for Incamination of Work in Progress* (Faber and Faber, London)
Breton A, 1972 *Manifestoes of Surrealism* (University of Michigan Press, Ann Arbor)
Brown N O, 1974 *Closing Time* (Vintage Books, New York)
Cioran E M, 1976 *The Trouble with Being Born* (Viking Press, New York)
Derrida J, 1973 *Speech and Phenomena* (Northwestern University Press, Evanston, Ill.)
Derrida J, 1974 *Glas* (Editions Galilee, Paris)
Derrida J, 1976 *Of Grammatology* (Johns Hopkins University Press, Baltimore, Md)
Descartes R, 1911 *The Philosophical Works of Descartes* translated by E S Haldane, G R T Ross (Cambridge University Press, London)
Dummett M, 1973 *Frege: Philosophy of Language* (Harper and Row, New York)
French M, 1976 *The Book as a World: James Joyce's Ulysses* (Harvard University Press, Cambridge, Mass)
Heller E, 1974 *Franz Kafka* (Viking Press, New York)
Horkheimer M, 1972 "Authority and the family" in *Critical Theory* (Seabury Press, New York)
Husserl E, 1970 *Logical Investigations* (Humanities Press, New York)
Joyce J, 1934 *Ulysses* (Modern Library, New York)
Joyce J, 1959 *Finnegans Wake* (Viking Press, New York)
Jung C G, 1959 *The Archetypes and the Collective Unconscious* (Princeton University Press, Princeton, NJ)
Jung C G, 1972 *Mandala Symbolism* (Princeton University Press, Princeton, NJ)
Keys J, 1974 *Only Two Can Play This Game* (Ballantine, New York)
Marx K, 1967 *Capital* (International Publishers, New York)

Marx K, 1973 *The Grundrisse* (Penguin Books, Harmondsworth, Middx)

Marx K, Engels F, 1970 *The German Ideology* (International Publishers, New York)

Mauss M, 1967 *The Gift* (Norton, New York)

Norris M, 1976 *The Decentered Universe of Finnegan's Wake: A Structuralist Analysis* (Johns Hopkins University Press, Baltimore, Md)

Olsson G, 1975 *Birds in Egg* (Department of Geography, University of Michigan, Ann Arbor)

Sartre J-P, 1966 *Being and Nothingness: An Essay on Phenomenological Ontology* (Washington Square Press, New York)

Seidel M, 1976 *Epic Geography: James Joyce's Ulysses* (Princeton University Press, Princeton, NJ)

Spencer Brown G, 1972 *Laws of Form* (Bantam Books, London)

Vico G, 1948 *The New Science* Eds T G Bergin, M H Fisch (Cornell University Press, Ithaca, NY)

Whitehead A N, Russell B, 1913 *Principia Mathematica* (Cambridge University Press, London)

Wittgenstein L, 1922 *Tractatus Logico-Philosophicus* (Routledge and Kegan Paul, London)

Generative and Cognitive Models of Biological Pattern Formation

B C GOODWIN
University of Sussex

1 Introduction

My intention in this essay is to describe the emergence of a new view of biological pattern formation which links this area of study very much more closely to human pattern-forming activities than has been the case in the past. During most of this century, biologists have tended to make the assumption that, somehow or other, detailed studies in genetics, biochemistry, and biophysics would eventually provide explanations of the processes which generate limbs in insects, feathers on birds, spiral patterns in the arrangement of leaves on plants, and spots on ladybird backs. This expresses a reductionist belief which is now foundering badly and is being replaced by a view of biological process which seeks to understand pattern formation in terms of rules or laws operating at levels above the molecular and the genetic (in the sense of products of the primary genetic material, DNA). Furthermore, these rules are biological, not physical, although they in no sense violate the laws of physics and chemistry. It is here that this new approach to morphogenesis differs quite sharply from the view of the most outstanding student of biological form in this century, D'Arcy Wentworth Thompson. His study *On Growth and Form*, published in 1917, sets forth the thesis that form can only be understood through mathematics, and that the forces which operate in the genesis of biological structure are essentially physical. That mathematics and form or order belong together few would dispute, but D'Arcy Thompson's view tends to eliminate the biological as a distinct and autonomous realm of nature; that is, his reduction of biological structure to the operation of mathematical and physical laws fails to recognize the biological origins of the constraints which generate this structure. It is biological process which 'discovers' rules, expressible in mathematical form, these rules giving rise to order and pattern. This process is both orderly and creative. Furthermore, I will argue that it may also be seen to be cognitive. Thus biological pattern formation assumes characteristics which link it closely with the processes which generate pattern and order in human society. And this is, I think, why I have been asked to contribute a paper to this conference.

2 The failure of the reductionist view of pattern formation

One of the most distinctive characteristics of biological process is its capacity to generate a great diversity of structures, forms, and patterns. The evolutionary process generates species of distinct morphology and behaviour, the developmental process generates individuals of characteristic form from eggs or buds, the process of living manifests itself in behaviour patterns such as hunting, feeding, talking, building, etc, typical of the individual and its species. In recent decades the dramatic success of such subjects as genetics, molecular biology, and neurophysiology in analyzing biological activities in terms of units such as genes, molecules, and neurons encouraged the view that a satisfactory understanding of biological pattern formation would arise from the detailed study of the properties and behaviour of these units, order and complexity arising from their interaction. However, this analytical programme of reduction and resynthesis works satisfactorily only when there is an extremely simple and direct relationship between the units of a system and its higher-level behaviour, as in a gas where the momentum or the kinetic energy of the molecules can be averaged to determine the pressure or the temperature of the gas. Of course there must always be *some* relationship between the properties of the units which are construed to exist within a complex system and the behaviour of the system itself. The problem is that if the units themselves are complex, in the sense that macromolecules or neurons are complex, then there are very many different ways in which higher-order behaviour can arise. The reductionist programme is then faced with the virtually impossible task of exploring all the possible interaction patterns available and selecting those which conform to observed higher-order behaviour. Given that one never has complete knowledge of the properties of the units, so that the relevant behaviour may well be missing from the computation to begin with, it is clear that this is not a very reliable strategy to pursue in the study of biological pattern formation at the macroscopic level, that of the species, the individual, and its behaviour.

An alternative approach, which has always been an important strategy in science, is to observe the behaviour of the system of interest, to record its regularities, and then to see if it is possible to devise simple formal rules which act as axioms from which the behaviour of the system may be deduced. These formal rules then represent the constraints within the system which underly its orderly behaviour. It may happen that they can never be reduced to certain categories of behaviour of simpler units, as the inverse-square rule or law of gravitational attraction could never be reduced to the mechanical properties of matter, much to the discomfiture of seventeenth-century mechanical philosophers. However, scientists rapidly accommodate themselves to such eventualities, and quite soon even go so far as to believe that a phenomenon such as gravitational attraction is in some sense explained by the law, whereas it is only described. What is explained by the use of the rule is, for example, planetary motion. Newtonian mechanics is a generative theory in the sense that it allows one to generate patterns (trajectories which are conic sections; for example, ellipses, parabolae, or hyperbolae) by means of formal operations constrained by rules (the calculus, with the inverse-square law of attraction), and these patterns fit the observed behaviour of the planets.

This is not a reductionist theory, since the phenomena can be explained in terms of units and rules which correspond to the level of the observables themselves. Reductionism entered science largely with the adoption of the atomic hypothesis in the seventeenth century. It is an extremely useful hypothesis for the explanation of certain microscopic phenomena in physics, chemistry, and biology; but not, I submit, for the understanding of biological pattern formation.

3 Cognitive biology

In facing the problem of pattern and order in biological process, I believe that biologists will be induced to adopt a very different view of organisms and their evolution from the reductionist and materialist one which has prevailed throughout this century. This will bring biology much closer to the ideas expressed by Whitehead (1929) in his philosophy of organism, and the idealist approach to the understanding of form which originated in the West with Pythagoras. Developmental biologists are now beginning to describe the appearance of characteristic structures such as limbs, somites, feathers, etc in terms of systems obeying formal rules whose molecular interpretation is left undescribed and is irrelevant for the explanation of the phenomena of interest (French et al 1976). These rules are not in the category of natural law, as the physicist tends to regard the law of gravitational attraction. They are rules which have been arrived at by the evolutionary process as a solution to the problem of reliably and repeatably generating particular types of form. And they are of course inherited, passed on from generation to generation.

What sort of system is this which employs rules to generate useful structures and behaviour patterns, and which can transmit the rules to its progeny? I have argued that such rules constitute knowledge, and that a system which uses knowledge is a cognitive system (Goodwin, 1976a, 1977). This comes from an extension of an argument presented by Chomsky (1972) in a linguistic context. In his analysis of linguistic competence, Chomsky presents evidence for an instinctive, unlearned capacity for generating correct sentence structure or syntax, a capacity which emerges in the course of the human developmental process. The rules or constraints which constitute linguistic competence define the processes which generate the correct surface structure of sentences from their deep structure, such as structure-dependent operations in sentence transformation. Possession of these rules, that is, possession of the structural (anatomical) and functional (physiological) constraints which are the embodiments of the rules, is equivalent to having the knowledge required for speaking correct sentences. This knowledge is not learned, but is innate, inherited as part of the human genotype. Chomsky's (1972) contention is that "knowledge of language results from the interplay of initially given structures of mind, maturational processes, and interaction with the environment". Innate structures are thus seen to constitute elements of knowledge. I have simply used this proposition in a more extended form to suggest that the basic attribute of living organisms is their possession of knowledge about aspects of the world, knowledge which renders them competent to survive and to reproduce in the environment to which they are adapted or which they know.

I have defined knowledge as a useful description of some aspect of the world, giving the possessor the competence to behave in a manner which contributes to its survival and reproduction (Goodwin, 1976a). The fact that we are dealing with descriptions means that there are codes or sets of codes which relate them to that which is described. The unravelling of such codes, which is the equivalent of learning to read an unknown language, together with the solution of the problem how the knowledge is transmitted reliably from generation to generation, has been a major preoccupation of contemporary biology. Coded knowledge is located largely in the DNA, which acts as a primary memory store for the organism, this knowledge being in the form of hypotheses which need to be translated into active form for testing. However, there is a great deal of 'tacit' knowledge in other structures. The elucidation of the translation and assembly process from the coded linear sequences in the DNA to active three-dimensional proteins which function as tests of genetic hypotheses by revealing their meaning, constitutes one of the triumphs of twentieth-century biology.

I used the term 'meaning' above in relation to the translation and testing of genetic hypotheses, and it needs some clarification in this context. In coded form as it occurs in the DNA, the information for a particular protein such as the enzyme β-galactosidase (required for the catabolism of the nutrient lactose in microorganisms) or a crystallin (a protein which forms the transparent lens of the eye) cannot be tested because it exerts no action upon the organism or its environment. Before it can be tested, the information in the DNA must be translated into a form in which it exerts a particular type of force and acts within a particular context. Thus the β-galactosidase converts lactose into glucose and galactose when it operates within the context of the bacterial cell (which defines particular conditions of pH, osmotic concentration, substrate level, etc); while a crystallin transmits light rays in a particular way within the context of the eye. These activities may be said to constitute tests of meaning of the coded hypotheses in the hereditary material, involving the interpretation of the information. This interpretation takes place within a particular context, which in part determines the pattern of forces which operate during the testing operation. We then arrive at a distinction between information and knowledge. The technical definition of information involves only selection (for example, specifying one out of a set of possibilities), but says nothing about meaning, which I take always to involve activity in real space-time. Thus knowledge differs from information in that it not only involves selection of alternative possibilities, but also includes instruction for action which, operating in a particular context, conveys meaning.

4 Generative processes

In the rather detailed discussion given above, it is clear that every aspect of the behaviour of what I have called a cognitive system is compatible with physical and chemical laws. However, such a system transcends the rules of physics and chemistry in that, besides obeying these, its behaviour is constrained by other rules which are the embodiment of particular types of knowledge of which it makes use. This allows such systems to operate in domains which, while available to systems obeying the laws of physics and chemistry, are relatively improbable; that is, cognitive systems can stabilize behaviour in physically and chemically improbable states by means of particular rules of action which they have embodied in parts of their own structure, such as catalysis of chemical reactions by enzymes so that relatively high rates of metabolic transformation can occur at low temperatures. By thus regulating their own activities through the imposition upon themselves of specific rules or constraints, biological systems have managed to discover and exploit an immense range of behavioural and morphological patterns. To give an architectural example: although rectangular stones occur in nature they are very rare; and structures in which they are piled on top of one another are much rarer still. However, the art of the stonemason and the builder consists in following some very simple rules about shaping stone and assembling it, and these rules then permit the construction of an immense variety of highly improbable structures, from Stonehenge to Chartres Cathedral.

The essence of order and pattern is adherence to laws or rules; and the characteristic of cognitive systems is that they operate in terms of rules which stabilize useful temporal and spatial patterns. The process whereby such rules and the variety of their applications is discovered is described as creative in a human context, and I would suggest that the evolutionary process shares this property. We do not yet know how to describe this creative potential of evolution, which generates organisms of greater and greater complexity constrained by the necessity that this be relevant, meaningful in its context; that is, that it be biologically successful. [But see Saunders and Ho (1976) for a very thoughtful and interesting paper on this subject.] Such generative processes appear to have the general property of proceeding from symmetry to asymmetry, which involves an increase in complexity; but then a new symmetry is generated which resolves the complexity into higher-order simplicity without, however, losing the lower-level complexity. Thus in the evolution of the human hand, the development of the opposable thumb involved the breaking of a structural and dynamic symmetry in the organization and behaviour of primate digits. The grasping action of the primate hand wherein all the digits act in unison, so well adapted to swinging in trees and grasping certain types of object, is transformed into a much more complex structure with great independence of action of the thumb. However, the human uses a series of coordinating activities for the hand which involve higher-order symmetries such as the coming together of the first finger and the thumb in the typical action of picking up a small object, or the opposed wrapping of thumb and fingers around a stick. These symmetries have a bilateral element rather than the simpler unilateral action of the primate, giving a unity of movement and action to the more complex structure.

Thus we arrive at the view that organisms are cognitive systems which engage in and are subject to generative processes, ones which involve the appearance of relevant novelty and are thus intrinsically creative. This links biology with the human sciences in the study of knowledge-using, knowledge-generating systems. I believe that the key to success in the enterprise of trying to learn the language of these systems, discovering the rules which generate their distinctive spatial and temporal patterns, is the structuralist insistence upon observing the phenomena and classifying their regularities without reducing the analysis to a lower level. Once the regularities are described and the rules have been formulated, then it is possible to discover consistencies which link the different levels of a cognitive system and provide the continuity which phenomenologically is always there from the beginning. This includes a continuity between biological process and mind of a type which joins Man to Nature in a manner which transcends the Darwinian synthesis by establishing a cognitive as well as an historical bond. Since a process capable of generating knowledge, such as evolution, manifests not only creativity but also intelligence, the capacity to learn (for example, to solve problems), we find that this union with Nature involves some of our highest attributes. The value of such a view is not simply that it may help us to understand both Nature and ourselves better; but the realization that we share a common enterprise may encourage a more cooperative attitude to the biosphere.

References
Chomsky N, 1972 *Problems of Knowledge and Freedom* (Fontana, London)
French V, Bryant P J, Bryant S V, 1976 "Pattern regulation in epimorphic fields" *Science* **193** 969-981
Goodwin B C, 1976a *Analytical Physiology of Cells and Developing Organisms* (Academic Press, London)
Goodwin B C, 1976b "On some relationships between embryogenesis and cognition" *Theoria to Theory* **10** 33-44
Goodwin B C, 1977 "Cognitive biology" in *International Workshop on the Cognitive Viewpoint* Eds M deMey, R Pinxten, M Poriau, F Vandamme (University of Ghent Press, Belgium) pp 396-400
Saunders P T, Ho M W, 1976 "On the increase in complexity in evolution" *Journal of Theoretical Biology* **63** 375-384
Thompson D, 1917 *On Growth and Form* (Cambridge University Press, London)
Whitehead A N, 1929 *Process and Reality* (Cambridge University Press, London) p 210

Efficient Calibration of an Urban Model with Dynamic Solution Properties

M BATTY
University of Reading

Introduction

In the development of urban models during the last two decades, questions of feasibility have always been to the fore. So many models have remained at the level of mere proposals because the problems of data and computer time which they imply cannot be resolved within the bounds imposed on model development. Although it is perhaps too sweeping to condemn all failures in operational model design as being due to lack of awareness or lack of understanding of these problems, many exciting proposals have remained as mere speculation because of these problems. For example, the San Francisco Housing Market Model (Brewer, 1973) was overly ambitious in this sense, and the National Bureau of Economic Research urban simulation models are so large and demanding of data and computer time, that they will never be fully researched numerically, let alone made operational on a widespread scale (Kain, 1975). Of course, these questions are changing rapidly with the continual development of new generations of computers. Nevertheless, the quest for greater efficiency leading to successful model design is no different than in any other area of applied science, and the benefits of greater efficiency are of wider import than mere reductions in computer use. Indeed, greater efficiency brings in its wake a greater understanding of model structure, and it is clear that greater consistency in model design and hence tighter theory is a result of the search for greater efficiency.

Although efficient algorithms are required for many of the models already proposed but operationally infeasible, the greatest progress in model design appears to have been made, not surprisingly, in relation to models which are already feasible. For example, the line of models originating with Lowry's (1964) Pittsburgh model has generated a good deal of work concerning questions of efficiency. Garin's (1966) initial reformulation, the debate over locational constraints procedures (Echenique, 1968; Batty, 1976; Banister, 1977; Williams, 1977), and the reformulations due to Baxter and Williams (1975) and Berechman (1976) are among several contributions seeking greater improvements in model structure and operationality. Furthermore, the existence of such work is not solely because of this style of model's popularity; it relates to the fact that such models are still difficult to calibrate and solve if formulated for systems of several hundred zones, and if augmented by consistent procedures for meeting constraints. In short, existing procedures for calibrating the model to meet its constraints and optimise its goodness of fit are efficient and feasible for modestly sized problems but are inappropriate for large ones. Therefore it is the purpose of this paper to introduce a reformulation of the model which enables much faster procedures to be developed, and the results which follow demonstrate that it is possible to calibrate such models in only one tenth of the time required at present.

The emphasis in this paper is on the results of such experiments, for the detailed reformulation is dealt with elsewhere (Batty, 1978). However, this paper will begin by stating the conventional model and analysing the dynamic or iterative properties of the procedures traditionally used in its solution. By exploiting these dynamic properties, which are referred to hereafter as pseudodynamic processes, a reformulation of the model can be made which enables much more efficient calibration and solution. Traditional methods of meeting constraints by biproportional factoring and of optimising the goodness of fit by unconstrained optimisation can be easily embedded into this reformulation, and most of this paper is based on experiments with these procedures applied to a simple problem based on data taken from the London Traffic Survey: LTS (LCC, 1964). The biproportional methods are explored first and then two methods for unconstrained optimisation—Gauss's algorithm and Newton's method—are presented. An integrated algorithm based on constraints and optimisation procedures is then assembled and tests are made on the trial LTS problem, and on a larger problem in Central and West Berkshire. In general, the results show dramatic improvements over existing practice and suggest a number of directions for future research.

Solution of static models with dynamic properties
Conventional urban models originating from Lowry's (1964) work seek to predict the location of population and its related employment, on the basis of a given pattern of employment that is not population orientated. Traditionally, this split of employment into two components has been based on the basic–nonbasic categorisation and, as such, can be rationalised through economic base theory. However, such an interpretation is not essential and it is of more relevance to assume that the division purely reflects exogenous and endogenous employments, however defined (Massey, 1973). In most applications, as in this one, the division has been based on exogenous employment comprising the primary and secondary industries, and endogenous employment comprising the tertiary sector. The model is best presented in terms of its *equilibrium conditions*, which characterise the locational patterns at a particular cross-section in time, and from these the *equilibrium relations* or reduced form can be derived. The first condition is stated as

$$p_j = \lambda \sum_i e_i t_{ij} ,$$ (1)

where p_j is population in zone j, e_i is employment in zone i, t_{ij} is the probability of working in i and living in j, and λ is a scalar—the inverse activity rate—which converts employment into population. The second condition is given as

$$e_k^s = \gamma \sum_j p_j s_{jk} \, , \tag{2}$$

where e_k^s is the endogenous or service employment in zone k, s_{jk} is the probability of living in j and requiring services in k, and γ is a scalar—the population-serving ratio—which scales population to service employment. The third condition is the identity

$$e_k \equiv e_k^s + e_k^b \, , \tag{3}$$

where e_k^b is exogenous or basic employment. Equation (3) simply closes the system. Note that without loss of generality it can be assumed that there are I employment and population zones which are equivalent; that is, $i, j, k = 1, 2, ..., I$.

The model implied by equations (1) to (3) is clearly linear, and its equilibrium relations or reduced form can be easily displayed by substituting for p_j in equation (2) from (1) and then substituting the result for e_k^s into equation (3). Thus

$$e_k = \gamma \lambda \sum_i e_i \sum_j t_{ij} s_{jk} + e_k^b \, . \tag{4}$$

Equation (4) is the basis of a system of linear equations which, if appropriately defined, is always solvable. It is possible to solve such systems for $\{e_i\}$, with known $\{e_k^b\}$, $\{t_{ij}\}$, $\{s_{jk}\}$, γ, and λ, either directly by standard matrix inversion (Garin, 1966; Harris, 1966; Batty, 1976), or indirectly by various iterative schemes. For example, iterative solution of equations (1) and (2) starting with $e_i = e_i^b$ generates the series of increments of population and employment equivalent to the Leontieff expansion of equation (4); this is the scheme characterising the Garin–Lowry model. In contrast, starting with $e_i = \bar{e}_i$, where the scroll denotes observed employment, was the scheme used by Lowry (1964), and in general this latter scheme will give different results if augmented by locational constraints. All these methods, however, can be seen as special cases of matrix iterative analysis (Varga, 1962), which seeks to develop efficient solutions to linear systems by directly operating on the equilibrium relations rather than on the equilibrium conditions.

A particular version of matrix iterative analysis suitable to the model under study is based on the so-called Jacobi split, which involves iterating equation (4) in the following fashion:

$$e_k(r+1) = \gamma \lambda \sum_i e_i(r) \sum_j t_{ij} s_{jk} + e_k^b \, , \tag{5}$$

where r represents the index of iteration: the formal derivation of equation (5) is given elsewhere (Batty, 1978). It is very clear that if

$e_i(0) = e_i^b$, as in the Garin–Lowry model, equation (5) generates the related series of increments of service employment, whereas if $e_i(0) = \bar{e}_i$, then the series generated is similar to that given by Lowry's original model. However, in operating on equation (5) rather than on equations (1) and (2), the appropriate series is generated cumulatively rather than in distinct increments, and this is similar to the reformulation by Baxter and Williams (1975). Of interest here is the idea that the matrices $\{t_{ij}\}$ and $\{s_{jk}\}$ might also vary with the process of solution—in short that they might depend upon the iteration r. Equation (5) can now be written as

$$e_k(r+1) = \gamma\lambda\sum_i e_i(r)\sum_j t_{ij}(r)s_{jk}(r) + e_k^b ,\qquad(6)$$

and it becomes clear that iteration on equation (6) will not in general converge to give the equilibrium conditions as will equation (5). If, however, the probability interaction matrices become stable at some future time R say, that is, $\{t_{ij}(R)\} \rightarrow \{t_{ij}\}$, and $\{s_{jk}(R)\} \rightarrow \{s_{jk}\}$, then repeated iteration on equation (6) with these stable matrices will yield solutions which converge towards the equilibrium conditions and relations. These notions are easy to demonstrate (see Batty, 1978) and the general ideas concerning such pseudodynamic processes and their convergence also have a temporal interpretation. Indeed, the idea that equation (5) or (6) can be used as procedures not only for distributing new activity but also for redistributing existing activity, that is activity already distributed, is appealing and has also been exploited in dynamic modelling (Batty, 1977).

The methods referred to so far are essentially solution techniques for systems of linear equations, but say nothing about the methods necessary to enable the model to meet given constraints and to optimise the goodness of fit. The problem involving locational constraints and the fit of the model is referred to generally as the problem of calibration, and in conventional practice has been largely separated from notions concerning the solution of the model. Before methods for calibration are outlined, it is necessary to firm up the structure of the model in this regard by defining the factors and parameters whose values have to be determined by the calibration. These factors and parameters relate to the interaction probability matrices and thus it is necessary to define them at this point. In this type of model the probability of working in i and living in j is usually based on a constrained gravity model of the form

$$t_{ij}(r) = \frac{B_j(r)D_j \exp\{-\mu_1(r)d_{ij}\}}{\sum_j B_j(r)D_j \exp\{-\mu_1(r)d_{ij}\}} ,\qquad \sum_j t_{ij} = 1 .\qquad(7)$$

D_j is a measure of the locational attraction of the residence zone j, in this case population, and d_{ij} is a measure of spatial impedance between i and j, here based on distance. The factor $B_j(r)$ is a weight applied to D_j, which is to be adjusted during the process of calibration so that the given constraints on population can be met. That is, $B_j(r)$ must be chosen to ensure that

$$\lambda \sum_i e_i(r) t_{ij}(r) \leqslant p_j^{\max} ,$$

(8)

where $p_j^{\max}$ is the maximum allowable population in zone j. The parameter $\mu_1(r)$ in equation (7) is a friction of distance parameter, which controls the overall effect of distance and thus the amount of interaction generated by the model. $\mu_1(r)$ must be chosen to satisfy its maximum-likelihood estimator, which is the mean amount of interaction observed in the system given by $\overline{C}$. This implies that $\mu_1(r)$ must be determined so that

$$\sum_i e_i(r) \sum_j t_{ij}(r) d_{ij} \bigg/ \sum_i e_i(r) = \overline{C} .$$

(9)

In fact, the calibration problem is usually more flexible than that implied by equations (8) and (9), for it is normally required only to converge to these constraints as the model converges to the equilibrium conditions.

In an analogous fashion, factors and parameters characterising the spatial demand for services must be chosen in relation to the gravity model used to estimate $s_{jk}(r)$. Then

$$s_{jk}(r) = \frac{A_k(r) F_k \exp\{-\mu_2(r) d_{ij}\}}{\sum_k A_k(r) F_k \exp\{-\mu_2(r) d_{ij}\}} , \qquad \sum_k s_{jk}(r) = 1 .$$

(10)

F_k is the measure of service-centre attraction in zone k, measured here by observed service employment, and the factor $A_k(r)$ is chosen so that

$$\gamma \lambda \sum_i e_i(r) \sum_j t_{ij}(r) s_{jk}(r) \leqslant e_k^{s\max} ,$$

(11)

where $e_k^{s\max}$ is the maximum amount of service employment allowable in zone k. The parameter $\mu_2(r)$ is chosen so that the mean amount of travel estimated by the model is equal to the observed mean $\overline{S}$. Then

$$\sum_i e_i(r) \sum_j t_{ij}(r) \sum_k s_{jk}(r) d_{jk} \bigg/ \sum_i e_i(r) = \overline{S} .$$

(12)

As in the case of the residential location model, equations (11) and (12) are usually only to be met in the given limit for r.

In previous developments of this type of model, solution and calibration have been tackled separately. Typically the model has been solved first, then the sets of factors $\{B_j(r)\}$ and $\{A_k(r)\}$ determined, and finally the parameters $\mu_1(r)$ and $\mu_2(r)$ chosen. In essence, the solution procedure for the model is nested within the procedure used to determine the constraint factors, which in turn is nested within the procedure used to choose the parameter values. By their very nature, each procedure requires iteration and, although some efforts have been made to speed up these procedures (Batty et al, 1974), these traditional methods still require a large amount of computer time and this prohibits their use on large problems. The major idea of this paper is that it is possible to devise integrated solution-calibration procedures which involve matching the iterations required by solution, factor calibration, and parameter calibration to the iterations characterising the methods of matrix iterative analysis. However, such a matching is only possible using equation (6) for solution. Such a use implies that at each iteration r, new factors and parameter values are computed which hopefully enable the model to come nearer to satisfying equations (8) and (9), and (11) and (12), and ultimately satisfy these when r reaches its given limit. Because equation (6) allows all activity generated so far to be redistributed, it is possible to change the factors and parameters so that the model is steered towards results which meet simultaneously the equilibrium conditions and constraints on location capacities and travel. In essence, the calibration problem then becomes the search for stable matrices $\{t_{ij}\}$ and $\{s_{jk}\}$; an elaboration of these points is contained in the complementary paper by the author (Batty, 1978). Note, however, that it is not possible to solve the model on the equilibrium conditions and achieve this integrated solution–calibration because it is necessary to move towards the constraints by recalibrating existing activity. Equations (1) and (2) in iterative solution, starting with $e_i = e_i^b$, only generate new increments of activity. The idea of redistribution contained here is similar to that pursued by Baxter and Williams (1975) in their treatment of automatic calibration.

In the sequel, it is proposed to develop the constraints procedures separately from the procedures used to choose the parameter values, largely because there are many applications which require only one or the other. Thus first, the conventional biproportional factoring procedures will be tested in relation to the iterative solution, and then the various optimisation procedures, based on Gauss's algorithm and Newton's method, will also be tested separately. Other methods of calibration could be developed in this integrated way, for example those developed by Coelho and Williams (1977), but the ultimate emphasis in the paper is on the results of assembling an integrated algorithm embedding biproportional procedures and optimisation methods into matrix iterative analysis. All the methods of this paper have been tested on a ten-sector-zone model based on London Traffic Survey data (LCC, 1964) and, in the event, this trial problem has turned out to be an excellent one for testing the kinds of model design pursued here. The results are generalised later to a sixty-three-zone model based on Central and West Berkshire data, and in all cases the number of iterations has been limited to thirty: as will be seen, this limit is sufficient for all the tests developed in this paper.

Constraints procedures based on biproportional factoring

To present the conventional biproportional procedure, first define two sets of zones, Z^p and Z^s, which contain the set of constrained residential and service-centre zones respectively. At the start of the model's operations when $r = 0$, $Z^p = Z^s = \Omega$ (the empty set), and the factors $B_j(0) = 1$, $\forall j$, and $A_k(0) = 1$, $\forall k$. At the end of each iteration a test is made to see whether a residential and/or service-centre zone should be constrained; if this is the case, new factors are computed. Then for any residential zone j, if ʼ

$$\lambda \sum_i e_i(r) t_{ij}(r) \geqslant p_j^{\max} , \qquad \text{zone } j \to Z^p . \tag{13}$$

The operation described in equation (13) is performed for all zones j, and on this basis if a zone belongs to the constrained set Z^p, a new factor $B_j(r+1)$ is computed from

$$B_j(r+1) = B_j(r) \frac{p_j^{\max}}{\lambda \sum_i e_i(r) t_{ij}(r)} , \qquad j \in Z^p . \tag{14}$$

The same kind of operation is performed in relation to service-centre zones: for any zone, k, if

$$e_k(r+1) - e_k^b \geqslant e_k^{s \max} , \qquad \text{zone } k \to Z^s , \tag{15}$$

and for all the zones belonging to Z^s after equation (15) has been tested, new factors $A_k(r+1)$ are computed from

$$A_k(r+1) = A_k(r) \frac{e_k^{s \max}}{e_k(r+1) - e_k^b} , \qquad k \in Z^s . \tag{16}$$

Note that zones which have not entered the constrained set are associated with factors which have remained unchanged from the first iteration, and are thus still equal to unity.

A number of points about this process need to be made. The term biproportional was first used generally by Bacharach (1970) in connection with the RAS method of adjusting an input–output table. To demonstrate that this method of factoring is equivalent to the row–column adjustment of a matrix such as an input–output table, it is necessary (as in this first set of test runs) to assume that the parameters are constant and independent of time. Then for the residential location model $\mu_1(r) = \mu_1$, $\forall r$, and it is now necessary to define the matrix to be biproportionally adjusted as the matrix of trips $T_{ij}(r)$. From equation (7) it is clear that, on iteration r, the work trips $T_{ij}(r)$ are computed from

$$T_{ij}(r) = e_i(r) t_{ij}(r) = a_i(r) e_i(r) B_j(r) D_j \exp(-\mu_1 d_{ij}) , \tag{17}$$

where the factor $a_i(r)$ is defined as

$$a_i(r) = 1 \bigg/ \sum_j B_j(r) D_j \exp(-\mu_1 d_{ij}) . \tag{18}$$

By substituting for $B_j(r+1)$ from equation (14) into the equation for $T_{ij}(r+1)$ analogous to (17), it is easy to show that

$$T_{ij}(r+1) = \left\{ \frac{e_i(r+1)}{\sum_j T_{ij}(r) \left[p_j^{\max} \bigg/ \sum_i T_{ij}(r) \right]} \right\} \left\{ \frac{p_j^{\max}}{\sum_i T_{ij}(r)} \right\} T_{ij}(r) , \tag{19}$$

where the two terms in the large brackets represent the appropriate proportional factors applied to the rows and columns of the trip-matrix elements $T_{ij}(r)$ to determine $T_{ij}(r+1)$. Note that the process implied by equation (19) assumes that $T_{ij}(r)$ is first factored with respect to the columns, and the resulting matrix is then factored with respect to the rows: the operations have been collapsed into a single equation although usually these are separated in more formal statements of the method (see, for example, Bacharach, 1970, or Evans, 1970).

Clearly what the procedure does is to scale up or down the appropriate locational attractors at the origin and destination towards the intended constraint values which are known. For example, in terms of the destination scaling operations implied by equations (14) and (16), the factors can be seen as weights which reduce or increase the attraction of the destinations to the location of activity. And such reductions or increases are required to move towards the intended constraint levels. The process is similar to the one suggested in economic equilibrium models of the Walrasian variety, in which prices are reduced or increased according to whether excess demands are negative or positive (see, for example, Scarf, 1973). The other point worth noting is that once a constraint has been violated, the above procedure ensures that the constraint will eventually be met. This is achieved by testing to determine whether a zone should enter the constrained set if a violation occurs, and, once in the set, the zone can never leave. The factoring is then determined on the basis of zones in the constrained set. It is an elementary point that constraint levels must be achieved once a violation occurs, otherwise convergence would never be possible.

The central question, of course, is whether or not the process will converge. As mentioned above, proofs are only available for the totally constrained problem in which all rows and columns of the matrix are factored. A number of related proofs are now available (McGill, 1975) and it does seem intuitively obvious that these could be extended to a partial set of row or column constraints. The process of averaging implicit in equation (19), for example, is such that eventually the intended constraint levels are likely to be met, although convergence in such partially constrained problems is likely to be much slower than in the totally constrained. Difficulties might be encountered if the structure of values in the original matrix reflected some loop or cycle, but in problems of this type this is not possible. However, an extension of the various proofs already available to partially constrained problems would be useful as these methods are employed quite extensively in urban modelling.

The speed of convergence is more of a problem because both theory and practice suggest that it is extremely slow. In methods of this sort, which are essentially trial and error, slow convergence is to be expected, but Robillard and Stewart (1974) show that the slowness is also a function of the size of the problem. Clearly this is because it takes more time in

larger matrices for the row and column factoring to be felt throughout
the system. But the speed of convergence which Robillard and Stewart
demonstrate is horrific: they show that for a totally constrained problem
of 100 zones, a conservative estimate for the percentage error in the total
trip estimates to converge to within five digits precision from iteration to
iteration is that 10^7 iterations would be required. This is an upper bound
for the number, and it would most certainly be less than this, but this
does give a frightening indication of the problem to be faced. In practice,
Cripps and Foot (1969) found the same problem in their Bedfordshire
model, and the constraint procedure was abandoned owing to the slowness
of its convergence. To speed up convergence, Robillard and Stewart try
to anticipate the final values of the factors by using Taylor's theorem to
expand their mathematical form about existing values, truncating at terms
of the first order, and thus solving the associated system of linear
equations—which is, in essence, the Newton–Raphson method. This
technique, however, poses some real problems because of problem size,
and thus they resort to a matrix iterative method which they suggest
should be complementary to the conventional biproportional procedure.
Although somewhat discouraging, their work is interesting and is probably
worthy of further investigation in future research, in the context of this
model. There may be other algorithms of potential interest, such as
Scarf's (1973) techniques based on simplicial search; these too await
further research.

   Finally, it is worth noting that the way the matrix iterative solution
procedure is structured enables the constraints procedure to be applied as
the system actually develops. Zones which reach their constraint limits
first are constrained first and other locations are then affected by the fact
that such constraints have been violated. Thus this is an improvement on
previous methods in which the complete solution has been used as a basis
for computing the two sets of factors. It also speeds up the procedure
during the early iterations. In the test example to be described below,
the constraints were set at $1 \cdot 2$ times the level of the observed values of
population and service employment.

Applications to the London Traffic Survey problem
A number of different variations on the biproportional scheme were tested
in terms of the model, the first being the original method as implied by
equations (13) to (16), the second being the introduction of a parameter
which anticipates the level of constraint violation (based on the stage
reached in the generative process), and the third being based on fitting a
polynomial function to the series of factors produced and subsequent
extrapolation of their values. To demonstrate the relative efficiency of
these methods, it is necessary to define a set of statistics which measure
convergence. Two types of statistic were used: a measure of the convergence
of the factors themselves from iteration to iteration, and a measure based

on the stability of the final activity distributions from iteration to iteration. Both statistics were suitably normalised with respect to some known value to give them a percentage or ratio interpretation, and they are applicable only to the set of constrained zones. Then for the two sets of factors, $\{B_j(r)\}$ and $\{A_k(r)\}$, the two appropriate statistics are defined as

$$\theta^p(r) = \sum_{j \in Z^p} \frac{|B_j(r) - B_j(r-1)|}{B_j(r)} \quad , \quad \text{and} \quad \theta^s(r) = \sum_{k \in Z^s} \frac{|A_k(r) - A_k(r-1)|}{A_k(r)} \, .$$

Note that as the equilibrium values of these factors are not known, the ratios imply only local, not global, convergence. To alleviate this problem, and to include a measure of the spatial distributions predicted which are also affected by the amount of activity generated, the two statistics for the population and service-employment distributions are defined as

$$\xi^p(r) = \sum_{j \in Z^p} \frac{|p_j(r) - p_j(r-1)|}{p_j^{\max}} \quad , \quad \text{and} \quad \xi^s(r) = \sum_{k \in Z^s} \frac{|e_k^s(r) - e_k^s(r-1)|}{e_k^{s\max}} \, .$$

Acceptable convergence limits for these statistics appear to be in the order of 10^{-2}. This means that from iteration to iteration there is a 1% change in the total values of the factors and/or the activity distributions. If all the zones were constrained, this would imply that on average the factor or activity was changing by $0 \cdot 1\%$, which can still be quite large absolutely for large populations or employments. For example, in a zone with a constraint limit of 200000 persons, a limit of 10^{-2} would imply that on average this zone would still be changing by 200 persons on each iteration. In the following analysis, the results of all the methods developed will be shown by a summary table in which the maximum number of iterations for any of the four statistics presented above to come within limits 10^{-1}, 10^{-2}, and so on, are recorded. This table does not record the speed of convergence very accurately but the original method and the best method will be presented in more detail using convergence graphs.

As a baseline comparison, a doubly constrained version of the model in which all population and service zones were constrained to their observed values was first run, and the acceptable limits of 10^{-2} were reached in fourteen iterations. By the twenty-eighth iteration, the limits of 10^{-5} had been reached. The original method was then run: it was not known in advance which constraints would be violated, but ultimately (by iteration 30) 6 out of 10 population zones and 9 out of 10 service zones were constrained. The tenth service zone is, of course, constrained automatically owing to the fact that there is a fixed total service employment to allocate; so in practice all the service zones were constrained. The performance of the original method was quite poor in that the limit of 10^{-1} had only been reached by the twenty-eighth iteration, and the slowness of the convergence is illustrated by a plot of the two sets of statistics on log–log graphs in figure 1. It is clear that the biproportional procedure, although converging, 'wanders around' quite a bit because it is

only using information based on individual constraints and not their
interrelations. In operating this model, activity is being generated at the
same time as the correct levels of factors are being sought, and thus a run
was attempted in which the factors were only computed after the ninth
iteration, a point at which 99% of the total activity associated with the
test problem had been generated. By iteration 30, the 10^{-1} limits had not
been met, thus it was clear that the method based on matrix iterative
analysis is immediately superior to conventional methods. Yet an
examination of the factors themselves reveals that their form is remarkably
regular. Figure 2 shows a plot of the two sets of factors, and from this it
is clear that if the point at which zones become constrained could be
anticipated in some way, then the procedure would certainly be speeded up.

A fairly obvious idea, involving this notion of anticipation, is to scale
the amount of activity in proportion to its final total whenever a constraint
is violated. For example, say that on the third iteration a constraint was
violated but only 70% of the total activity in the model had been
generated. On the assumption that if nothing were done about the
constraint violation until most of the activity, say 99%, had been generated,
it would be likely that this zone would receive more activity in proportion
to the remaining 30% of activity to be generated. Thus by scaling the
zone up after the third iteration by the ratio of total activity to be
generated to activity generated, an estimate of the eventual severity of
this constraint could be computed. In general, on iteration r of the model,
the proportion of activity generated so far is given by $[1-(\lambda\gamma)^{r+1}]$ and the
remaining activity is clearly $(\lambda\gamma)^{r+1}$. Thus the activities predicted so far
must be scaled by $[1-(\lambda\gamma)^{r+1}]^{-1}$ at each iteration to anticipate the amount
of activity eventually locating in any zone. Then for the residential

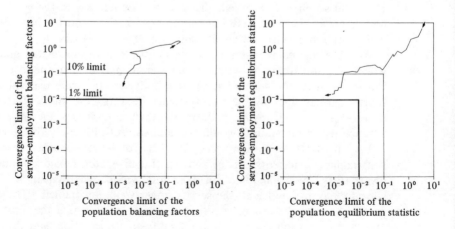

Figure 1. Convergence of the original biproportional method.

location model, equations (14) and (16) are replaced by

$$B_j(r+1) = B_j(r)\frac{p_j^{\max}[1-(\lambda\gamma)^{r+1}]}{\lambda\sum_i e_i(r)t_{ij}(r)} \quad , \qquad j \in Z^p \; , \tag{20}$$

and

$$A_k(r+1) = A_k(r)\frac{e_k^{s\;\max}[1-(\lambda\gamma)^{r+1}]}{e_k(r+1)-e_k^b} \quad , \qquad j \in Z^s \; . \tag{21}$$

Equations (20) and (21) can also be interpreted as a factoring scheme in which the constraints to be met are reduced to a level appropriate to the generative stage within which the model is, by the percentage of activity generated so far.

This method can only be applied when a constraint has actually been violated, because if all activities were scaled, there might be unnecessary violation of some constraints. In essence the method is reasonably successful in that in the early iterations it reduces the value of factors to a level closer to their ultimate values and thus speeds up the process slightly. Two versions of the method were tried: first the scaling procedure was applied throughout all 30 iterations of the model; and second, the scaling procedure was tested for sensitivity by applying it only after $[1-(\lambda\gamma)^{r+1}] \leqslant 0\cdot01$. It was not felt that this latter variation would give results any different from the original method, but in fact it makes a small difference owing

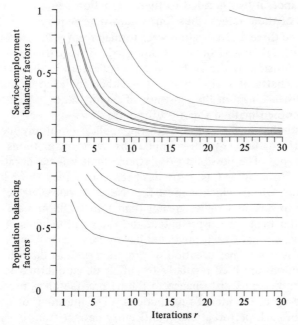

Figure 2. Convergence of the biproportional factors (using the original method).

to the scale of activities involved. The method is operated over the whole sequence (30 iterations) and enables the limits of 10^{-2} to be reached on iteration 30, whereas although the second version does not, it is a very slight improvement on the original method as the later tabulation shows. Clearly 30 iterations for a small problem is too slow, and therefore a third set of methods based on the anticipation of the final factor values was devised.

The regular pattern of change in the values of the constraint factors graphed in figure 2 suggests immediately the possibility of fitting single and independent polynomial functions to a sequence of these values, and then extrapolating their equilibrium or limit values. A variety of functions could be developed based on different orders of polynomial applied at different stages of the iteration but, as in all these methods, some balance between the advantages and disadvantages incurred by the technique must be sought. No exhaustive set of tests was begun in the search for an optimal polynomial fit but common sense and the number of iterations which characterise the speed of the previous methods suggest that a quadratic form would be fairly relevant to test. For each set of factors $\{B_j(r)\}$ and $\{A_k(r)\}$ different from unity, a quadratic of the form

$$B_j(r) = b_0 + b_1 r^{-1} + b_2 r^{-2} ,$$

was fitted. Then as $r \to \infty$, $B_j(r) \to b_0$ which represents the equilibrium value. To fit such a function, three sequential values of $B_j(r)$ are required but, in this instance, it was decided to fit the function based on average first-differences of these values, thus four values were required. In the case of $\{B_j(r)\}$, the three derived values were formed from $\frac{1}{2}[B_j(r) + B_j(r+1)]$, $\frac{1}{2}[B_j(r+1) + B_j(r+2)]$, and $\frac{1}{2}[B_j(r+2) + B_j(r+3)]$. This particular version had already been tested by the author and his colleagues in the Area 8 modelling study (Batty et al, 1974) and it was then found to be useful in smoothing localised 'kinks' in the sequence of factor values, which tend to throw a nonsmoothed method slightly off course.

There are a number of difficulties with the application of any method such as this to the natural sequences implied by averaging methods of the biproportional type. The possibility of extreme limit values—negative or positive—exists: to counter this, $B_j(r)$ has been constrained to be between 0 and 1, the range within which it must lie. Negative values are set arbitrarily close to zero and values greater than 1 to 1. In no case so far have values greater than 1 been predicted, and the small number of cases where negative values have been predicted have posed no problems. The second problem is one of perturbation in processes such as this where polynomial functions are used regularly to anticipate equilibrium values— there is bound to be some disturbance to the natural factoring process which will show up in the model's predictions. The question, of course, is whether or not such perturbations significantly detract from the progress generated by the method. In this case, after four iterations of the model, if four values of the factors different from unity have been computed using the biproportional procedure, a polynomial is fitted, and a new value for use on the next model iteration is extrapolated. This new value, however, is associated with the last iteration, and thus it is used only to produce the value of the factor associated with the next iteration; consequently, it is never used in the polynomial fitting four iterations later. Thus if the extrapolated value is off course, it will be slightly modulated before use in future curve fitting and this reduces the degree of perturbation. Other possibilities are worthy of note: for example, it might be better to fit a polynomial of a higher order after a greater number of iterations, and to do this less frequently. It may be possible to overlap the fitting, thus continuously updating the limit value if a sufficiently good limit value can be initially established. A good deal of fairly basic work remains to be done in this area but, on the basis of the results reported here, it does appear to be a reasonably useful way to speed up the convergence of the biproportional process in problems of this kind.

Different ways of applying this quadratic fitting procedure were tested in the context of the model. The method was applied to factor values based on the anticipated generation described above in the second method, and on the original method. It was also applied to the total number of iterations and to the iterations only after the ninth, when 99% of activity has been generated. Thus four varieties were tested in all, and all four come to within the 10^{-3} limits by the twenty-eighth iteration, thus endorsing the relative and expected superiority of these methods. Table 1 records the relative convergence of all the methods introduced so far, and it is clear that the polynomial method, in which the factors are anticipated over the whole set of iterations, is probably the fastest of all the partially-

Table 1. Convergence of various biproportional constraints procedures in terms of maximum number of model iterations required.

Type of constraints procedure	Convergence limits of the statistics				
	10^{-1}	10^{-2}	10^{-3}	10^{-4}	10^{-5}
Doubly-constrained	10	14	21	23	28
Partially-constrained (original method)	28	–	–	–	–
Anticipated generation (second method)					
all iterations	25	30	–	–	–
after iteration 9	25	–	–	–	–
Polynomial method (third method)					
no anticipation					
all iterations	16	23	28	–	–
after iteration 9	19	23	28	–	–
anticipation					
all iterations	15	20	27	–	–
after iteration 9	17	23	27	–	–

constrained methods. This is to be expected and a detailed illustration of the convergence of this method is presented in figure 3, where the directness of the line of convergence must be contrasted to that of figure 1 to gauge the performance. However, the degree of perturbation is also surprising, as is the fact that this perturbation does not seem to have much effect on

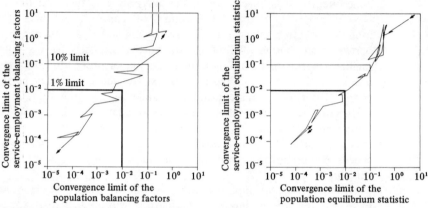

Figure 3. Convergence of the polynomial-anticipated biproportional method.

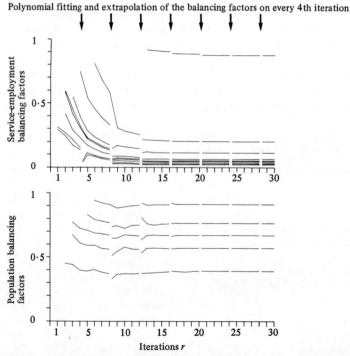

Figure 4. Convergence of the biproportional factors using the polynomial-anticipated method.

the direction of the convergence. Another illustration of this point is given in figure 4, where the values of the factors predicted by the biproportional and polynomial extrapolation are plotted. The discontinuities in the graphs are quite clear but the order of magnitude of the factors is established earlier than in the original method (compare with figure 1), and by the thirtieth iteration these values are quite stable.

In general, the constraints on service-centre location tend to dominate the overall convergence in this test problem. The statistics associated with convergence of the factors, and distributions associated with services, take longer to come within given limits than do the statistics relating to residential location, and this is owing to the fact that ultimately all service zones are constrained in the solution. There is not much difference between the factor statistics and distribution statistics, although the factor statistics appear to be marginally slower in their convergence. On balance, the polynomial methods are clearly best, but in the integrated algorithms to be presented later a variety of these methods will continue to be tested because the integration of calibration and constraints procedures might lead to unforeseen advantages or disadvantages. At this point, the constraints procedures will be left and the emphasis will be on the calibration of the model without constraints, in preparation for the discussion of an integrated algorithm embodying the best elements of both procedures.

Calibration procedures based on unconstrained optimisation
The main characteristic of the biproportional constraints procedures described above is the singular lack of any technique for measuring interdependence between each factor and between the sets of factors. Such interdependence clearly exists, but the difficulty of accounting for it is primarily owing to the size of the problem involved. In this test problem, the number of interdependent row and column factors is 36: 6 destination constraints in the residential sector and 10 in the service sector are ultimately required, and 10 origin constraints in each sector are prespecified. Thus, to assess interdependence between 36 factors involves the systematic analysis of a 36×36 matrix of relations, and in most schemes in which some form of expansion or extrapolation of equilibrium values is required, a 36×36 matrix would have to be inverted or its inversion approximated. The work of Robillard and Stewart (1974) and the results of Cesario's (1973) research were sufficient to detract from exploring such methods at this stage. In contrast, the calibration problem involves a much smaller number of parameters, 2 in this case, and usually it is much more feasible to develop methods which emphasise their interdependence. In this section, the general basis of the techniques to be applied will be presented, and the two related techniques that are developed will be structured in terms of the specific test problem.

In calibrating urban models, it is generally assumed that there are more statistics measuring the goodness of fit or numerical structure of the

model than there are parameters whose values it is required to determine.
Assume, therefore, that there are M statistics (or equations) and K
parameters (unknowns), where $M \geqslant K$. Construct the mth statistic, f_m,
from the deviation between some aspect of the model's prediction and its
associated observation and calculate f_m^2, thus ensuring that this squared
deviation statistic is always positive. Each statistic is dependent upon the
K parameters, μ_k, $k = 1, 2, ..., K$, as is the composite function $F(\mu)$, where
μ is the $1 \times K$ row vector of parameters. This function is defined as

$$F(\mu) = \sum_m f_m^2 \, . \tag{22}$$

The calibration problem is thus one in which the sum-of-squares function
in equation (22) is to be minimised by a judicious choice of parameters μ.
The necessary conditions for a minimum can be stated by differentiating
equation (22) with respect to μ_k and setting the result equal to zero.
Then

$$\frac{\partial F(\mu)}{\partial \mu_k} = 2\sum_m f_m \frac{\partial f_m}{\partial \mu_k} = 0 \, , \qquad k = 1, 2, ..., K \, , \tag{23}$$

and the second-order conditions can be stated in a similar way. However,
it is possible to expand equation (23) about a known set of parameter
values, $\mu_k(r)$, using Taylor's theorem, and thus produce an approximation
to equation (23) which provides the basis of a method for finding μ_k.
This, of course, is the basis of many such algorithms, but the least-squares
function has certain special characteristics which enable interesting and
useful approximations to be derived. Approximating the expansion of
equation (28) to the first-order leads to

$$\frac{1}{2} \frac{\partial F(\mu)}{\partial \mu_k} \approx \sum_m \left\{ f_m(r) \frac{\partial f_m(r)}{\partial \mu_k(r)} + \sum_l \left[\frac{\partial f_m(r)}{\partial \mu_k(r)} \frac{\partial f_m(r)}{\partial \mu_l(r)} + f_m(r) \frac{\partial^2 f_m(r)}{\partial \mu_k(r) \partial \mu_l(r)} \right] \epsilon_l(r) \right\}$$

$$\approx 0 \, , \qquad k = 1, 2, ..., K \, . \tag{24}$$

If it is assumed that this approximation is correct, it is possible to write
the system of equations implied by equation (23) in matrix terms and
solve directly. Then

$$\tfrac{1}{2} \nabla F' = \mathbf{J}_r' f_r' + \{\mathbf{J}_r' \mathbf{J}_r + \mathbf{G}_r\} \epsilon_r' = 0 \, , \tag{25}$$

where $\mathbf{J}_r$ is an $M \times K$ Jacobian matrix of first derivatives of the function
$\partial f_m(r)/\partial \mu_k(r)$, f_r is a $1 \times M$ row vector of function values $f_m(r)$, $\mathbf{G}_r$ is a
$K \times K$ matrix of second-order terms $\sum_m f_m(r) \partial^2 f_m(r)/\partial \mu_k(r) \partial \mu_l(r)$, and ϵ_r is
a $1 \times K$ row vector of error terms on the parameters; all these variables
are specified for the rth iteration. ∇F is the $1 \times K$ gradient row vector
of the first derivatives of the least-squares function, $F(\mu)$, defined at its
optimal point where the gradient is zero.

Two possible schemes for solving equation (25) suggest themselves. If it is now assumed that the approximation to $\nabla F'$ is good enough using only first-order information, then it is possible to assume that $G_r = 0$, and make a further approximation of the following form

$$J_r' f_r' + J_r' J_r \epsilon_r' = 0 \,. \tag{26}$$

Solving equation (26) for the error vector ϵ_r gives

$$\epsilon_r' = -(J_r' J_r)^{-1} J_r' f_r' \,, \tag{27}$$

and equation (27) is then used as the basis of an iterative scheme in which new parameters $\mu_k(r+1)$ are chosen from $\mu_{r+1} = \mu_r + \epsilon_r$ until ϵ_r becomes less than some limit vector. The algorithm implied by equation (27) is called Gauss's algorithm and it is clear that the system can be seen as equivalent to the notion of nonlinear regression. Indeed equation (27) has the same structure as the equation for computing the parameter values in a linear regression. Of interest is the fact that if $M = K$, the system reduces to one in which the number of statistics is equal to the number of unknown parameter values (Kowalik and Osborne, 1968), then

$$\epsilon_r' = -J_r^{-1} f_r' \,, \tag{28}$$

and equation (28) is clearly the Newton–Raphson equation which has been used quite extensively in conventional applications of these types of urban model (Batty, 1976). Gauss's algorithm would be linearly convergent in the neighbourhood of the optimum owing to the fact that only first-order information is used, whereas if equation (25) were solved directly, the implied algorithm would be quadratically convergent. Then

$$\epsilon_r' = -(J_r' J_r + G_r)^{-1} J_r' f_r' \,, \tag{29}$$

and it is obvious that the iterative scheme based on equation (29) involves more computation than that in equation (27). One might also expect equation (29) to give better convergence than (27), but this involves the trade-off between speed and computer time per iteration and this will be discussed quite fully in the sequel.

A much clearer interpretation of equation (29) can be made if a slightly different form of derivation is used. Consider the direct expansion of the least-squares function $F(\mu)$ about some known value $F(\mu_r)$ on iteration r. Then using Taylor's theorem and expanding to terms of the second order leads to

$$F(\mu) \approx F(\mu_r) + \sum_k \frac{\partial F(\mu_r)}{\partial \mu_k(r)} \epsilon_k(r) + \frac{1}{2} \sum_k \sum_l \epsilon_k(r) \epsilon_l(r) \frac{\partial^2 F(\mu_r)}{\partial \mu_k(r) \partial \mu_l(r)} \,, \tag{30}$$

where $\epsilon_k(r)$ is the error term associated with the parameter $\mu_k(r)$. As before, assuming that the approximation in equation (30) is good, equation (30) can be written in matrix terms as

$$F(\mu) = F(\mu_r) + \epsilon_r \nabla F_r' + \tfrac{1}{2} \epsilon_r H_r \epsilon_r' \,, \tag{31}$$

where H_r is the $K \times K$ matrix of second-order partial derivatives known as the Hessian (Simmonds, 1976). Equation (31) directly includes the second-order information which, when combined with the first-order information given by equation (23), provides the necessary and sufficient conditions for a minimum. This is guaranteed if the Hessian matrix is positive definite, that is, if the third term on the right-hand side of equation (31) is positive. At the minimum, the derivative of equation (31) with respect to the error vector ϵ_r must be equal to zero, that is

$$0 = \nabla F_r' + H_r \epsilon_r' , \tag{32}$$

and the solution for ϵ_r' follows directly from equation (32):

$$\epsilon_r' = -H_r^{-1} \nabla F_r' . \tag{33}$$

In this instance, equation (33) forms the basis of the iterative scheme, and the algorithm is referred to as Newton's method. This is quite different from Gauss's algorithm or the Newton–Raphson method although, if the function is appropriately defined, the two methods can be the same.

To note the equivalence of Newton's method and the scheme given by equation (29), all that need be done is to find forms for $\nabla F_r'$ and H_r in terms of the original deviation statistics f_m. Then differentiating $F(\mu)$ to get $\nabla F_r'$ leads to

$$\nabla F_k(r) = \sum_m f_m(r) \frac{\partial f_m(r)}{\partial \mu_k(r)} ,$$

and a second differentiation gives

$$H_{kl}(r) = \sum_m \left\{ f_m(r) \frac{\partial^2 f_m(r)}{\partial \mu_k(r) \partial \mu_l(r)} + \frac{\partial f_m(r)}{\partial \mu_k(r)} \frac{\partial f_m(r)}{\partial \mu_l(r)} \right\} .$$

Comparison with equation (23) demonstrates that

$$\nabla F_r' = J_r' f_r' , \tag{34}$$

and

$$H_r = -(J_r' J_r + G_r) . \tag{35}$$

Substitution for $\nabla F_r'$ and H_r from equations (34) and (35) into (32) gives equation (29), which shows that Newton's method is equivalent, in this instance, to the second-order Gaussian scheme. In the work reported below, the first-order method based on equations (27) or (28) is referred to as Gauss's algorithm in contrast to the second-order method of equation (29) or (33) which is Newton's algorithm. It is proposed to test both but, from a priori considerations, it would appear that Newton's algorithm would be faster overall owing to its quadratic convergence in the neighbourhood of the optimum. Moreover, the information provided by the Hessian is most useful in that global convergence can be assured through the criterion of positive-definiteness. Divergence of Newton's method away from the

optimum in the early stages of the algorithm can also be avoided, since if
the Hessian indicates divergence, such divergence can be minimised by
forcing the Hessian to be positive-definite. Such techniques are given by
Himmelblau (1972) but they were not required in this case.

The application of Gauss's and Newton's algorithms involved matching
the iterative structure of this model with the iterative structure of the
algorithms. The function $F(\mu)$ was particularly straightforward in that the
two parameters $\mu_1(r)$ and $\mu_2(r)$ are associated with the two mean statistics
based respectively on the predicted work trips and service demands. These
mean trip lengths on iteration r are defined as $\overline{C}(r)$ for work trips and
$\overline{S}(r)$ for service demands, and their observed values at the base date are $\overline{C}$
and $\overline{S}$ as specified previously. At each iteration r, these means are

$$\overline{C}(r) = \sum_i e_i(r)\sum_j t_{ij}(r)d_{ij} \Big/ \sum_i e_i(r)$$

$$= \sum_i \sum_j T_{ij}(r)d_{ij} \Big/ \sum_i \sum_j T_{ij}(r) , \qquad (36)$$

and

$$\overline{S}(r) = \sum_i e_i(r)\sum_j t_{ij}(r)\sum_k s_{jk}(r)d_{jk} \Big/ \sum_i e_i(r) = \sum_j \sum_k S_{jk}(r)d_{jk} \Big/ \sum_j \sum_k S_{jk}(r) , \qquad (37)$$

where $S_{jk}(r)$ are the service demands from j to k, and $T_{ij}(r)$ are the work
trips from i to j as introduced above. It is clear that the deviation
statistics which form the basis of the least-squares function can now be
stated for this problem as

$$f_1(r) = \overline{C}(r) - \overline{C} , \qquad f_2(r) = \overline{S}(r) - \overline{S} , \qquad (38)$$

and the elements of the Jacobian—the first derivatives of the functions in
equation (38)—are

$$J_{1k}(r) = \frac{\partial \overline{C}(r)}{\partial \mu_k(r)} , \qquad J_{2k}(r) = \frac{\partial \overline{S}(r)}{\partial \mu_k(r)} , \qquad k = 1, 2 . \qquad (39)$$

The elements of the gradient vector $\nabla F_k(r)$ and the Hessian matrix $H_k(r)$
immediately follow from equations (38) and (39), and these are stated as

$$\nabla F_k(r) = [\overline{C}(r) - \overline{C}]\frac{\partial \overline{C}(r)}{\partial \mu_k(r)} + [\overline{S}(r) - \overline{S}]\frac{\partial \overline{S}(r)}{\partial \mu_k(r)} , \qquad k = 1, 2 , \qquad (40)$$

$$H_{kl}(r) = [\overline{C}(r) - \overline{C}]\frac{\partial^2 \overline{C}(r)}{\partial \mu_k(r)\partial \mu_l(r)} + \frac{\partial \overline{C}(r)}{\partial \mu_k(r)}\frac{\partial \overline{C}(r)}{\partial \mu_l(r)}$$

$$+ [\overline{S}(r) - \overline{S}]\frac{\partial^2 \overline{S}(r)}{\partial \mu_k(r)\partial \mu_l(r)} + \frac{\partial \overline{S}(r)}{\partial \mu_k(r)}\frac{\partial \overline{S}(r)}{\partial \mu_l(r)} , \qquad k = 1, 2 . \qquad (41)$$

The derivatives of the mean-trip-length functions are quite straightforward
and have been stated generally by Evans (1971). They are not presented
here, largely because their presentation would be somewhat lengthy and

would contribute little to the central argument. In the computer program developed for these algorithms, these derivatives are computed from their analytic forms, although whether or not this can be done depends upon the model structure within which they are embedded. This is a problem which will be examined in the following section for all the elements of the two calibration algorithms have now been described, and it is now necessary to focus upon specific applications to the test problem.

Iterative optimisation of the pseudodynamic process
In applying Gauss's and Newton's algorithms, the quest is to find a set of parameters, μ_1 and μ_2, for which $F(\mu) = 0$, thus implying that $\overline{C}(r) = \overline{C}$, and $\overline{S}(r) = \overline{S}$, where r is being used now to denote the iteration at which equilibrium is reached. In previous models, the equilibrium form of the general model has been tested inside the iterative schemes implied by the two algorithms, but in this context, the idea is to match the iterative schemes implied by the algorithms with the matrix iterative analysis of the model itself. This is the same logic as matching the biproportional procedure to the model's iterations, and constraints and calibration will be matched in this way in the integrated algorithm to be discussed below. As in the constraints procedures, the idea is to calibrate the model during the generative and distributive processes which build up the model's predictions, thus correcting the direction towards which the calibration is proceeding by feeding back information about the state of the system to the calibration process. A similar idea was used by the author (Batty, 1977) to calibrate a related model structure, although in that instance the incremental rather than cumulative form of the process was used and backtracking was necessary.

   The question once again is whether or not the calibration procedure will converge. Convergence can only be assured if it can be demonstrated that the Hessian is positive-definite, which would imply that the response surface generated by the model in terms of the least-squares function is strictly convex. Such a proof does not appear possible in general terms, although in all the tests so far the Hessian has been positive-definite. However, Evans's (1971) work with a unidimensional function implies that the surface is certainly unimodal, and probably convex in the region where one is most likely to search. In other words, convexity is not assured but, in the area where the function varies most, it appears convex. There are several different ways in which these algorithms can be matched to the model's iterative process and three types, which are henceforth called 'Structures', have been applied. In Structure 1, each model iteration which consists of generating and distributing population from the input employment, and service employment from population, is considered to be quite separate. At the end of each iteration, the parameter error vector ϵ_r is computed using the information about trip lengths predicted solely during that iteration. In this structure, $\overline{C}(r)$ is computed from $t_{ij}(r)$ which is then used in the computation of $\overline{S}(r)$, but $\overline{C}(r)$ depends only upon $\mu_1(r)$, not upon $\mu_2(r)$, whereas $\overline{S}(r)$ depends on both. In other words, population depends upon employment generated from the previous iteration but not upon the employment generated on the current iteration. The structure of activity relationships is sequential not simultaneous, although in the long-term equilibrium, activities will be simultaneously related. In examining this structure, it is clear that the Jacobian matrix $\mathbf{J}_r$ is lower triangular, that is

$$
\mathbf{J}_r = \begin{bmatrix} \dfrac{\partial \overline{C}(r)}{\partial \mu_1(r)} & 0 \\[2ex] \dfrac{\partial \overline{S}(r)}{\partial \mu_1(r)} & \dfrac{\partial \overline{S}(r)}{\partial \mu_2(r)} \end{bmatrix} ,
$$

and thus its inversion is slightly easier than if it were full. Although this makes little difference for a 2×2 matrix, it does demonstrate that the Newton–Raphson method might be preferable to all others for large models with many sectors linked in this type of recursive or sequential way. For overdetermined systems, of course, or for Newton's algorithm, this property is not important.

Perhaps the most important feature of this sequential ordering of computations relates to the fact that any simultaneity which might ultimately exist in the model, does not occur in any iteration. Thus constraint factors which are determined at the end of each iteration are assumed constant during an iteration and do not vary with respect to the parameters. As Evans (1971) has shown, if the constraint factors do vary with the parameters, as is the case in the conventional static model in which the model and its constraints procedure are embedded into the calibration, large sets of simultaneous equations have to be solved to get the derivatives. In fact, in the Area 8 model, the derivatives were computed numerically to avoid this problem, but by formulating the model in the manner of this paper, analytic derivatives can be used. These points also pertain to the other two methods used. In Structure 2, the idea is to overlap the iterations and to use information from a previous iteration if this is the latest information available. In Structure 1 the derivative of $\overline{C}(r)$ with respect to the service-centre parameter $\mu_2(r)$ is zero, but with respect to the previous value of this parameter, $\mu_2(r-1)$, it is positive. Thus the Jacobian matrix $\mathbf{J}_r$ now becomes

$$
\mathbf{J}_r = \begin{bmatrix} \dfrac{\partial \overline{C}(r)}{\partial \mu_1(r)} & \dfrac{\partial \overline{C}(r)}{\partial \mu_2(r-1)} \\[2ex] \dfrac{\partial \overline{S}(r)}{\partial \mu_1(r)} & \dfrac{\partial \overline{S}(r)}{\partial \mu_2(r)} \end{bmatrix} ,
$$

and this implies the idea of a periodic update of information in terms of
the relationship between employment from a previous iteration and
interaction in a current iteration.

This notion of updating the information about the pattern of interaction
on the system can be taken even further. In a sense, the organisation of
the two activity generations and distributions in one iteration is fairly
arbitrary, and there is no reason why the relationship of population to
employment to new population needs to reflect the computations
associated with an iteration. It is possible to overlap the iterations even
more tightly than in Structure 2, and to compute the error vector ϵ_r
afresh after each activity has been generated and distributed. This idea is
developed in Structure 3: retaining the index r as characterising a
conventional iteration, assume first that population $p_j(r)$ has just been
generated and distributed from employment $e_k(r)$. Then a new error
vector, ϵ_r^1, is computed using trip-length derivatives of which the following
Jacobian matrix, $\mathbf{J}_r^1$, is an example:

$$\mathbf{J}_r^1 = \begin{bmatrix} \dfrac{\partial \overline{C}(r)}{\partial \mu_1(r)} & \dfrac{\partial \overline{C}(r)}{\partial \mu_2(r-1)} \\ \dfrac{\partial \overline{S}(r-1)}{\partial \mu_1(r-1)} & \dfrac{\partial \overline{S}(r-1)}{\partial \mu_2(r-1)} \end{bmatrix}.$$

From this information two errors, $\epsilon_1^1(r)$ and $\epsilon_2^1(r)$, are calculated: a new
parameter value for $\mu_1(r)$ is not required as it is not needed until the next
iteration. However, $\mu_2(r)$ is calculated as $\mu_2(r) = \mu_2(r-1) + \epsilon_2^1(r)$, and
this is used in the calculation of service demands and employment. After
these services have been generated and distributed, a new error vector is
calculated from the new information of which the following Jacobian, $\mathbf{J}_r^2$,
is representative:

$$\mathbf{J}_r^2 = \begin{bmatrix} \dfrac{\partial \overline{C}(r)}{\partial \mu_1(r)} & \dfrac{\partial \overline{C}(r)}{\partial \mu_2(r-1)} \\ \dfrac{\partial \overline{S}(r)}{\partial \mu_1(r)} & \dfrac{\partial \overline{S}(r)}{\partial \mu_2(r)} \end{bmatrix}.$$

A new parameter, $\mu_1(r+1)$, calculated as $\mu_1(r+1) = \mu_1(r) + \epsilon_1^2(r)$, is now
introduced. A new parameter for $\mu_2(r)$ is not required yet, and it is clear
that in this process, although both parameters could be changing after
each activity has been dealt with, it is only relevant to change the
parameter for which the next activity is being computed. Thus in the
above scheme, $\epsilon_1^1(r)$ and $\epsilon_2^2(r)$ are pieces of information which are
incidental to the process and are not actually used directly. In short, the
information appearing in the Jacobians above (and, of course, the second-
derivative functions which are not shown) is that which *directly* affects
the distribution of activities.

In these three structures, the two algorithms are applied to response surfaces which are varying at each iteration. The degree to which each structure relates each iteration to the previous one is, however, a way of gradually moving from one response surface to the next. In the case of Structure 1, each iteration is quite separate and each response surface is regarded as different from the previous one, although it is generally assumed that the previous parameter values are good starting points for the new search. In Structures 2 and 3 the links are much stronger, and in the case of Structure 3 the closest possible link is used. In fact, the logic behind this updating of response surfaces in Structures 2 and 3 is not unlike the Gauss–Seidel method of matrix iterative analysis, which is based on using information once created for the prediction of new information (Varga, 1962). Indeed, many of the techniques of this paper depend upon the notion of using information in this way, once it has been predicted. Moreover, the fact that analytic derivatives are easier to compute for these types of sequential structure reduces computation time, although it should be noted that this is only the case if the model is subject to locational constraints. If not, analytic derivatives for the simultaneous equilibrium are also possible. A diagrammatic illustration of these three structures in relation to the model's iteration process is presented in figure 5.

Three structures and two algorithms give rise to six possible applications of the unconstrained optimisation methodology. In general, it would appear that Newton's method would be more efficient than Gauss's, and that structures which were based on updating response surfaces from iteration to iteration would be preferable: that is, Structure 3 would be more efficient than Structure 2, which would be more efficient than Structure 1. Thus overall, Newton's method applied to Structure 3 would seem most efficient from purely theoretical considerations. However, Newton's method takes 47% more computer time per model iteration than does Gauss's algorithm, and this added time is almost entirely accounted for by the evaluation of the second derivatives. In contrast, there is hardly any difference in terms of computer time between the three structures: Structures 1 and 2 are almost identical, and Structure 3 takes 3% longer than these to compute. Thus the final choice of algorithm will rest on a trade-off between efficiency of the method and computer time taken. As in the constraints procedures outlined above, the efficiency of the method is measured by two statistics based on comparisons between successive iterations. These statistics are based on the change in the mean trip lengths from iteration to iteration, suitably normalised by their observed values. For the residential location model, the appropriate statistic $\eta^\mathrm{p}(r)$ is defined as

$$\eta^\mathrm{p}(r) = \frac{|\overline{C}(r) - \overline{C}(r-1)|}{\overline{C}} ,$$

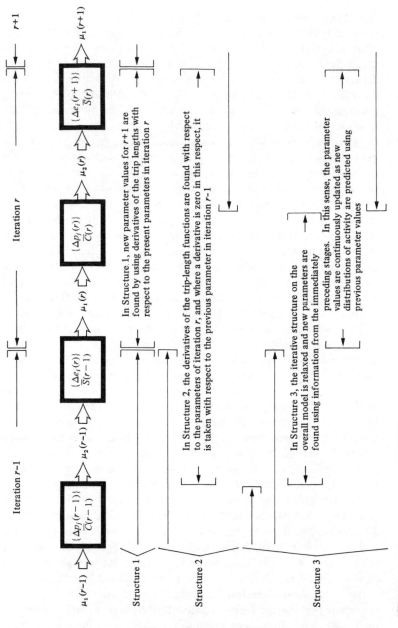

Figure 5. Calibration structures.

and for the service-centre model, $\eta^s(r)$ is defined as

$$\eta^s(r) = \frac{|\overline{S}(r) - \overline{S}(r-1)|}{\overline{S}} \ .$$

Appropriate convergence limits for these statistics have been fixed at 10^{-3} rather than 10^{-2} as in the case of the constraint factors. These statistics refer to the total system, and a $0 \cdot 1\%$ change from iteration to iteration implies that for an observed mean trip length of 10 time/distance/cost units, precision to two decimal places has been obtained. In fact the results presented below show that much greater accuracy can be obtained for calibration independent of the constraints procedure, and it may be that greater precision, up to 10^{-4} say, should be specified: this will clearly depend on the context and the resources available to build the model.

The results of the six applications—each algorithm applied to each structure—are recorded in table 2, which shows the number of iterations required for each of the two statistics, $\eta^p(r)$ and $\eta^s(r)$, to come within the specified limits. Clearly one of these statistics will dominate the convergence, in that it will take longer for this statistic to converge, and the one that dominates in this way is picked out in bold type in the table. The immediate impression from table 2 is that there is little to distinguish the algorithms if the number of iterations to reach a change of 10^{-7} is examined. However, there are some differences in terms of the speed of convergence before this limit is reached. The residential statistic converges faster at first up to the 10^{-3} limit but from then on the service statistic is faster. Up to 10^{-3} there is little question that Gauss's algorithm is faster for every structure, but from then on until the limit of 10^{-7} is reached, there is little to choose, although Newton's algorithm probably has the edge.

Table 2. Convergence of the calibration procedures in terms of the numbers of model iterations required to reach given limits.

Convergence limit	Method [a]											
	Gauss's algorithm						Newton's algorithm					
	structure 1		structure 2		structure 3		structure 1		structure 2		structure 3	
10^{-1}	3	2	3	2	3	2	5	2	5	2	5	2
10^{-2}	5	3	5	5	5	5	8	3	8	4	8	4
10^{-3}	6	5	6	6	6	6	9	7	9	8	9	8
10^{-4}	10	11	10	11	10	11	9	11	10	10	10	10
10^{-5}	14	15	14	15	14	15	14	15	14	15	14	15
10^{-6}	19	19	19	20	19	20	19	19	19	20	19	20
10^{-7}	23	25	23	25	23	25	24	25	23	25	25	25

[a] Note that in each column of the table, the number of iterations associated with the service statistic is presented first, then the number associated with the residential statistic. The dominant statistic is set bold in each pair of statistics.

With regard to the three structures, there is hardly any difference in terms of speed, although in the case of Newton's algorithm, Structures 2 and 3 are marginally superior to Structure 1. However, given the relative crudeness of this type of comparison, it is hardly a basis for choice. In terms of the acceptable limit of 10^{-3} Gauss's algorithm is superior, but in view of the general ambiguity of these results, it was decided to test all six methods in the integrated algorithm described below.

In results such as these the basis for choice must be in terms of other factors and, because Newton's algorithm takes 47% more computer time, Gauss's algorithm is to be preferred. In fact, the Newton–Raphson version of Gauss's algorithm has already been used extensively for models such as these, but the improvement in the applications described here over present practice is quite remarkable. In terms of Gauss's algorithm, only six model iterations are required to come to within the 10^{-3} limit and, at this point, only just enough activity has been generated by the model in terms of its generative process. If we use any of these methods, an excellent calibration can be achieved in ten iterations of the model, and this must be contrasted with something of the order of at least seventy in conventional applications (Batty, 1976). Moreover, this dramatic increase in speed results from a very different interpretation of the properties of the model, and it also opens up the model structure to the incorporation of other information which might be considered important to its process. For example, although not incorporated here, the model allows for the possibility that prior information affecting interaction can be used to start the model's distributive processes: the search for stable matrices of interaction need not be based on purely external criteria but on the idea that the model's pseudodynamic process is an approximation to the way the system has actually evolved and must be treated as such.

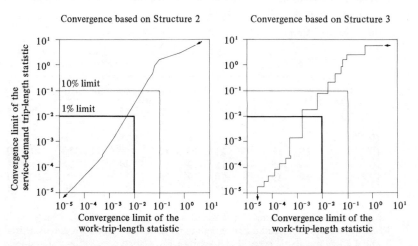

Figure 6. Convergence of the Newton method on Structures 2 and 3.

To conclude this section, it is worthwhile illustrating some detailed results from the tests so that a deeper impression of the speed of these various algorithms and their structure is given. In figure 6 the two statistics of convergence are plotted on log–log graphs for Newton's algorithm applied to Structures 2 and 3. The speed of convergence and directness of path in Structure 2 is clear and the stepped effect in Structure 3 is owing to the fact that the convergence statistics are computed each time the algorithm is applied, which in this case is twice in each iteration of the model. In fact, Structures 2 and 3 have quite similar paths of convergence if the stepped effect is ignored. The detailed computations of intermediate variables in the algorithm, such as derivatives, are shown in figure 7 for Newton's algorithm applied to Structure 2. The signs of the first derivatives of the mean-trip-length functions are negative as expected from theory (see Evans, 1971), and the second derivatives of the least-squares functions are also plotted. These partial derivatives are interesting in that the self-derivatives are some one hundred times as large as the cross-derivative, thus implying that the Hessian is positive over the range of values shown. Moreover, the first derivatives of the mean-trip-length functions with respect to each other's parameters are small relative

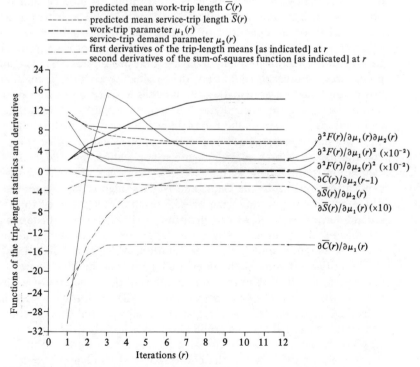

Figure 7. Convergence of the trip-length functions by using Newton's method on Structure 2.

to the same derivatives taken with respect to their own parameters, thus implying that the connections between the residential and service sectors of the model are much weaker than connections within these sectors. Finally, the well-known inverse relationship between parameter value and mean trip length is illustrated by figure 7. The trip lengths converge to their observed values from above and the parameters converge from below, and the graph also illustrates the relative speed of this convergence in terms both of the residential and of the service sectors. At this point it is necessary to test these calibration algorithms further in the context of the various constraints procedures outlined above, and to this end the integrated algorithm will now be presented.

An integrated algorithm for constrained solution and calibration
From the test results already reported for the individual analyses of constraints and calibration procedures, it is not clear which methods are best, owing to conflicting evidence in terms of the criteria used. For example, some indications are available that the polynomial methods appear best in terms of the constraints procedures, but when the two sets of methods—calibration and constraints—are both matched to the model's iterative structure, a new problem is constituted. It may be that the two procedures will or will not reinforce one another and so it was decided to test a variety of combinations of methods already introduced, on the general assumption that the results of the individual procedures could not be transferred to this problem involving joint procedures. Three constraints procedures were developed: first, the original procedure; second, the procedure based on anticipating the model's activity generation over all iterations; and third, the polynomial method based on anticipation over all iterations. The six methods of calibration based on the three structures and two algorithms outlined above were applied with each of these constraints procedures, making eighteen applications in total. As in the calibration results, the essential difference in computer time for these applications related to the Gauss and Newton algorithms, where the difference in computation time of 47% results from the need to evaluate second-derivatives in Newton's algorithm. The differences in terms of calibration structures and constraints procedures amounted to no more than 4% computer time per model iteration, which is not significant.

The initial test runs of the integrated algorithm, in which new parameters and factors were computed during or at the end of each model iteration for use in the next, were based on the test problem used in the individual analyses. However, it was eventually realised that the locational constraints specified for this problem were so tight that the observed mean trip lengths were not consistent with the range of possible solutions to the model. In other words the constraints and trip lengths could not be simultaneously satisfied and, because of the way in which the two procedures operate, the biproportional procedure will always dominate the unconstrained optimisation algorithm. In this sense, the initial problem proved to be an excellent test problem in that it was used to continually refine and check the integrated algorithm in the hope that a solution might exist. However, the lack of a solution was realised when (in desperation!) the number of model iterations was increased to one hundred, and the results showed the parameter in the residential sector tending to infinity. This is a particularly interesting result in models of this kind, it being, in this case, due largely to the relatively poor performance of the model on the test problem; it demonstrates that a set of constraints and trip lengths can be specified which, in terms of the model's performance, cannot be met. Furthermore, the problem could be particularly important in the context of using this type of structure in more formal problems of policy optimisation. It results from the relationship between the various sectors which, in the equilibrium, are simultaneously related and it is certainly an area worthy of further research. An additional point also suggests itself: had the constraints and calibration problem been set up as an unconstrained optimisation procedure in the manner suggested in the work of Robillard and Stewart (1974), the nonexistence of a solution might never have been found because the lack of convergence may then have been attributed to the method and not to the model as applied to the problem.

Because of these difficulties a new test problem was defined by relaxing the locational constraints, placed on the LTS data, in such a way that a solution is ensured. The four statistics defined earlier in relation to the constraints procedure, and the two in relation to calibration, were used to measure the convergence of each of the test runs. To summarise all this information three tables will be presented for the limits 10^{-1}, 10^{-2}, and 10^{-3}, and in each table, the maximum number of iterations required to

Table 3. Convergence of the integrated algorithm to the limit 10^{-1}.

Calibration algorithms		Biproportional procedure [a]					
		the original 'Furness' procedure		the procedure with anticipated activity generated		the polynomial procedure	
Gauss's	Structure 1	3	21	3	18	3	21
algorithm	Structure 2	3	21	4	18	4	18
	Structure 3	3	21	4	18	4	18
Newton's	Structure 1	5	21	5	18	9	15
algorithm	Structure 2	5	21	5	18	10	24
	Structure 3	5	21	5	18	11	18

[a] Note that in tables 3, 4, and 5, the maximum number of iterations to reach the limit in terms of the two trip-length statistics, $\eta^P(r)$ and $\eta^s(r)$, is presented first in each column, followed by the maximum number in terms of the biproportional factor statistics, $\theta^P(r)$, $\theta^s(r)$, $\xi^P(r)$, and $\xi^s(r)$.

meet the limit on the calibration statistics, $\eta^p(r)$ and $\eta^s(r)$, and the maximum on the constraint statistics, $\theta^p(r)$, $\theta^s(r)$, $\xi^p(r)$, and $\xi^s(r)$, will be shown. The speed of convergence can be extracted by following through each of the three tables in sequence, and it is possible to note the differences in convergence of the calibration and constraints procedures. Table 3 shows the results for each of the eighteen methods for the limit 10^{-1}, and it is fairly clear from this, that Gauss's algorithm is faster than Newton's. In table 4, which gives the number of iterations required to reach 10^{-2}, Gauss's algorithm still has the edge. However, the picture begins to change in table 5: for the limit of 10^{-3}, it is clear from table 5 that Gauss's algorithm is still marginally better, but after that point, that is after iteration 15 of the model, Newton's algorithm is clearly faster and is essential when tables 3 and 4 are analysed in terms of the constraints procedures.

In terms of the three structures, it is clear that Structure 1 is best up to the 10^{-1} limit but after that Structures 2 and 3 appear better. As previously, the evidence does not favour strong conclusions, but Structure 3 probably has the edge. For the three constraints procedures, however, the evidence is much firmer: the anticipation method is best up to the

Table 4. Convergence of the integrated algorithm to the limit 10^{-2}.

Calibration algorithms		Biproportional procedure					
		the original 'Furness' procedure		the procedure with anticipated activity generated		the polynomial procedure	
Gauss's algorithm	Structure 1	5	-	5	-	10	28
	Structure 2	4	-	5	-	11	28
	Structure 3	5	-	5	-	10	28
Newton's algorithm	Structure 1	8	-	8	-	13	27
	Structure 2	8	-	8	-	10	27
	Structure 3	8	-	8	-	10	26

Table 5. Convergence of the integrated algorithm to the limit 10^{-3}.

Calibration algorithms		Biproportional procedure					
		the original 'Furness' procedure		the procedure with anticipated activity generated		the polynomial procedure	
Gauss's algorithm	Structure 1	11	-	8	-	26	-
	Structure 2	11	-	8	-	11	-
	Structure 3	11	-	8	-	11	-
Newton's algorithm	Structure 1	12	-	13	-	14	-
	Structure 2	12	-	13	-	14	-
	Structure 3	12	-	13	-	15	-

10^{-1} limit but after that the polynomial method is the only one which is able to meet the prespecified limit of 10^{-2}. On balance, for a large problem Newton's method is probably superior and almost certainly the polynomial version of the biproportional constraints procedure will be required. The operation of this scheme using Structure 2 or Structure 3 appears to give better results than on Structure 1, and this conclusion is quite consistent with theoretical arguments which also suggest the same.

Polynomial fitting and extrapolation of the balancing factors on every 4th iteration

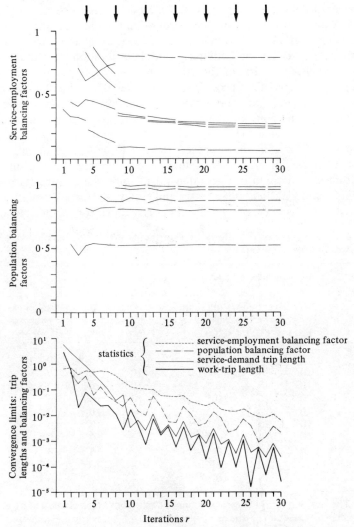

Figure 8. Convergence of the integrated algorithm based on Newton–Structure 3-polynomial methods.

C

By iteration 30, the Newton method applied to Structure 3 with the polynomial procedure is noticeably faster than any of the others, and therefore the results from this application will be presented in more detail.

Figure 8 shows the convergence of the biproportional factors themselves for the service and residential sectors and also contains a plot of the statistics $\theta^s(r)$, $\theta^p(r)$, $\eta^s(r)$, and $\eta^p(r)$. These graphs have many of the characteristics of the individual analyses presented earlier and, although the orders of magnitude of the biproportional factors have been established by the 15th iteration, the polynomial method tends to perturb these values at every 4th iteration, thus accounting for the oscillations in the convergence statistics. Another important feature of the algorithm is the fact that up to about the 10th iteration, the calibration algorithm converges at a similar speed to that of the same algorithm applied independently of the locational constraints procedure. But after this point the convergence begins to slow and, from about the 15th iteration on, the calibration is dominated by the constraints procedure: both procedures converge at much the same speed. This is a particularly essential point in that the advantages of the calibration procedure tend to be lost in the later iterations as the constraints procedure begins to dominate, and thus the algorithm as structured is highly dependent upon the constraints procedure. The implication must be that better and faster constraints procedures are required and this is clearly another important area for further research.

Table 6. Convergence of the integrated algorithm at every 10th iteration based on the Newton-Structure 3 version.

Number of iterations	Convergence statistics					
	service-centre-location submodel			residential-location submodel		
	$\eta^s(r)$	$\theta^s(r)$	$\xi^s(r)$	$\eta^p(r)$	$\theta^p(r)$	$\xi^p(r)$
10	10^{-2}	10^{0}	10^{0}	10^{-1}	10^{-1}	10^{-1}
20	10^{-3}	10^{-1}	10^{-1}	10^{-3}	10^{-2}	10^{-2}
30	10^{-3}	10^{-2}	10^{-2}	10^{-4}	10^{-2}	10^{-3}
40	10^{-4}	10^{-2}	10^{-3}	10^{-5}	10^{-3}	10^{-3}
50	10^{-4}	10^{-3}	10^{-3}	10^{-5}	10^{-3}	10^{-3}
60	10^{-5}	10^{-3}	10^{-4}	10^{-6}	10^{-4}	10^{-4}
70	10^{-5}	10^{-4}	10^{-4}	$-$	10^{-4}	10^{-4}
80	10^{-6}	10^{-4}	10^{-5}	$-$	10^{-5}	10^{-5}
90	$-$	10^{-5}	10^{-5}	$-$	10^{-5}	10^{-5}
100	$-$	10^{-5}	10^{-6}	$-$	10^{-6}	10^{-6}

Note: The lack of a record in certain columns of the above table, indicated by a -, implies that the relevant statistic had converged to 10^{-6} but no further convergence limit was specified in the computer printout, which gave results only to six decimal places.

To establish formally the eventual speed of convergence, this particular version of the integrated algorithm has been run for 100 iterations, and in table 6 the long term convergence properties of the model are demonstrated by recording the limit reached on every 10th iteration for each of the six statistics. Table 6 shows that the convergence is fairly regular: in terms of the calibration statistics one additional decimal point of accuracy is gained after about every 15th iteration after iteration 30, and for the biproportional factor and distribution statistics, this gain in precision is achieved after about every 20th iteration. Overall, in this example, it is possible to say that 10^{-1} accuracy is achieved within 20 iterations, 10^{-2} within 30, 10^{-3} within 50, 10^{-4} within 70, and 10^{-5} within 90. Clearly the convergence would be different for a larger problem, and by way of conclusion to this analysis, the results of applying the integrated algorithm to the Central and West Berkshire model will now be presented.

For the sixty-three zone model of Berkshire, test runs were made both for the calibration procedure without locational constraints (unconstrained)

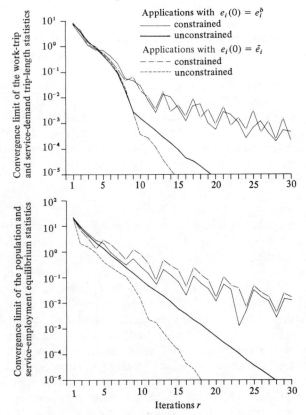

Figure 9. Convergence of the Central and West Berkshire model.

and with such constraints. Furthermore, tests were made starting the matrix iterative solution of the model from the normal input, basic employment $e_i(0) = e_i^b$, and from the observed distribution of employment $e_i(0) = \tilde{e}_i$. A total of four runs was thus generated and the results are shown in figure 9 for the statistics $\frac{1}{2}[\eta^s(r) + \eta^p(r)]$ and $\frac{1}{2}[\xi^s(r) + \xi^p(r)]$. It is clear that the convergence is generally slower than in the LTS test problem but, by iteration 30, all these statistics had converged to the limit 10^{-1}, and in the case of the calibration statistics to 10^{-3}. In fact, in the unconstrained runs, the version starting with $e_i(0) = \tilde{e}_i$ converges to the limit 10^{-5} within 15 iterations for the calibration and within 18 iterations for the distribution statistics. This is in contrast to similar limits obtained within 20 iterations for calibration and 28 iterations for the distribution starting with $e_i(0) = e_i^b$. Thus it is clear that to calibrate the model unconstrained, it is preferable to start with the observed vector of employment and to operate on this. Figure 9 also shows that this advantage is lost when the constrained version of the model is applied, for the constraints procedure tends to dominate the convergence, and the perturbations due to the polynomial smoothing become characteristic. The biproportional factor statistics, $\theta^s(r)$ and $\theta^p(r)$, are not shown in figure 9, but these statistics also come to within 10^{-1} in 30 iterations for the constrained runs, and, although this is not an acceptable limit, some runs to 50 iterations show that the limit of 10^{-2} is reached at about 38 iterations. This confirms that in large models the integrated algorithm is far superior to any available technique, for the fastest method previously reported required over 80 runs of a thirty-four zone model to reach a limit of 10^{-1} (Batty et al, 1974). Yet this example once again reinforces the obvious point that better methods of dealing with locational constraints in such models are required if computer time is to be further reduced, and it is certain that further improvements can be made.

Conclusions

The constraints procedure based on biproportional factoring remains the most problematic element in the integrated algorithm, and future research will have to be addressed to the search for faster methods. Although the use of methods of expansion or extrapolation based on assessing the interdependence of the system appear slow from the work of Robillard and Stewart (1974) and Cesario (1973), it may be possible to develop certain gradient procedures which anticipate the equilibrium values of the factors more closely than the polynomial method. Such techniques would not involve any matrix inversion, which is the stumbling block in the method of Robillard and Stewart, although other problems, such as the way in which these methods would fit into the matrix iterative analysis, would have to be faced. Other approaches involving extrapolation may also be useful: Murchland's (1977) small-error analysis of the gravity model reveals that the convergence of the error in the balancing factors, using biproportional factoring, is linear in the neighbourhood of the optimum. The method which he has devised, based on this analysis, is under test at present and although preliminary results do not suggest that it is any faster than the polynomial method, it is likely to be a valid alternative to the methods presented here.

It is also possible, however, that entirely different sorts of procedures might be more appropriate to the problem. Scarf's (1973) algorithm, for example, which is used to generate solutions to the general economic equilibrium model, is based on systematic sampling of the possible solutions according to known properties of the solution space; and it does appear that such methods might be relevant to the problem as implied by McGill (1975; 1976). More formal optimisation methods may be worthy of development as well. Coelho and Williams (1977) have interpreted a variety of urban models based on spatial interaction as problems in nonlinear programming, and they demonstrate how efficient solutions can be produced using standard and readily available algorithms. For example, the iterative structure of such programming procedures could be matched to the solution procedure using the matrix iterative formulation as developed here. Thus the linearity of the constraints, to which such programs are subject, could be preserved despite the nonlinearity of the final equilibrium relations. These matters are all for future research but prospects for even further improvements in the efficiency of calibration are quite good.

Finally, this paper has illustrated a classic idea in applied scientific research: that problems involving model efficiency and solution can best be tackled not by ad hoc improvements, but by reformulation of the model structure, since this enables a deeper appreciation of the model's inner workings to be gained. Such ideas are sorely absent from the field of urban modelling, where the emphasis is mainly on substantive questions or on technique. But structure is of the essence and what limited research does exist always seems to yield fresh insights. For example, Stonebraker's (1972) simplification of Forrester's (1969) *Urban Dynamics* model, and Paelinck's (1970) analysis of urban processes, represent excellent researches into model structure, motivated by questions of efficiency and parsimony. Urban modelling has become dominated by excessively complex and often 'messy' model structures in the past, and the time seems ripe for a greater concentration on simplicity and feasibility. It is to this end that the ideas developed in this paper are addressed.

References
Bacharach M, 1970 *Biproportional Matrices and Input-Output Change* (Cambridge University Press, Cambridge)
Banister C E, 1977 "A method for incorporating maximum constraints into the Garin-Lowry model" *Environment and Planning A* 9 787-793
Batty M, 1976 *Urban Modelling: Algorithms, Calibrations, Predictions* (Cambridge University Press, Cambridge)

Batty M, 1977 "Pseudo-dynamic urban models", unpublished paper, Department of
    Geography, University of Reading
Batty M, 1978 "Operational urban models incorporating dynamics in a static
    framework" in *Spatial Interaction Theory and Planning Models* Eds A Karlqvist,
    L Lundqvist, F Snickars, J W Weibull (North-Holland, Amsterdam) pp 227–252
Batty M, Bourke R, Cormode P, Anderson-Nicholls M, 1974 "Experiments in urban
    modelling for county structure planning" *Environment and Planning A* 6 455–478
Baxter R, Williams I, 1975 "An automatically calibrated urban model" *Environment
    and Planning A* 7 3–20
Berechman J, 1976 "Interfacing the urban land-use activity system and the
    transportation system" *Journal of Regional Science* 16 183–194
Brewer G D, 1973 *Politicians, Bureaucrats and the Consultant: A Critique of Urban
    Problem Solving* (Basic Books, New York)
Cesario F J, 1973 "Parameter estimation in spatial interaction modelling" *Environment
    and Planning* 5 503–518
Coelho J D, Williams H C W L, 1977 "The design of land use plans through locational
    surplus maximisation" WP-202, School of Geography, University of Leeds, Leeds
Cripps E L, Foot D H S, 1969 "A land-use model for subregional planning" *Regional
    Studies* 3 243–268
Echenique M, 1968 "Urban systems: towards an explorative model" WP-7, Centre for
    Land Use and Built Form Studies, University of Cambridge, Cambridge
Evans A W, 1970 "Some properties of trip distribution methods" *Transportation
    Research* 4 19–36
Evans A W, 1971 "The calibration of trip distribution models with exponential or
    similar cost functions" *Transportation Research* 5 15–38
Forrester J W, 1969 *Urban Dynamics* (The MIT Press, Cambridge, Mass)
Garin R A, 1966 "A matrix formulation of the Lowry model for intra-metropolitan
    activity location" *Journal of the American Institute of Planners* 32 361–364
Harris B, 1966 "Note on aspects of equilibrium in urban growth models" Department
    of City and Regional Planning, University of Pennsylvania, Philadelphia, Penn.
Himmelblau D M, 1972 *Applied Nonlinear Programming* (McGraw-Hill, New York)
Kain J F, 1975 "Development of a computer model of urban housing markets" in
    Urban Development Models Eds R Baxter, M Echenique, J Owers (The Construction
    Press, Lancaster) pp 85–99
Kowalik J, Osborne M R, 1968 *Methods for Unconstrained Optimisation Problems*
    (Elsevier, New York)
LCC, 1964 *London Traffic Survey: Volume I: Existing Traffic and Travel
    Characteristics in Greater London* (London County Council, County Hall, London)
Lowry I S, 1964 "A model of metropolis" RM-4035-RC, Rand Corporation, Santa
    Monica, Calif.
Massey D B, 1973 "The basic: service categorisation in planning" *Regional Studies*
    7 1–15
McGill S M, 1975 "Balancing factor methods in urban and regional analysis" WP-124,
    School of Geography, University of Leeds, Leeds
McGill S M, 1976 "Theoretical properties of biporportional matrix adjustments"
    WP-113, School of Geography, University of Leeds, Leeds
Murchland J D, 1977 "Convergence of gravity model operations" in *Proceedings of
    the Fifth Annual Meeting of Planning Transport Research and Computation:
    Transportation Models Seminar*, PTRC, London
Paelinck J H P, 1970 "Dynamic urban growth models" *Papers of the Regional Science
    Association* 24 25–37
Robillard P, Stewart N F, 1974 "Iterative numerical methods for trip distribution
    models" *Transportation Research* 8 575–582

Scarf H, 1973 *The Computation of Economic Equilibria* (Yale University Press, New Haven, Conn.)

Simmonds D, 1976 *Nonlinear Programming for Operations Research* (Prentice-Hall, Englewood Cliffs, NJ)

Stonebraker M, 1972 "A simplification of Forrester's model of an urban area" *IEEE Transactions on Systems, Man and Cybernetics, SMC-2* 468–471

Varga R S, 1962 *Matrix Iterative Analysis* (Prentice-Hall, London)

Williams I N, 1977 "A method for solving spatial allocation models with maximum constraints", unpublished paper, Martin Centre for Architectural and Urban Studies, University of Cambridge, Cambridge

Life-cycle Factors and Housing Choice in the Private Sector: A Temporal Economic Study Using Path Analytic Approaches

D BONNAR
Scottish Development Agency†

1 Introduction

This paper examines the influence of life-cycle stage on the purchase decisions of households in the private housing market. The concept of the life cycle plays an important part in our understanding of the demand for housing, and the implications of this demand for urban ecology and residential mobility. Much of the early work on urban ecology which took place at the University of Chicago in the 1920s suggested that the city functions like an organism, sorting and shifting the population into appropriate ecological niches. Urban development was seen to be a response to subsocial processes of invasion and succession whereby land uses in more central locations invade and force out land uses in adjacent more peripheral locations. However, as the study of urban ecology developed, there was a reaction to the absence of any explicit references to the more social aspects of behaviour or to the influence of individual choice. Later students of human ecology reformulated the processual elements of the earlier models and Johnston (1971) suggests that the invasion and succession model can be replaced by one based on the life cycle,

> "In many ways the family cycle model is merely an extension of the invasion and succession model and is fused with it if the housing markets are used as the organising elements."

Models of residential mobility based on the life cycle have been proposed by numerous authors (for example Lansing et al, 1964). These suggest that intraurban migration arises from the bringing together of households with their space requirements, and that this has a specific spatial dimension. Critical life-cycle stages are hypothesised as follows:

(1) A pre-child phase wherein after marriage both parents are working, have low levels of saving and will therefore live in rented accommodation in accessible (city centre) locations.

(2) The childbearing stage puts pressure on the household's existing amount of space and creates a demand for more spacious accommodation.

---

† The views expressed in this paper are those of the author and not necessarily of the Agency.

With the wife no longer working, accessibility is less important and, in association with increased space consumption, there is a tendency for the family to purchase a dwelling in the suburbs. These tendencies are consolidated during the child-rearing and child-launching stages.
(3) The post-child phase sees the departure of children to establish their own households, which will tend to be in central rented accommodation. While the children commence the cycle, the parents, having reduced space needs, will adjust their house consumption accordingly. After the death of one spouse, the survivor will move to live with a married child. Johnston (1971) suggests that this life-cyclical process is the source of the concentric life-cycle pattern found in studies of urban ecology.

Rossi (1955), in a study of the social psychology of residential mobility, suggested that household movement was a stimulus–response phenomenon, the stimulus to move arising from stress induced by space shortages. These space shortages were due, in the main, to objective life-cycle factors. The life-cycle model thus presents a picture of a smooth adjustment process of households being matched to their space needs. However, this picture is evidently an incomplete one since there are obvious factors other than space requirements which influence demand in the private housing market. This is evident from some of the studies noted above. For example, Rossi observes that not all households with objective space needs actually undertake mobility. Other research work has observed that a move to a smaller dwelling does not always accompany the post-child phase (Winnick, 1957), and that different life-cycle stages have different rates of mobility (Harris and Clausen, 1967). However, perhaps the biggest omission of the life-cycle model is that it fails to identify the nature of the relationship between life-cycle stage and the effective demand for housing in the market place.

There are two main schools of thought on the nature of the relationship. Some writers (Alonso, 1964; Cullingworth, 1965) suggest that households in the more expansive stages of the cycle have higher propensities to consume housing than those in the stages where household sizes are smaller. On the other hand, some authors have suggested that the households with peak space needs are also likely to be the ones with the smallest budget constraints. For example, it has been suggested that the peak demand for housing space coincides with the period of maximum household earnings, allowing space demands to be satisfied (Robson, 1975). On the other hand, Doling (1976) suggests that life-cycle stage is related to effective demand and hence to residential mobility because of the wealth which has accrued to the household during its expansion. He suggests that a major element of this expansion is in the form of existing housing property which can be capitalised and used for the purpose of purchasing a dwelling which satisfies the household's space needs. The differences in the two concepts of demand relate to different emphases on the modus operandi of life-cycle stage in the housing market, that is, whether the effect is by virtue of the space preferences of households or through its relation to income and wealth.

It is evident that the nature of the relationship between life-cycle stage and the consumption of housing is not as straightforward as the life-cycle model would imply. The precise effect of the life-cycle is all the more difficult to identify owing to the highly complex character of the housing market, in which a multiplicity of factors condition the relationship between household demand and housing supply.

2 Problems of housing market analysis

There are numerous difficulties involved in any study of the housing market, which stem both from the nature of the good 'housing' and from the method by which house purchases are financed. Some of these problems are particularly relevant to the issues raised in this paper. First, a house must be understood not only as a consumption good but also as a capital good which is durable and which delivers a flow of services—for example, space, shelter, and accessibility—over time. This quality of housing gives it potential as an investment good. The life-cycle model ignores this aspect of housing demand and considers housing only as a supply of the service of accommodation. The nature of the demand for housing will therefore vary according to the relative importance to the purchaser of housing as a consumption good and as an investment good. The characteristics of this mix will of course depend upon the rate of return available from housing and from other investment goods. An important relationship in this regard is the expected rate of change in house prices relative to the price of other commodities and other investment goods. This could have the effect of altering the nature of the relationship between house purchase for consumption and for investment reasons, and could evidently affect the relationship between household mobility and life-cycle stage. On the other hand, if the demand for housing is elastic with respect to price then if house prices rise faster than other goods we would expect a shift in the composition of the average bundle of goods purchased with an increased demand for goods other than housing. However, as Whitehead (1974) observes, since house purchase is normally financed through an intermediate institution (usually a building society), the price which is relevant to the buyer is not simply the asking price but is the cost of credit and there need not be perfect covariation between fluctuations in asking price and fluctuations in the cost of financing the purchase.

Similarly, since housing is not simply a consumption good but is also an investment good, higher rates of inflation, if they are expected to continue, will increase demand since households will be attempting to maximise consumption, not only because of space needs but out of the desire to use housing as a hedge against inflation. This aspect is of particular importance in the British housing context where interest payments on loans for house purchase can be offset against income tax. The combination of inflation and the existence of tax relief make it attractive to spend as much as possible on housing. For example, Harrington (1972) shows that if the annual rate of inflation is 6% then an individual paying around 8% for money borrowed from a building society and paying income tax at a rate of 32% will in fact, once tax relief has been taken into account, be paying a net real rate of interest which is negative. The Nationwide Building Society (1970) commissioned a survey of new purchasers and found that 35% gave investment as the main reason for buying. However, Redwood (1974) suggests that when high rates of inflation are accompanied by high rates of unemployment there is a reluctance for purchasers to take on the financial burden of the maximum possible mortgage which would be allowed on the basis of their salary, for fear of being unable to service the loan in the future owing to redundancy. Whatever the effects on demand, it is evident that during 1969–1972 the average price of new houses purchased by mortgages rose faster than the average price of consumer goods as measured by the retail price index (figure 1). Figure 1 also demonstrates that the average price of new mortgaged houses varied in relation to average earnings—a situation with evident consequences for effective housing demand over time.

The second factor having implications for the demand for housing is the lending activity of the financial institutions. Because of the large amount of finance required for house purchase, it is necessary for the vast majority of purchasers to supplement their existing wealth with a loan to be repaid with interest over several years. Building societies dominate the activity of lending for house purchase, and have provided over 80% of the amount advanced as mortgages for house purchase in recent years. Building societies operate by lending a borrower a multiple of his income, using the house to be purchased as security for the loan. However, in order to lend money to house purchasers, building societies must themselves borrow money from investors and they are therefore in competition with other

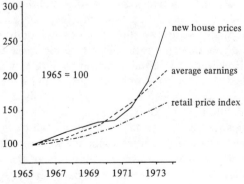

Figure 1. Inflation trends.

forms of investment, such as unit trusts and national savings. If the
interest rates offered by societies are competitive then their deposit levels
will rise and they will have more money available to lend for house
purchase. Such a situation obtained in the period after 1969 when both
private and institutional investors deposited large amounts with the building
societies. This resulted from a coincidence of factors, namely rising
incomes and increasing propensities to save, allied with uncertainty on the
stock market and generally falling rates of interest. However, this situation
reversed in 1972 when the building societies lost deposits to other forms
of investment and to consumption as the general level of interest rates fell
further behind the rate of inflation (Whitehead, 1974), bringing about a
mortgage famine coupled with very high levels of house prices.

In periods when deposits are high the building societies can adopt more
generous lending policies, for example by offering higher multiples of a
borrower's income, by including wife's earnings for mortgage purposes or
by extending the length of loan repayments, although policy can vary from
one society to another. Between 1969 and 1971, the British building
societies in total increased the amount of new advances from £1587
million to £2741 million, and increased the number of mortgage advances
from 460000 to 653000. This period was of course characterised by
unprecedented rates of house price inflation. Richardson (1971) contends
that the lending policies of building societies are central to the determination
of housing consumption. Indeed he goes so far as to maintain that because
of the taxation advantages referred to above and because of the investment
nature of housing, most households will tend to borrow the maximum
allowed. In this situation, where building societies either constrain
individuals to borrow a certain maximum multiple of their income or
where borrowers automatically borrow as much as they can, estimation of
demand from analysis of the relationship between price and income will
be spurious since such estimates will measure the effects of building
society policy rather than individual propensities to consume housing (Ball
and Kirwan, 1975). Byatt et al (1973), on the other hand, insist that
house expenditures do not simply reflect building society policy but are
true reflections of individuals' demand functions and they cite as evidence
the fact that when areas with low average house prices are compared to
areas with high average prices then the ratio of average mortgage to
income is also lower. However, the period analysed by Byatt et al was
1967–1968 and 1970 and it is doubtful whether they would conclude
that "the availability of building society funds ... (has) ... only a minor
influence" in the light of the post-1970 experience.

The fact that building societies are lending institutions which borrow
short and lend long might mean that they consider the long-term earning
prospects of the individual as well as his earnings at the time of the mortgage
application. Such a policy would lend credence to Barbolet's (1969)
suggestion that building societies discriminate against manual workers

when lending money as they are prepared to offer higher loan-to-income ratios to nonmanual workers, whom they consider to have better earning potential. Societies can also exercise a degree of benevolence in their lending, for example in discriminating in favour of first-time buyers.

The heterogeneous character of the housing commodity and the possible shift in the mix of the bundle of goods which the purchaser buys as a house, as changes occur in the context in which the housing market operates, have important welfare implications. In effect, the flow of housing services qua accommodation to the population within a housing market area will not simply depend on the propensity to consume housing qua accommodation as the life-cycle model suggests. As MacLennan (1977) observes,

> "In condition of slowly rising absolute and relative prices, then it was perhaps legitimate to abstract time from urban housing market models. However, under period of rapid inflation such as in the United Kingdom since 1968, it appears that rapid wealth transfers can occur in the urban housing market."

It would seem, then, that the role of life-cycle stage in the demand for housing space and hence intraurban migration should be analysed not only in relation to its effect on income and on housing wealth, but also in terms of possible changes which might be expected to occur in the relation between life cycle and demand as the context in which the housing market operates changes. In the analysis which follows, we will examine the influence of life-cycle stage on the purchase of housing in rapidly changing market conditions.

3 Data base
The data to be analysed consist of the details of the sales of the dwellings built by one large builder in the South East of England over the period 1965–1973. The transactions involved dwellings in nine different estates grouped in a semicircle on the south and west of London. Estates at greater and lesser distances were omitted to ensure that differences in distance from central London were kept relatively small. In any one year and on any one estate, a variety of house sizes were built in terraced, semidetached, and detached units and there is no significant tendency to build houses of different types and sizes on different estates. Thus for any one year, the range of house prices reflects differences in the average dwelling size from one price group to another and price in any one year is a good proxy for dwelling size.

The building company has a quota arrangement with one building society and the mortgage details of house sales are analysed in this paper. Information was collected of the mortgage, income, age, marital status, number of children, previous tenure, and occupation as well as the price

paid for the house. Figure 2 shows a comparison between the annual
average house price in the sample and the trend in the prices of new
houses mortgaged by the Nationwide Building Society in the South East
of England. It can be seen that the prices in our sample experienced a
very similar trend to those in the much larger Nationwide sample.

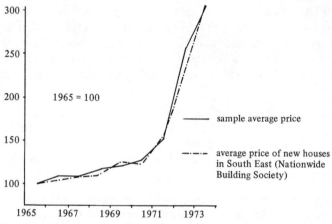

Figure 2. House price trends.

4 Fluctuations in building society performance

As we observed above, building societies have fluctuating performances in
the attraction of funds, relative to the competitiveness of other institutions
in the finance market. The success of any building society in attracting
funds is indicated by its net receipts, that is, its share and deposit receipts
minus its withdrawals of principal. The trend in the annual net receipts
for the building society examined in this study is shown in figure 3. Also
shown are the changes in the rate of interest in the building society's
share accounts—in line with the recommendation of the Building Societies
Association—grossed up at the standard rate of income tax. Figure 3 also
shows the comparable trends in the rates of interest offered by competitors
of the building societies in the finance market. It can be seen that the
rates of increase in net investment receipts are highest in those years when
the building society's share interest rate is significantly higher than
competing areas, that is, in 1967 and between 1970 and 1972.

These increased rates in the net inflow of funds were used partly to
increase the society's rates of investment and cash to total assets (the
liquidity ratio) but also to increase the total amount advanced for
mortgages as shown in figure 3. The trend in funds advanced for mortgages
lagged somewhat behind that of the net inflow of funds. Figure 3 also
shows the trend in the number of mortgages advanced, which showed
significantly less volatility than the amount of money advanced. When
the number of advances is broken down by new and existing dwellings,

the former are shown to exhibit greater stability than the latter, indicating the inelasticity of new housing supply. The fact that the number of advances remained relatively constant obviously affected the average mortgage size and this is shown in figure 3.

When we note that this process was common to all building societies, the implications for house price inflation are evident. The fluctuations in the net flow of funds could also have implications for lending policy and could alter the extent into which space demand as indicated by life-cycle stage is translated into effective demand.

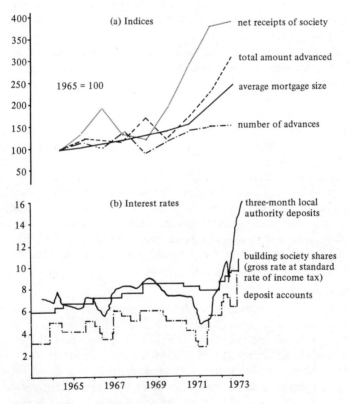

Figure 3. Building society performance.

5 Methodology

There are two major methodological problems involved in an assessment of the role of life-cycle stage in the process of housing choice. The first difficulty that we encounter is the definition of life-cycle stage, which is evidently not simply a linear function of age. The second problem relates to the need to identify the extent to which life-cycle stage acts directly, that is by virtue of its effect on the propensity to consume housing, or indirectly by virtue of its effect on budget factors (namely income and wealth).

5.1 Measurement of life-cycle stage

There have been numerous studies of residential mobility which have employed different indices of life-cycle stage and which claim to confirm the life-cycle hypothesis. For example, Pickvance (1974) uses marital status as an index of life-cycle stage although conceding its crudeness. Fredland (1974) employs a quadratic function of age whereas many factorial ecologies have identified factors which although variable in composition are regarded as representing life-cycle stage.

The main problem in defining a measure which corresponds to the concept is that clearly not all households pass through the sequence of critical stages. For instance some individuals never marry whereas some married households do not have children. Speare (1970) points out that age is not an appropriate index because it need not necessarily correlate with life-cycle stage, and he suggests that a composite index of marital status and age be employed. However, in this paper the main characteristic of the life-cycle concept on which we are concentrating is its association with space needs. Consequently life-cycle stage is measured in dummy variable form by giving the variable the value 0 for single households, households about to be married, and married households with no children where the age is less than forty. The value of 1 is given to those married households with one or more children. By omitting those households aged over forty with no children we are excluding from the analysis those who are in the post-child phase and whose space needs are in accordance with those of the first life-cycle group. However, Doling (1976) suggests that the income and wealth characteristics of the post-child group are such as to distinguish them from the pre-child group, which implies that they should be separated for analytical purposes.

5.2 Path analysis

As pointed out above, the methodology employed must be capable of separating out and measuring the effects of life cycle occurring through propensity to consume and those effects arising from budget differences. Path analysis is an approach which allows us to estimate the way in which any independent variable which we have specified has a direct effect on housing demand or whether its influence occurs through the action of other factors. For example, Barbolet (1969) has suggested that occupational status (that is, whether manual or nonmanual) affects the amount which building societies are prepared to lend. Path analysis allows us to assess whether and by how much occupational status has a direct causal effect on the amount of mortgage borrowed or whether any effect occurs through the fact that manual workers have different incomes on average from white-collar workers.

Duncan (1966) has observed that any a priori causal interpretation of data rests on a minimum of two assumptions: (1) concerning the ordering of the variables in the causal model, (2) concerning the variables which are not taken into account and which require to be represented as uncorrelated residuals. Thus, our first task is to postulate a causal model. In this study two models will be presented in increasing order of complexity, which are designed to answer certain unresolved questions posed in the earlier discussion.

6 Occupational status and mortgage allowance

The first path-analytic approach is designed to investigate whether economic status does in fact affect mortgage allowance directly, or whether the effect is an indirect one through income, and also to elaborate the principles of path analysis. We can present the relationship between status, income and mortgage in the form of a path diagram (figure 4).

This diagram obeys the conventions of path analysis (Duncan, 1966), that is, there is an assumption of at least a weak causal order among the variables, and arrows lead from determining to dependent variables. Thus in figure 4 the hypothetical causal system involving economic status, income, and amount of mortgage advance is presented. It is suggested that whether the individual is manual or nonmanual affects his income rather than vice versa, and also that income and status affect mortgage rather than vice versa. If our causal system is linear, additive, and unidirectional, then any changes in a variable X_j which are brought about by changes in the variable X_i through both direct and indirect paths can be denoted by a linear function having the form

$$X_j = C_{ji} X_i ,$$

where C_{ji} is the 'effect coefficient'. One of our tasks is to separate the indirect and direct components of this coefficient.

In figure 4, E_1, E_2, and E_3 are disturbance terms representing the effects of unmeasured variables such that the causal relations can be expressed by simultaneous equations;

$$X_1 = b_{12 \cdot 3} X_2 + b_{13 \cdot 2} X_3 + E_1 ,$$
$$X_2 = b_{23} X_3 + E_2 ,$$
$$X_3 = E_3 .$$

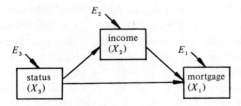

Figure 4. Expected causal paths.

The final equation indicates that X_3 depends only upon influences outside the causal model. This system of equations is known as a recursive system because there is no reciprocal causation between any two variables, for example, income can affect mortgage but mortgage cannot affect income. On the assumption that the disturbance terms in each equation are uncorrelated with each other and also with all of the determining variables that appear in their equations, these recursive equations have the property that unbiased estimates of the b values can be obtained from simple least-squares methods of estimation, that is, by the use of a regression model incorporating estimates of the determining and dependent variables (Blalock, 1967a). The size of any causal path is found by taking each lower-order variable in the causal system and regressing it against the higher-order variables as independent variables, for example the present problem is approached by fitting two regression models, the first of which has mortgage as the dependent variable and status and income as predictors, the second of which has income as the dependent variable with status as the independent variable. In general, if the causal system contains n variables then $(n-1)$ regressions will usually be required.

In the path analysis literature two approaches to the measurement of causal paths appear. The first approach favours the use of standardised regression coefficients whereas the second emphasises the benefits of unstandardised coefficients. By convention (Wright, 1960) the former are referred to as 'path coefficients' while the latter are termed 'path regression coefficients'. The benefit accruing from the use of standardised coefficients is that meaningful comparisons can be made between variables measured on different scales. In this approach each variable is measured on a scale whose unit is the standard deviation of that variable in the sample population (Duncan, 1969), that is, the path coefficient allows us to assess how much of the variance in the dependent variable is accounted for by an independent variable through direct and indirect paths. The second benefit relates to the assessment of unmeasured variables which, as Wright (1960) points out, can only be dealt with in standardised form.

However, there is a problem associated with path coefficients which limits their utility in comparing populations. This difficulty arises from the fact that the path coefficient is a function of the standard deviation of the determining variable (other determining variables being held constant). Thus, when comparing the effects of a particular variable on other variables *between* populations, one should note that if a variable has a low standard deviation in one population then the path coefficients leading from this variable will be relatively small (Blalock, 1967b). However, the change in the dependent variable produced by a unit change in the determining variable may well be the same in both populations, that is, the 'causal laws' linking the two variables may be the same (Blalock, 1964). The constancy of the causal law would be evidenced by the similarity of the path regression coefficients.

In the present study there are reasons for using both types of coefficient. The path coefficient allows us to compare the contribution of variables measured on different scales within a population whereas the path regression coefficient allows us to look for similarity in causal processes between populations. The direct and indirect contributions of one variable to the variation in another is found from the path coefficient. The path coefficient also allows us to examine the paths leading from unmeasured variables, and hence to evaluate the usefulness of our models.

These approaches can be demonstrated in relation to the causal system displayed in figure 4. The paths from economic status can be divided into that having a direct effect on the amount of mortgage and that having an indirect effect via income. These effects are found from the path coefficients (p_{ji}) as follows:

direct effect $= p_{13}$,
indirect effect $= p_{12}(p_{23})$.

The procedure for estimating the path regression coefficients, c_{ji}, is similar. Algorithms for tracing paths are given by Duncan (1966) and Turner and Stevens (1959) for path coefficients and path regression coefficients respectively.

A simplified interpretation of the data would suggest that economic status has an effect on the size of the mortgage ($r_{13} > 0$). However, it will be seen that part of the correlation between status and mortgage is spurious, that is, it can be accounted for by the indirect path. The direct importance of occupational status to the amount of mortgage borrowed for any one year can be assessed from the values of p_{13} in table 1. From this table it can be seen in the years 1965 and 1966 that the variance in mortgage accounted for by the direct path was greater than that via the indirect path, that is, for these years most of the correlation between occupational status and mortgage size was due to the direct influence of status rather than being explicable by the relation between status and income.

Thus, it would seem that in 1965 and 1966 the occupational status of the purchaser played a significant part in determining the amount of mortgage advanced, even when the fact that status has an effect on income (confer p_{23} values), with nonmanual purchasers having higher incomes, is allowed for. When the criterion of significance employed by Duncan (1969) is used, that is, when coefficients whose absolute values are less than their standard errors are eliminated, it is evident that all of the direct paths from status are at least weakly significant except in 1968 and 1971. However, subsequent to 1966, with the exception of 1969, there is a general trend for the relationship between mortgage and status to derive from the indirect path through income.

The reduction in the direct importance of status in 1967 can be attributed to the fact that the net receipts of the building society were at a record level, allowing manual incomes to be assessed more favourably. However, in 1968 this situation reversed but the response of the society was not to reduce the effectiveness of manual workers' incomes for borrowing purposes. Instead, it was to reduce the number of lower-income manual workers entering the submarket. This is evidenced by comparing the c_{23} values for 1968 and 1967. This trend was continued in 1969 where the differences in income between manual and nonmanual workers was reduced still further ($c_{23} = 150\cdot08$). Consequently, the indirect effect of status in 1969 was the lowest for the study period although the direct effect was significant. It should be noted that 1968 and 1969 were years in which the building society share rate was not competitive with other forms of investment, with a resultant reduction in net receipts. However, although the net receipts of the society fell in 1968, the amount advanced for mortgages on newly built dwellings *increased* and the effect was to increase mortgage relative to income ($c_{12} = 1\cdot74$) in this submarket.

After 1969 the building society was once again competitive for funds although in 1970 the size of mortgage relative to income (with status held

Table 1. Path coefficients (p) and path regression coefficients (c) for model 1.

Year	p_{12}	p_{13}	p_{23}	Direct effect	Indirect effect	r_{13}
1965	0·57	0·22	0·33	0·22	0·19	0·41
1966	0·61	0·17	0·23	0·17	0·14	0·31
1967	0·58	0·08[a]	0·27	0·08	0·16	0·24
1968	0·73	0·01[b]	0·19	0·01	0·14	0·15
1969	0·61	0·10[a]	0·11[a]	0·10	0·07	0·17
1970	0·46	0·09[a]	0·23	0·09	0·10	0·19
1971	0·57	0·01[b]	0·35	0·01	0·20	0·21
1972	0·70	0·07[a]	0·26	0·07	0·18	0·25
1973	0·73	0·09[a]	0·25	0·09	0·18	0·27

Year	e_1	e_2	c_{12}	c_{13}	c_{23}
1965	0·73	0·94	1·32	401·80	255·35
1966	0·74	0·97	1·53	398·17	335·32
1967	0·79	0·96	1·58	210·95[a]	249·87
1968	0·69	0·98	1·70	19·38[b]	222·91
1969	0·78	0·99	1·35	300·10[a]	150·08[a]
1970	0·72	0·97	0·95	231·75[a]	268·06
1971	0·82	0·94	1·32	19·04[b]	397·82
1972	0·69	0·97	1·65	319·33[a]	508·99
1973	0·65	0·97	1·90	467·58[a]	479·17

[a] Value shown is less than 1 s.e.   [b] Value shown is greater than 1 s.e. but less than 2 s.e.
All other coefficient values are greater than 2 s.e.

constant) was the lowest of the study period ($c_{12} = 0 \cdot 95$) but rose consistently after this. After 1970 the importance of the direct effect of status was consistently lower than that through the indirect effect, particularly in 1971 when the building society experienced a rapid increase in net receipts.

Thus, Barbolet's (1969) thesis does appear correct in that in the British housing market there is a relationship between the amount of mortgage advanced and the occupational status of the applicant and that this does not simply result from the fact that manual workers have lower incomes. However, the direct influence of status on mortgage has declined over the years both in absolute terms (when we take house price inflation into consideration), as shown by the c_{13} values, and relative to the indirect effect (cf p_{13} and p_{23} values). The direct relationship between occupational status and the amount of mortgage borrowed is not consistent, however, and seems to be related to the way the building society chooses to deal with changes in its competitive position in the finance market.

7 The adequacy of the model

The degree to which the model outlined in figure 4 explains the variation in mortgage size can be assessed by examining the estimates of the residual paths E_1 and E_2. The estimates of the residual paths will approach zero if all of the variations in mortgage size and income are explained within the model, and if all variables are measured without error. The closer the residual-path estimate approaches $1 \cdot 0$, the less adequate is the model. Table 1 shows the sizes of the residual paths, where e_1 and e_2 are the relevant estimates.

It can be seen that variation in mortgage is better explained by the model than variation in income and that the 'fit' is not constant from year to year. This is to be expected, since there are other factors affecting mortgage size which we have not included. For example, the older the borrower the less likely, other things being equal, will be his prospects of obtaining a mortgage of a given size. Second, the housing career of the individual may be important. For example, borrowers with existing capital (possibly in the form of a previous house) may need to borrow less. These characteristics might not be independent of occupational status.

A second causal system designed to include some of these features of demand is proposed in figure 5. The dependent variable is price paid for the dwelling (including land cost), which, it is suggested, is a good proxy for the quantity of housing space consumed. The two factors previously discussed (status and income) are also included as these have been seen to affect mortgage prospects, and hence in all probability the price which can be paid. Previous tenure is also included in the model because of its possible implications for expenditure on house purchase owing to the use of assets derived from the sale of a previous dwelling.

    The model suggests that the previous tenure of the purchaser is affected by his occupational status: several studies have noted that white-collar workers are more eager to own, and thus may be more likely to be previous owners. The model also posits a relationship between status and income. It is also suggested that life-cycle stage affects previous tenure; it would seem probable that the later the stage in the life cycle the more likely is previous owner-occupation. However, it has also been suggested that stage in the life cycle is related to income (Robson, 1975) and this is shown by the appropriate path in figure 5. A path is also shown between income and previous tenure. This assumes a link between present income, past income and hence previous tenure, although it is realised that this does not take account of sudden increases in income which may be a prelude to an adjustment of housing consumption. Nor does it account for the fact that previous renters may need higher incomes because of their lack of assets. However, the path-analytic procedure allows us to test the validity of any proposed causal link.

    As we have discussed, the life-cycle hypothesis assumes that, other things being equal, larger families consume more space. However, in this study, because of the nature of the sample of houses, house price is a good proxy for space consumed. Thus, we are positing a path leading from the life-cycle variable to price.

    The curved two-headed arrow in figure 5 represents an unanalysed correlation, that is, we are recognising that there may be a statistical association between status and the life-cycle variable, but that this association is noncausal, and derives from influences outside the model. Table 2 presents the path coefficients estimated by regression procedures. It is now possible to assess the role of life-cycle stage in the causal structure which we have hypothesised. The effects of life cycle can be

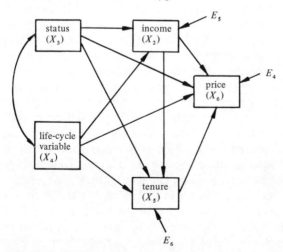

Figure 5. Second proposed causal system.

decomposed into four categories. There is, first, the effect which the life-cycle variable exerts on price directly; second, the effect which occurs via the path through tenure to price; third, a similar path through income; and fourth the effect due to the analysed correlation between life cycle and the other exogenous variable, occupational status.

The basic path analysis theorem can be expressed mathematically as

$$r_{ij} = \sum_q p_{iq} r_{jq}$$

(Duncan, 1966), that is, the correlation between two variables i and j is equal to the sum of the paths which lead directly from any variable q to X_i. Thus in figure 5, the correlation between life-cycle stage and price can be represented as the sum of

(a) the direct effect, p_{64},
(b) the indirect effect via tenure, $p_{65}(p_{54})$,
(c) the indrect path via income, $p_{24}(p_{62} + p_{65}p_{52})$,
(d) the 'common cause' effect, $r_{34}[p_{62}p_{23} + p_{65}(p_{52}p_{23} + p_{53})]$.

The sizes of these paths are represented in table 3 by path coefficients. The significance of any coefficient is assumed to be nil where the standard error of the coefficient is greater than its magnitude and to be weak where the coefficient is less than twice the standard error. From table 2 we can

Table 2. Path coefficients for model 2.

Year	p_{64}	p_{65}	p_{63}	p_{62}	p_{54}	p_{53}	p_{52}	p_{24}	p_{23}
1965	−0·04[b]	0·36	0·11[a]	0·59	0·70	0·03[b]	0·10[a]	0·29	0·28
1966	−0·02[b]	0·49	0·05[b]	0·45	0·53	−0·09[b]	−0·01[b]	0·23[a]	0·01[b]
1967	0·03[b]	0·42	0·15[a]	0·49	0·56	0·02[b]	0·00[b]	0·14[a]	0·20[a]
1968	0·06[b]	0·43	−0·01[b]	0·57	0·50	0·03[b]	0·09[b]	0·50	0·15[a]
1969	−0·01[b]	0·25	−0·12[a]	0·69	0·17[a]	−0·18[a]	0·15[a]	0·48	0·03[b]
1970	0·19	0·46	0·03[b]	0·26	0·30	−0·28	0·10[a]	0·31	0·28
1971	−0·04[b]	0·50	−0·01[b]	0·35	0·57	0·01[b]	−0·22	0·33	0·28
1972	0·09[a]	0·27	0·10[a]	0·58	0·32	0·11[a]	−0·13[a]	0·22	0·23
1973	0·10[a]	0·26	0·08[a]	0·64	0·50	−0·04[b]	−0·16[a]	0·20[a]	0·20[a]

	e_4	e_6	e_5	r_{46}	n
1965	0·60	0·67	0·91	0·42	74
1966	0·73	0·84	0·97	0·34	69
1967	0·72	0·83	0·98	0·28	95
1968	0·50	0·83	0·84	0·59	83
1969	0·61	0·95	0·87	0·38	56
1970	0·76	0·91	0·91	0·42	103
1971	0·81	0·84	0·89	0·33	123
1972	0·71	0·94	0·95	0·31	128
1973	0·68	0·87	0·96	0·33	80

[a] and [b] as in table 1.

see that life cycle as measured by the dummy variable is generally *insignificant*. In fact, most of the covariation between price and life-cycle stage, as measured by the life-cycle dummy, is *spurious*. For most years, the correlation between life cycle and price occurs through the indirect path via tenure, that is, most of the correlation between life cycle and price occurs because the later stage of the life cycle is associated with previous ownership and this is the main source of the effect on price (table 3). However, in 1968, 1969, and 1972 the main source of the relation between the life-cycle dummy and housing consumption is due to the fact that those in the later stage of the cycle tend to have larger incomes.

Doling (1976) presents evidence that heads of household under the age of forty who have children are more likely to pay a higher price for housing than those without children, and are more likely to be previous owners. This leads Doling to suggest that although "the demand by young families with children for more space is undoubtedly influenced by their changed family structure, the factor which allows them to act in the market appears to be that of increased wealth" since "the higher purchasing power of previous owners appears to match the housing choice of families at different stages in the life cycle". However, Doling looked at only one year and in fact it would appear that both income and housing wealth differences are important, with the relative importance of each being variable over time. We can examine the year-by-year interrelationships of life-cycle stage by examining the path regression coefficients which are presented in table 4. The slope coefficients of the bivariate regression of the dummy variable on price (b_{64}) and the correlation coefficients (r_{46}) are also shown.

When 1965, 1966, and 1967 are compared, it can be seen that there is a general reduction in the strength of the relationship between price and life-cycle stage as seen from the b_{64} and r_{46} values. The decline in the overall life-cycle–consumption relationship between 1965 and 1967 resulted principally from the reduction in the importance of the indirect path via

Table 3. The role of life-cycle stage evaluated by path coefficients.

Year	Direct effect	Indirect effect via previous tenure	Indirect effect via income	Shared effect	r_{46}
1965	−0·04	0·25	0·18	0·03	0·42
1966	−0·02	0·26	0·10	0·00	0·34
1967	0·03	0·23	0·07	−0·05	0·28
1968	0·05	0·22	0·31	0·01	0·59
1969	−0·01	0·04	0·35	0·00	0·38
1970	0·19	0·14	0·10	0·01	0·42
1971	−0·04	0·29	0·08	0·00	0·33
1972	0·09	0·09	0·12	0·01	0·31
1973	0·10	0·13	0·19	0·01	0·33

income as can be seen from table 3. The explanation for the decline in
the role of this path is partly due to the decreased role of the path from
income to price (cf c_{62} values in table 4). This occurred because there
was a slight reduction in the rates of average mortgage to average income
as shown in table 5, coupled with a rise in average house prices, which
thereby increased the relative importance of assets in house purchase.
This occurred even though the building society was competitive for funds
and there was a consequent increase in the size of the average mortgage
granted. However, the increase in price was such as to reduce mortgage as
a percentage of price, as shown in table 5. Furthermore, part of the

Table 4. Path regression coefficients for model 2 (levels of significance as in table 2).

Year	c_{64}	c_{65}	c_{63}	c_{62}	c_{54}
1965	−88·1	818·1	248·9	1·6	0·7
1966	−38·5	801·7	87·7	1·0	0·5
1967	47·8	711·2	271·9	1·2	0·5
1968	168·2	1382·0	−34·1	1·6	0·5
1969	−33·9	766·4	−420·3	1·9	0·2
1970	441·0	1060·4	65·9	0·5	0·3
1971	−101·5	1269·6	−26·5	0·9	0·6
1972	745·3	2486·7	777·7	2·2	0·3
1973	826·8	3057·2	728·9	3·0	0·4

	c_{53}	c_{52}	c_{24}	c_{23}	b_{64}
1965	0·03	0·00012	232·2	236·1	887·3
1966	−0·09	−0·00002	160·2	5·9	518·8
1967	0·02	0·00000	95·3	147·6	441·1
1968	0·03	0·00008	516·9	160·8	1731·5
1969	−0·21	0·00014	507·3	32·6	1091·9
1970	−0·31	0·00009	352·2	344·9	980·8
1971	0·01	−0·00021	343·2	298·2	841·3
1972	0·09	−0·00005	466·8	473·2	2419·0
1973	−0·03	−0·00006	364·3	404·1	2839·0

Table 5. Relation of mortgage to income and house price.

Year	Average mortgage/ average income	Mortgage as percentage of price
1965	2·85	76·82
1966	2·70	75·85
1967	2·69	72·28
1968	2·78	76·99
1969	2·62	75·90
1970	2·59	72·48
1971	2·73	70·39
1972	2·89	58·66
1973	2·98	55·96

increase in net receipts which took place in 1967 was used, not for increased lending, but to increase the liquidity rates of the society from $13\cdot3$ in 1966 to $17\cdot3$ in 1967.

In 1968 and 1969 the influence of life-cycle stage on housing consumption was due mainly to the indirect effect of income and in 1969 the tendency for households later in the life-cycle stage to be previous owners is the least significant of the study period (cf p_{54}).

In 1968 the total amount advanced by the society increased, probably in response to the high liquidity level which had been reached in 1967 and which was reduced to $12\cdot5$ in 1968. Consequently, there was a 15% increase in the average mortgage granted and also an increase in the average size of mortgage relative to income (cf table 5). These two factors, coupled with the fact that average house prices rose by only 8%, meant that mortgage formed a larger percentage of house price on average and that income was a more important determinant of price. The large income difference between the life-cycle stages in 1968—the later group having incomes higher by an average of £516·90—and the fact that the building society was granting mortgages which were a relatively high factor of income, meant that the indirect path via income was the main cause of the life-cycle–consumption relationship. The reduction in the competitiveness of the building society for funds in 1968 had the effect of reducing somewhat the amount of mortgage relative to income to $2\cdot62$, as shown in table 5. This reduced the importance of income effects relative to previous tenure effects (cf p_{62} and p_{65} values), meaning that previous owners paid an average £1060·40 more for a house.

The only year in which the later life-cycle group shows a significant difference in the propensity to consume housing independent of income and previous tenure differences is 1970. One possible reason for this could be that, in 1970, house prices were rising more slowly than either incomes or the retail price index and this could have reduced the role of housing as an investment good such that a purchaser's consumption was more likely to reflect his space needs. This hypothesis is partly substantiated by the fact that mortgage size as a factor of income fell to $2\cdot59$ even though the building society was competitive for funds.

However, this situation was short-lived, and in 1971 the income factor increased to $2\cdot73$. This situation probably arose because of the substantial increase in net receipts which allowed the society to lend freely. At the same time, the acceleration of the general inflation rate coupled with stable building society interest charges reduced the real payments for a mortgage considerably and made house purchase an attractive investment. This increase in demand resulted in rising house prices and the average price of the sample increased by 19% between 1970 and 1971. Thus, although mortgages increased in relation to income, the rise in prices meant that the ownership of assets, in the form of an existing house, increased in importance. Previous ownership increased the price paid by an average of £1269·60 (cf c_{65} values in table 4).

In 1972 and 1973, the net receipts of the society increased substantially over the 1971 level and the amount advanced for new mortgages rose considerably. Previous ownership on average increased the price paid by £2486·70 in 1972 and by £3057·20 in 1973. However, the increasing income factor, which reached almost three in 1973, made income the most important determinant of price paid (cf p_{65} and p_{62} values in table 3). Life-cycle differences had only a weak effect on the propensity to consume housing and the main impact was through indirect paths.

8 Conclusion

This paper has shown that the impact of life-cycle stage on housing consumption is largely a result of changes in income and accumulated wealth. However, the relative importance of these factors appears to be variable according to changes in the financial context in which the housing market operates and according to changes in the rates of general and house price inflation. The absolute effect of previous tenure on price paid increases through time. This is due partly to the fact that a building society offers only a percentage of total house price and, as house prices rise, the difference between mortgage and price also rises, thus improving the position of those with existing assets. It is also due to the fact that— even when the larger factors of income offered by societies are taken into consideration—the rate of increase of house price inflation was such that the size of the mortgage as a percentage of price decreased, thereby increasing the importance of nonmortgage elements.

Changes in housing market conditions have important welfare implications since there appears to be little evidence that the higher space demands of larger families can be translated into space consumption by virtue of increased propensities to consume housing. Thus, the opportunity for larger families to purchase larger houses of a particular quality depends on their having either higher incomes and—increasingly in importance—on the degree to which they have existing property.

It is also clear that occupational status has only a weak effect on the consumption of housing (cf p_{63} values). Thus the weak status effect on mortgage which was identified by the analysis of the first model is generally not translated into an effect on house price, perhaps owing to the tendency of manual workers to use personal savings in house purchase.

Acknowledgement. This paper forms part of a research programme undertaken in the Department of Geography, University of Reading for which the support of the SSRC is gratefully acknowledged.

References
Alonso W, 1964 "The historic and the structural theories of urban form: their implications for urban renewal" *Land Economics* **XL** (2) 227-231

Ball M, Kirwan R, 1975 "The economics of an urban housing market, Bristol Area Study" RP-15, Centre for Environmental Studies, London

Barbolet R H, 1969 "Housing classes and the socio-ecological system" UWP-4, Centre for Environmental Studies, London

Blalock H M, 1964 *Causal Inferences in Non-experimental Research* (University of North Carolina Press, Chapel Hill)

Blalock H M, 1967a "Causal inferences, closed populations and measures of association" *American Political Science Review* **61** 130-136

Blalock H M, 1967b "Path coefficients versus regression coefficients" *American Journal of Sociology* **72** 675-676

Byatt I C R, Holmans A E, Laidler D E W, 1973 "Income and the demand for housing: some evidence for Great Britain" in *Essays in Modern Economics: The Proceedings of the Association of University Teachers of Economics: Aberystwyth, 1972* Eds M Parkin, A R Nobay (Longmans, London)

Cullingworth J B, 1965 *English Housing Trends* Occasional Papers on Social Administration 13 (Bell, London)

Doling J, 1976 "The family life-cycle and housing choice" *Urban Studies* **13** 55-58

Duncan O D, 1966 "Path analysis: sociological examples" *American Journal of Sociology* **72** 1-16

Duncan O D, 1969 "Inheritance of poverty or inheritance of race" in *On Understanding Poverty* Ed. D P Moynihan (Basic Books, New York) pp 85-110

Fredland D R, 1974 *Residential Mobility and Home Purchase* (D C Heath, Lexington, Mass)

Harrington R L, 1972 "Housing—supply and demand" *National Westminster Bank Quarterly Review* May 43-54

Harris A I, Clausen R, 1967 *Labour Mobility in Great Britain 1953-1963* (HMSO, London)

Johnston R J, 1971 *Urban Residential Patterns* (Bell, London)

Lansing J B, Muell E, with Barth H, 1964 *Residential Location and Urban Mobility* Institute for Social Research, University of Michigan, Ann Arbor

MacLennan D, 1977 "Some thoughts on the nature and purchase of house price studies" *Urban Studies* **14** (1) 59-71

Nationwide Building Society, 1970 "Why do people move?" *Occasional Bulletin 99* Nationwide Building Society, London

Pickvance C G, 1974 "Life-cycle, housing tenure and residential mobility: a path analytic approach" *Urban Studies* **11** 171-188

Redwood J, 1974 "The UK housing market" *National Westminster Bank Quarterly Review* November 52-64

Richardson H W, 1971 *Urban Economics* (Penguin, Harmondsworth, Middx)

Robson B T, 1975 *Urban Social Areas* (Oxford University Press, London)

Rossi P H, 1955 *Why Families Move. A Study in the Social Psychology of Urban Residential Mobility* (Free Press, Glencoe, Ill.)

Speare A, 1970 "Home ownership life-cycle stage and residential mobility" *Demography* **7** (4) 449-458

Turner M E, Stevens C D, 1959 "The regression analysis of causal paths" *Biometrics* **15** 236-258

Whitehead C M E, 1974 *The UK Housing Market: An Econometric Model* (Saxon House, Farnborough, Hants)

Winnick L, 1957 *American Housing and Its Use* (John Wiley, New York)

Wright S, 1960 "Path coefficients and path regressions: alternative or complementary concepts" *Biometrics* **16** 189-202

The Functional Form of Migration Relations

C P A BARTELS
University of Groningen
H TER WELLE
Economic Technological Institute for Friesland

1 Introduction

In the literature on migration analysis many attempts have been made to estimate relationships that associate selected independent variables with aggregated interregional migration flows. The choice of the functional form in which the relationships are expressed is in general very weakly motivated. This paper concentrates more explicitly on the choice of a functional form, with the aim of obtaining a migration relation that provides an attractive tool to predict interregional migration flows.

We start with a short discussion of the best-known traditional approaches in this context. In general, these approaches lack a clear indication of theoretical reasons to prefer a certain form above others. It is indeed believed that convincing theoretical frameworks are difficult to construct. Therefore a more empirically orientated approach will be followed in this paper. This enables us to focus on a more general class of functions, with the traditional specifications as particular elements. A linear combination of transformed variables will be the point of departure. By means of linear least-squares and maximum-likelihood estimation procedures, a relationship may be selected that performs best for a specific data set. In this way an empirical test on the functional form of the relationship is obtained. The approach will be illustrated by means of data relating to interprovincial migration and associated variables for the Netherlands. Our results indicate that an optimal functional form is found which differs from the traditional additive and multiplicative specifications. For other data sets these conclusions may be different, and the procedure outlined below might be used to test the appropriateness of the traditional specifications.

2 Specification of a migration relation

As in many other migration studies we are concerned with the analysis of *aggregated gross interregional migration flows*. The aim is to indicate significant associated variables that are useful to predict migration flows with different values of the independent variables. This approach enables us to link migration to other variables in a more comprehensive model, which is in fact the ultimate aim of our research. A Markov approach that uses only past observations on the migration variable to generate predictions is considered less attractive for our purposes. Hence this latter approach will not be discussed further. Instead, we focus on relations that link the relative migration of region r to region r' with several associated variables. For relative migration we shall use the flow of migrants divided by the population in the region of origin, so that this variable can be interpreted as a migration probability (cf Drewe and Rodgers, 1973). An alternative would have been to use the population in the region of origin multiplied by that in the region of destination as the denominator (cf Somermeyer, 1971; Weeden, 1973). This procedure seems to be consistent only with a very specific functional specification of the migration equation, and is therefore not attractive for our more general approach.

With regard to the specification of the functional form of such a relationship and the introduction of the stochastic disturbances, the following approaches have been followed more or less frequently [cf Weeden (1973) for a discussion of some functional specifications]. The first approach involves a multiplicative relationship with a multiplicative lognormally distributed disturbance term. This relationship is based on notions expressed in gravity analysis. The migration relation may be expressed as

$$m_{rr'} = \alpha_0 \prod_{i=1}^{I} x_{i,rr'}^{\alpha_i} \epsilon_{rr'},$$ (1)

where

$m_{rr'}$ is the relative flow of migrants from r to r' (absolute flow divided by population in region r),

$x_{i,rr'}$ is the associated nonstochastic variable influencing the migration flow from r to r' and having positive values,

I is the number of associated variables selected a priori,

$\alpha_0, ..., \alpha_I$ are parameters to be estimated,

$\epsilon_{rr'}$ is the disturbance term with lognormal distribution, $E(\epsilon_{rr'}) = \exp(\tfrac{1}{2}\sigma^2)$, $\mathrm{var}(\epsilon_{rr'}) = \exp(2\sigma^2) - \exp(\sigma^2)$, and mutually independent.

Taking the natural logarithm on both sides of equation (1), we obtain

$$\ln m_{rr'} = \ln \alpha_0 + \sum_{i=1}^{I} \alpha_i \ln x_{i,rr'} + v_{rr'},$$ (2)

with

$$v_{rr'} = \ln \epsilon_{rr'}.$$ (3)

The disturbance terms $v_{rr'}$ in equation (2) are independently normally distributed, with $E(v_{rr'}) = 0$ and $\mathrm{var}(v_{rr'}) = \sigma^2$. Hence, traditional linear least-squares may be used to derive parameter estimates in equation (2). Examples of this approach can be found in Drewe and Rodgers (1973) and Klaassen and Drewe (1973).

It has to be noted that equation (1) allows for different specifications of the distance function. If $d_{rr'}$, the distance between r and r', enters as an explanatory variable, specification (1) implies a power function for the distance variable. If one prefers an exponential distance function, then exp $(d_{rr'})$ may be introduced as an explanatory variable. A general approach could use exp $[f(d_{rr'})]$ with f a function to be specified, for example, $f(d_{rr'}) = (\ln d_{rr'})^a$ or $f(d_{rr'}) = d_{rr'}^a$, with a to be chosen a priori or after some experimentation (cf Taylor, 1971).

Another remark with respect to this formulation concerns the assumptions on the disturbance term. The assumptions stated above are convenient to obtain a transformed model that obeys the traditional assumptions for linear regression analysis, and thus yields unbiased estimates of the parameters $\ln \alpha_0, \alpha_1, ..., \alpha_I$. The assumptions are less attractive, however, if one is interested in obtaining an unbiased predictor of the untransformed dependent variable. For this purpose alternative assumptions like $E(\epsilon_{rr'}) = 1$ and var $(\epsilon_{rr'}) = \sigma^2$ could be preferred, which complicate the estimation procedure. [For a more extensive discussion of this type of problem and references to the literature see Bartels (1979).]

The way in which the disturbance term is introduced above reflects the desire to use linear estimation procedures. If we instead employ a multiplicative relationship with an additive, normally distributed disturbance term, estimation of the parameters requires nonlinear procedures. The migration relation in this case equals

$$m_{rr'} = \alpha_0 \prod_{i=1}^{I} x_{i, rr'}^{\alpha_i} + v_{rr'}. \tag{4}$$

A third alternative states that the deterministic part of the migration relation is an additive function of the associated variables, while the normally distributed disturbance term also enters in an additive way. This specification might be considered as a first-order Taylor approximation of relation (4). The relationship may now be expressed as

$$m_{rr'} = \alpha_0 + \sum_{i=1}^{I} \alpha_i x_{i, rr'} + v_{rr'}. \tag{5}$$

Unbiased parameter estimates are again obtained by means of linear least-squares techniques. An example of this approach is given in Willis (1972).

As a final alternative, one could prefer to use some combination of the formulations considered above. An example is the relationship that incorporates additive components in a multiplicative specification.

$$m_{rr'} = \alpha_0 \prod_{i=1}^{I'} x_{i, rr'}^{\alpha_i} \left(\sum_{i=I'+1}^{I} \alpha_i x_{i, rr'} \right) \epsilon_{rr'}, \tag{6}$$

where I' is the number of variables that influence migration in a multiplicative way. A simple case of specification (6) is considered in Somermeyer (1971).

It is difficult to indicate on *theoretical grounds* which of the relationships has to be preferred a priori. A careful selection is important, however, since different forms may yield rather different parameter estimates, even with regard to their signs. One would like to have at one's disposal a theoretical set of conditions that generates a specific relationship for the probability to migrate at the level of a microunit. Consistent aggregation might then provide a relationship that may be estimated with aggregated data. The theoretical treatment might best proceed along the lines of utility theory, since this has received wide attention in different branches of economics. In order to obtain an appropriate description of mobility patterns, variables of a very different nature would have to enter the utility function. Besides, operationality of the approach requires additional assumptions, for example with regard to the functional form of the utility function which might be rather arbitrary. For these reasons, a theoretical analysis along these lines is not expected to provide a firmer base for our selection problem.

As an alternative procedure we shall follow a more *empirical statistical approach* in this paper. This approach aims to select a functional form that describes in an optimum way the relationship between the selected variables in a specific empirical context. Hence, no general statements concerning the ultimate functional form of a migration relation will be derived. Instead, we propose a general method of analysis that enables the analyst to select for each data set the most appropriate functional form within a certain class of functions. This extends the approach of Taylor (1971), who restricted his analysis to the specification of an optimal transformation of the distance variable in spatial-interaction models. The method will be described in the next section, together with the procedures that can be used to obtain parameter estimates.

3 A general transformation function
From the different specifications of the migration relations, equations (2) and (5) share some important properties. Both are linear in the parameters (with ln α_0 taken as a new parameter) and possess a disturbance term obeying traditional assumptions, namely constant variance, zero expectation, and independent normal distribution. In the sequel we indicate how these specifications relate to a more general class of functions.

In a rather illuminating paper Box and Cox (1964) propose a method to obtain such a normal, homoscedastic, linear model after some suitable transformation of the dependent variable. If one looks additionally for a simple regression model, a transformation of the independent variables may also be performed. In fact, relation (2) uses a logarithmic transformation of all variables to satisfy the conditions mentioned above. This transformation is a rather specific one, and we would like to consider a broader class of functions to extend the possibilities to derive an appropriate regression model.

Let us consider the following model

$$\hat{m}_{rr'} = \alpha_0 + \sum_{i=1}^{I} \alpha_i \hat{x}_{i,\,rr'} + v_{rr'} \tag{7}$$

with $\hat{m}_{rr'}$ and $\hat{x}_{i,\,rr'}$ denoting transformed variables and $v_{rr'}$ a disturbance term obeying the traditional assumptions. Following the original suggestions of Tukey (1957) and the extension of Box and Cox (1964) we consider the following family of power transformations:

$$
\hat{m}_{rr'} = \begin{cases} \dfrac{m_{rr'}^{\beta} - 1}{\beta}, & \beta \neq 0, \\[2mm] \ln m_{rr'}, & \beta = 0, \end{cases}
\tag{8}
$$

and similarly for $\hat{x}_{i,\,rr'}$, $i = 1, ..., I$. In equation (8) parameter β is a transformation parameter, to be determined further. Since all variables are restricted to possess strictly positive values in this paper, transformation (8) needs not to be extended with a parameter that modifies the range of observations. [A further discussion on this family of transformations is contained in Schlesselman (1971) and Wood (1974).]

Combining equations (7) and (8) we easily see that loglinear relation (2) is a special case of relation (7); that is, the transformation parameter β is assumed to be equal to zero. If no conclusive theoretical reasons are available to set β equal to zero, the best point of departure seems to be not to impose this a priori restriction on β but to attempt to estimate its value in the particular empirical context. If this estimation yields a value of β approaching zero, relation (2) is confirmed by the data and the multiplicative migration model constitutes an attractive point of departure. If β approaches one, linear relationship (5) results and the additive migration model is more appropriate. Other values of β would reveal that neither of these models is a good candidate in the present context.

It is obvious that the linear relation in transformed variables [relation (7)] allows for a wider specification than that provided by relation (2). Other types of transformation functions could perhaps be defined (cf Bartlett, 1947; Hoyle, 1973), although the power transformation seems to be attractive in the present context since it yields a test on linear and loglinear relationships. Within this class of transformations, an extension could be possible by allowing for different values of the transformation parameter β as applied to the different variables. One possibility would be to take transformation parameter β_1 for the dependent variable and parameter β_2 for all independent variables. This would generate the possibility of a semilogarithmic relation, for example. Another extension could use a number of different transformation parameters for the independent variables. One could even think of extending the model by allowing interaction terms to enter the specification, for example

$$
\hat{m}_{rr'} = \alpha_0 + \sum_{i=1}^{I} \alpha_i \hat{x}_{i,\,rr'} + \sum_{i=1}^{I}\sum_{i'=1}^{I} \beta_{ii'} \hat{\hat{x}}_{i,\,rr'} \hat{\hat{x}}_{i',\,rr'} + v_{rr'},
\tag{9}
$$

where ⌢, ≈, and $\hat{\approx}$ are associated with transformation parameters β_1, β_2, and β_3 respectively. Below, we shall start with a single transformation parameter β

D

as in relation (7). If a reasonable fit is obtained in this way, little need seems to exist to consider the more complicated cases with several different transformation parameters.

It will be shown below that unbiased estimates of the parameters in relation (7) may be easily obtained. Such parameter estimates do not always form the ultimate aim of the analysis, however, since one will frequently also be interested in the use of the estimated relationship for getting a prediction of variable $m_{rr'}$. From relation (7) and the assumptions on the disturbance term it follows that the parameter estimates can be used to obtain an unbiased predictor of the *transformed* dependent variable $\hat{m}_{rr'}$. But we are ultimately interested in the value which the untransformed dependent variable $m_{rr'}$ takes. A natural choice for a predictor of $m_{rr'}$ would seem to be

$$\widetilde{m}_{rr'} = \left[1 + b\left(a_0 + \sum_{i=1}^{I} a_i \hat{x}_{i, rr'} \right) \right]^{1/b}, \tag{10}$$

where $a_0, ..., a_I, b$ are unbiased estimates of $\alpha_0, ..., \alpha_I, \beta$ respectively, and $\widetilde{m}_{rr'}$ is a predictor of $m_{rr'}$.

However, the expected value of expression (10) is in general not equal to

$$\left[1 + \beta\left(\alpha_0 + \sum_{i=1}^{I} \alpha_i \hat{x}_{i, rr'} \right) \right]^{1/\beta}, \tag{11}$$

so relation (10) does not constitute an unbiased estimator of $m_{rr'}$.

In general it seems not easy to derive an unbiased predictor for the dependent variable. This property might be considered as a rather serious drawback of the present approach. However, for the special case where $\beta = 0$, the loglinear specification, expressions for unbiased predictors have been obtained in the literature (see Goldberger, 1968; Bradu and Mundlak, 1970). For the general case of β not equal to 0 or 1 the situation is much more complicated, and we are not yet able to present such unbiased predictors. We may only hope that the bias involved is not too large. It is obvious that this problem presents an interesting area for further research.

4 Parameter estimation of the transformed model
The general model proposed above constitutes a model nonlinear in the transformation parameter β. This characteristic implies that traditional linear least-squares analysis is not appropriate to obtain estimates for all parameters. However, numerical procedures can be used to derive nonlinear least-squares or maximum-likelihood estimates. Since the solution of numerical search techniques may depend on the values of the parameters chosen as the starting point, it is essential to have a good guess of an appropriate starting point available. For this purpose traditional linear least-squares may be used, since for fixed β a model linear in the remaining parameters is obtained. Linear least-squares may also be used

to obtain the standard errors of estimates of parameters α_0, ..., α_I in the optimum point, which is a more attractive procedure than calculation of asymptotic standard errors in the likelihood approach. The likelihood approach can be used to calculate a confidence interval for the estimate of β, as is shown below. Hence, a combination of linear least-squares and nonlinear maximum likelihood presents an attractive estimation procedure [cf also Zarembka (1968; 1974) for this approach].

With equation (7) written in matrix notation our model can be expressed as follows:

$$\hat{m} = \hat{X}\alpha + v, \tag{12}$$

where

$\hat{m}$ is the vector of observations on the dependent variable transformed according to equation (8),

$\hat{X}$ is the matrix of transformed values for the independent variables, including a column with elements equal to one,

α is the vector of parameters α_0, α_1, ..., α_I to be estimated, and

v is the vector of normally, independently distributed disturbance terms, each with zero mean and variance σ^2.

The *maximum-likelihood* method chooses those values of the parameters as estimates that maximise the likelihood, L, of the original observations. This equals the joint density of the original observations, which equals in this case:

$$L(\theta, m) = \left(2\prod\sigma^2\right)^{-N/2} \exp\left[-\frac{(\hat{m} - \hat{X}\alpha)^{\mathrm{T}}(\hat{m} - \hat{X}\alpha)}{2\sigma^2}\right]|J| \tag{13}$$

where

θ is the vector of parameters to be estimated (β, α_0, α_1, ..., α_I, σ),

m is the vector of observations on $m_{rr'}$,

N is the total number of interactions (migration flows) being studied,

J is the Jacobian of the inverse transformation from $\hat{m}_{rr'}$ to $m_{rr'}$.

The Jacobian, J, is defined by

$$J = \prod_{n=1}^{N}\frac{d\hat{m}_n}{dm_n} = \prod_{n=1}^{N} m_n^{\beta-1}. \tag{14}$$

Taking the logarithm of the likelihood

$$\mathcal{L}(\theta, m) = \ln L(\theta, m) \tag{15}$$

and substituting equation (14) results in the following expression for the concentrated log-likelihood function (except for a constant).

$$\mathcal{L}(\theta, m) = -\tfrac{1}{2}N \ln(\hat{m} - \hat{X}\alpha)^{\mathrm{T}}(\hat{m} - \hat{X}\alpha) + (\beta - 1)\sum_{n=1}^{N} \ln m_n : \tag{16}$$

In equation (16) use has been made of the maximum likelihood estimate of σ^2, obtained as

$$\hat{\sigma}^2 = \frac{(\hat{m} - \hat{X}a)^T (\hat{m} - \hat{X}a)}{N}, \tag{17}$$

where a is the maximum likelihood estimate of α. From equations (14) and (16) it is clear that the calculation procedure is simplified by working with the following normalised transformation:

$$\hat{\hat{m}}_{rr'} = \frac{\hat{m}_{rr'}}{J^{1/N}}, \tag{18}$$

where $\hat{m}_{rr'}$ is as defined in equation (8) and J is as defined in equation (14). With this transformation the function to be maximised simplifies into $-\frac{1}{2} N \ln (\hat{m} - \hat{X}\alpha)^T (\hat{m} - \hat{X}\alpha) = \psi(\alpha)$, which procedure amounts to minimising $(\hat{m} - \hat{X}\alpha)^T (\hat{m} - \hat{X}\alpha)$. This is a standard nonlinear least-squares problem. In our application we used a standard subroutine available in the NAG library [a library constructed by the Numerical Algorithm Group, version ICL 1900 System, subroutine EO4GAF; this routine finds a local minimum of $(\hat{m} - \hat{X}\alpha)^T (\hat{m} - \hat{X}\alpha)$ by means of an iterative technique due to Marquardt].

The estimation procedure suggested by the discussion above proceeds in several stages. First, for different fixed values of β, linear least-squares can be used to calculate the value of $(\hat{m} - \hat{X}\alpha)^T (\hat{m} - \hat{X}\alpha)$, and associated estimates for the remaining parameters. Mutual comparison of these values indicates a preliminary minimum. The estimated parameter vector $\hat{\theta}$ associated with this minimum can then be used as a starting point of the nonlinear least-squares problem, to investigate whether the minimum can be decreased in the neighbourhood of this starting point. With this procedure the ultimate choice of parameter β can be made, and used to obtain parameter estimates and confidence intervals by means of ordinary linear least-squares.

As outlined in Box and Cox (1964) a likelihood ratio test can be used to obtain an approximate 95% confidence interval for β. This makes use of the result that

$$\ln L(\theta_0, m) - \ln L(\theta_1, m) \sim \tfrac{1}{2}\chi_1^2, \tag{19}$$

where
θ_0 is the vector of maximum likelihood estimates for the parameters, and θ_1 is the vector of alternative estimates for the parameters.

At a 95% confidence level, the critical value of $\frac{1}{2}\chi_1^2$ is $1 \cdot 92$ and this may be used to indicate the values of β that satisfy.

$$\ln L(\theta_0, m) - \ln L(\theta_1, m) < 1 \cdot 92. \tag{20}$$

The procedure discussed above will be illustrated now with data for interprovincial migration in the Netherlands.

5 Empirical relations for interprovincial migration in the Netherlands

As an element of a rather comprehensive regional labour market model for the northern part of the Netherlands we were interested in having at our disposal, relations that might be used to obtain satisfactory predictions of (gross) interprovincial migration flows from a limited number of associated variables. The variables were required to have a strong intuitive appeal, as compared with additional insight derived from other studies in this field. In order to allow for different mobility characteristics for the northern population and the population of the rest of the country, two different estimations have been performed, with the use of cross-sectional data for 1975 (this is the most recent year for which detailed migration data are available). This characteristic distinguishes our approach from that followed by other studies of migration behaviour in the Netherlands. For example, Drewe and Rodgers (1973), Klaassen and Drewe (1973), and Somermeyer (1971) assume the same mobility characteristics for all migration flows. Since the aim is to integrate the estimated relations in a regional labour market model, we take as the dependent variable relative interprovincial migration flows of migrants belonging to the occupied labour force. The *first* migration relation relates relative migration from each of the eight nonnorthern provinces to each of the three northern provinces to some independent variables. This relation will be estimated consequently with twenty-four units of measurement. The *second* relation expresses relative migration flows from each northern province to each of the ten remaining provinces, which gives thirty units of measurement. Of course we could also have incorporated the intranorthern migration flows in both data sets, giving two sets of thirty data. This option has also been explored empirically and did not alter our results significantly. Hence we concentrate on the first-mentioned estimations.

The choice of an attractive set of independent variables is not a straightforward procedure in an analysis like the present one. Such a set has to incorporate several indicators of the attractiveness of migration from a certain region to another one, like

distance,

economic variables (labour market, incomes, cost of living, etc) [for an extensive discussion of economic variables influencing aggregate migration, see Greenwood (1975)],

indicators of the living conditions (housing, environment, cultural facilities, etc).

Some empirical estimation is required to select variables that perform well, that is, have the expected sign, have parameter estimates significantly different from zero, and yield a good fit (as measured in R^2 terms). Besides, we aim at including only a limited number of independent variables. Since it would have taken too much computational time to follow the complete scheme as outlined above for all possible combinations of variables, we started with a preliminary choice of a functional specification.

This amounted to taking the logarithmic relation and considering several combinations of variables in order to select an attractive set of independent variables (using the criteria as outlined above).

For migration *to the north*, ultimately the following independent variables were selected as the preferred ones:

1 the *physical distance* between the largest town in province r and r': $d_{rr'}$;

2 an indicator of the attractiveness of *the labour market* in r' as compared with r: this is measured by the ratio of the total demand for labour in r' and the demand for labour in r: $l_{rr'}$, and the use of this indicator assumes that the number of vacancies is proportional to the labour demand;

3 an indicator of the *housing* conditions in r' as compared with r: we used the ratio of the percentage of one-family houses as a possible indicator of differences in housing quality between r' and r: $h_{rr'}$.

With these variables the following general migration relation is postulated

$$\hat{m}_{rr'} = \alpha_0 + \alpha_1 \hat{d}_{rr'} + \alpha_2 \hat{h}_{rr'} + \alpha_3 \hat{l}_{rr'} + v_{rr'}, \tag{21}$$

with all variables defined as before, and a hat indicating a transformation according to equation (8) and the double hat indicating the normalised transformation [equation (18)].

For migration *from the northern provinces* the ultimate set of independent variables appeared to differ from that given above. Variable $h_{rr'}$, appeared to behave badly for this data set, whereas two other variables constituted better alternatives. The set of independent variables for these migration flows then consists of:

(1)   the *distance* variable: $d_{rr'}$;

(2)   the labour force variable: $l_{rr'}$;

(3)   an additional indicator of the labour market in r' as compared with r: this is measured by the ratio of *unemployment* percentages in r' and r: $u_{rr'}$;

(4)   an indicator of the attractiveness of the *natural environment* in r' as compared with r. The ratio of a weighted sum of different types of physical areas, taken per square kilometer, was thought to be an appropriate indicator of this dimension: $e_{rr'}$. As weights we used the inverse of the relative share of the surface of a certain type of physical area in the total surface for the Netherlands. Hence the weights express the expectation that physical areas which are relatively scarce will possess a high weight in the evaluation of their attractiveness by individuals.

These variables lead to the following general migration relation:

$$\hat{m}_{rr'} = \gamma_0 + \gamma_1 \hat{d}_{rr'} + \gamma_2 \hat{l}_{rr'} + \gamma_3 \hat{u}_{rr'} + \gamma_4 \hat{e}_{rr'} + v_{rr'}, \tag{22}$$

with all variables defined as before.

Although the selection of variables has been based already on a particular preliminary specification of the transformation function, namely the logarithmic one, it may quite well happen that this specification cannot be considered the optimal one in the empirical–statistical sense as used in this paper. Therefore, we used equations (21) and (22) as the point of departure to investigate which value of transformation parameter β may be considered to produce optimal results. We followed the procedure as outlined above. First, ordinary least-squares have been run for values of β from -1 to $+1$, varying with steps of $0\cdot2$. In the neighbourhood of $\beta = 0$ the search has been more detailed by performing the calculations also for $\beta = -0\cdot0001$ and $\beta = +0\cdot0001$. Results for the decision criterion $\psi(\alpha)$ are presented in table 1 for the different values of β. In figure 1 we present plots for the concentrated log-likelihood function, together with an indicator of the approximate 95% confidence intervals for β.

Table 1. Value of $\psi(\alpha) = -\frac{1}{2}N \ \ln(\hat{m} - \hat{X}\alpha)^{\mathrm{T}}(\hat{m} - \hat{X}\alpha)$ with varying transformation parameter.

β	Migration to the north	Migration from the north
Linear least-squares solution		
$-1\cdot0$	15	-48
$-0\cdot8$	20	-39
$-0\cdot6$	23	-30
$-0\cdot4$	29	-21
$-0\cdot2$	32	-12
$-0\cdot0001$	36	-5
$0\cdot0$	36	-5
$0\cdot0001$	36	-5
$0\cdot2$	39	$-0\cdot2$
$0\cdot4$	37	-3
$0\cdot6$	33	-10
$0\cdot8$	26	-19
$1\cdot0$	20	-28
Nonlinear least-squares solution		
$0\cdot245$	39	
$0\cdot229$		$-0\cdot1$

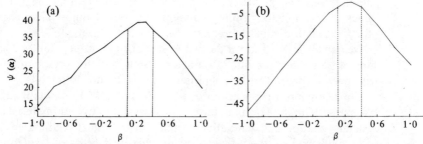

Figure 1. Log-likelihood (except for constant) for varying β; (a) migration to the north; (b) migration from the north. The dotted lines indicate confidence intervals.

For the first regression the preliminary optimum is found at the value $\beta = 0 \cdot 2$ by using successive linear least-squares solutions for different values of β. A check on this solution is given by the nonlinear least-squares algorithm, by using $\beta = 0 \cdot 2$ as a starting value and searching its neighbourhood for a possible better solution. The procedure gives as a solution $\beta = 0 \cdot 245$ with the criterion being equal to 39. These results suggest that for these data the transformation parameter β is best chosen as equal to $0 \cdot 2$. From figure 1(a) we see that the 95% confidence interval is rather small and extends from $0 \cdot 1$ to $0 \cdot 4$ approximately, indicating that β differs significantly from zero (the logarithmic transformation).

From the second regression the results are as follows. The linear least-squares solutions point again to $\beta = 0 \cdot 2$ as the best value for the transformation parameter. Using this as a starting value in the nonlinear least-squares algorithm yields as a solution, $\beta = 0 \cdot 229$, with the associated value of $\psi(\alpha)$ equal to $-0 \cdot 1$. Hence, the value of the criterion is roughly the same as for $\beta = 0 \cdot 2$.

The 95% confidence interval indicates that β differs significantly from zero, that is, the logarithmic transformation (the confidence interval extends from $0 \cdot 1$ to $0 \cdot 4$ approximately).

For migration equations (21) and (22) and both sets of data, the estimation results would indicate as an optimal value of the transformation parameter, a value close to $0 \cdot 2$. A 95% confidence interval around this value would exclude a zero value of β in both cases. However, decreasing the level of confidence somewhat would make it possible to include the $\beta = 0$ value in the confidence region. Also from table 1 we note that the relative increase in the criterion value is not that impressive if we go from a logarithmic transformation to a power transformation with a value of β equal to $0 \cdot 2$. So we may conclude that the optimal transformation is given by this latter value, but that the logarithmic transformation (that is, the multiplicative model) is a good second-best solution, and at least to be preferred above the additive specification [equation (5)].

6 Empirical properties of the different specifications
Let us first consider the *effects* of varying functional forms *on the parameter estimates*. We shall not discuss the results for all the different values of the transformation parameter but restrict ourselves to those associated with β equal to zero (in fact $0 \cdot 0001$ was used for computational convenience) and 1, and for β equal to its optimum value. Tables 2 and 3 summarise the main results. Parameter estimates with corresponding t values have been recorded for the migration flows to the north in table 2.

If we compare the specifications $\beta = 0$ and $\beta = 1$, a notable difference is apparent for the constant term. This has a positive estimate in the loglinear relation and a negative estimate in the linear relation. This has to be explained by the influence of the different types of transformation implied by these relations. Another difference is found in the coefficient estimate of the housing variable $h_{rr'}$. This possesses in both relations the expected positive sign, but is highly significant in the loglinear relation and highly nonsignificant in the linear relation. The distance factor has a highly significant negative coefficient, and the indicator of the labour markets $l_{rr'}$, a significant positive coefficient in both specifications. The goodness-of-fit as measured by the R^2 exhibits a remarkable improvement for the loglinear equation compared with the linear one.

If we consider the results for the optimal specification, where $\beta = 0 \cdot 245$, no notable differences with the logarithmic transformation can be found. Both the coefficient estimates for the independent variables and their t values are almost the same. Besides, only a minor improvement in goodness-of-fit, R^2, is obtained in the optimal specification with $\beta = 0 \cdot 245$. We may conclude that the loglinear specification gives an appropriate second-best solution.

For the second data set, the results are recorded in table 3. Again results are given for the specification obtained with $\beta = 0$, $\beta = 1$, and the optimal specification with a value $\beta = 0 \cdot 229$. As in the regressions discussed above, the constant term of the linear specification has a sign different from the sign of the constant term in the other specifications, owing to the transformation used.

A further notable difference is apparent for the environmental variable $e_{rr'}$. This has a negative coefficient estimate in the linear relation,

Table 2. Estimation results for selected transformation parameters: migration to the north ($N = 24$). The results in this table and in table 3 have been obtained by using normalised migration flows, as indicated in the text.

	Constant term	$\hat{d}_{rr'}$	$\hat{h}_{rr'}$	$\hat{l}_{rr'}$	R^2
$\beta = 0 \cdot 0001$	$0 \cdot 12$	$-0 \cdot 47$	$0 \cdot 17$	$0 \cdot 08$	$0 \cdot 90$
t value	$2 \cdot 99$	$-13 \cdot 14$	$3 \cdot 08$	$4 \cdot 26$	
$\beta = 1$	$-0 \cdot 25$	$-0 \cdot 44$	$0 \cdot 00$	$0 \cdot 23$	$0 \cdot 78$
t value	$-3 \cdot 28$	$-8 \cdot 18$	$0 \cdot 01$	$3 \cdot 45$	
$\beta = 0 \cdot 245$	$0 \cdot 07$	$-0 \cdot 41$	$0 \cdot 13$	$0 \cdot 12$	$0 \cdot 92$
t value	$1 \cdot 98$	$-15 \cdot 06$	$3 \cdot 02$	$5 \cdot 51$	

Table 3. Estimation results for selected transformation parameters: migration from the north ($N = 30$).

	Constant term	$\hat{d}_{rr'}$	$\hat{l}_{rr'}$	$\hat{u}_{rr'}$	$\hat{e}_{rr'}$	R^2
$\beta = 0 \cdot 0001$	$-0 \cdot 32$	$-0 \cdot 87$	$0 \cdot 23$	$-0 \cdot 41$	$0 \cdot 39$	$0 \cdot 87$
t value	$-4 \cdot 67$	$-12 \cdot 72$	$3 \cdot 81$	$-3 \cdot 79$	$3 \cdot 35$	
$\beta = 1$	$0 \cdot 45$	$-0 \cdot 65$	$-0 \cdot 00$	$-0 \cdot 07$	$-0 \cdot 06$	$0 \cdot 63$
t value	$2 \cdot 61$	$-6 \cdot 38$	$-0 \cdot 01$	$-0 \cdot 18$	$-0 \cdot 29$	
$\beta = 0 \cdot 229$	$-0 \cdot 14$	$-0 \cdot 81$	$0 \cdot 14$	$-0 \cdot 37$	$0 \cdot 26$	$0 \cdot 89$
t value	$-2 \cdot 34$	$-14 \cdot 30$	$3 \cdot 13$	$-3 \cdot 54$	$2 \cdot 67$	

although it does not differ significantly from zero. The same holds true for the labour market indicator $l_{rr'}$. The coefficient estimate of the unemployment variable $u_{rr'}$ has the expected negative sign in all equations but it is very insignificant in the linear relation, as indicated by the low t value.

From the results for $\beta = 0 \cdot 229$ and $\beta = 0$ we note that no impressive differences exist: the goodness-of-fit, as indicated by R^2, is approximately the same, and t values and signs of coefficients are similar.

However, the estimates of the coefficients of $\hat{l}_{rr'}$ and $\hat{e}_{rr'}$ still possess a remarkable difference for these relations. The linear relation would imply conclusions completely different from those derived from the other specifications, whereas its goodness-of-fit is relatively very low. If one is interested in general results (sign of coefficients, significance, high R^2), not much need seems to exist for discriminating between the optimal specification and the multiplicative gravity-type model. For a detailed analysis a transformation parameter equal to $0 \cdot 229$ is to be preferred, and the multiplicative relation can only be regarded as a good second-best alternative.

It appears from the results for both data sets that the choice of a linear or loglinear relation has a severe impact on the conclusions to be derived from a regression analysis. In some cases the sign of coefficients differs, whereas coefficients that differ significantly from zero in one specification do not possess this property in the other specification. This finding demonstrates the necessity of investigating explicitly what functional specification has to be preferred for describing the variations in a given data set appropriately.

We noted already that both data sets imply roughly the same optimal value for parameter β. Since we use numerical search routines one might wonder whether this optimal value is really associated with a global, rather than a local, optimum. In order to investigate the robustness of the estimates, we reran the nonlinear programme with quite different starting values. This resulted in convergence to the same values as found before. Of course, this finding does not indicate that all migration relations will have to be formulated with a power transformation using a value of β equal to $0 \cdot 2$. Although rather different data sets produced the same optimal β value, for other data sets one has not to expect a priori similar results. Hence, the whole process of estimation may best be repeated for each new set of data.

Above we considered the consequences of different functional specifications for parameter estimates, their significance and the overall goodness-of-fit. We now want to pay some attention to the properties of the residuals as generated by the different specifications.

A first point to consider is whether the optimal transformation indeed produces residuals that are closer to being normally distributed than residuals from other transformations. For this purpose the following test procedure has been followed. From the residuals we derive an estimated standard deviation. This is used to compare the empirical cumulative distribution function of the residuals with the cumulative distribution function associated with a normal distribution with a mean of zero and a standard deviation as calculated from the residuals. The maximum absolute difference between these two cumulative distribution functions may be used as a crude indicator of the appropriateness of the normality assumption. In fact, this indicator is known as the Kolmogorov statistic (cf Kendall and Stuart, 1973, page 469). The larger the value of this statistic, the greater the deviation of the observed distribution from the postulated normal distribution. For migration from the north its value equals $0 \cdot 138$ for $\beta = 1$, $0 \cdot 088$ for $\beta = -0 \cdot 0001$, and $0 \cdot 081$ for $\beta = 0 \cdot 229$ (the optimal value). For migration to the north we obtain $0 \cdot 1631$ for $\beta = 1$, $0 \cdot 010$ for $\beta = -0 \cdot 0001$, and $0 \cdot 095$ for $\beta = 0 \cdot 245$. Hence, we may conclude that in both cases the use of the optimal transformation parameter implies a substantially better approximation of the residuals to a normal distribution as compared with the linear specification. (If we apply a test procedure with a 5% significance level we cannot reject the hypothesis that the observed residuals are drawings from the postulated normal distribution in the six cases mentioned above.)

A second question to be investigated is whether the homoscedasticity assumption of the disturbances is more valid for the optimal transformation than for the linear specification. For this purpose we break our data down into three separate data sets; that is, migration to each of the three northern provinces (three sets of eight data) and migration from each of the three northern provinces (three sets of ten data), respectively. In order to test the null hypothesis that there is no difference among the variances of the three populations from which our data were drawn we employed a test statistic designed by Bartlett (cf Kane, 1968, page 373), which follows a chi-square distribution under the null hypothesis. For migration to the north, the value of this statistic equals $4 \cdot 67$ for the linear specification and $0 \cdot 05$ for the optimal transformation. For migration from the north we obtain a value of $0 \cdot 60$ and $1 \cdot 52$ respectively. Hence, the test statistic does not lead to a rejection of our null hypothesis in the four cases considered. Furthermore it does not appear that the use of the optimal transformation parameter implies a better approximation to the homoscedasticity assumption.

A third point we investigate is whether our optimal result satisfies the null hypothesis of no spatial autocorrelation among the disturbances. For this purpose ordinary least-squares residuals for the optimal transformation parameter have been used, and inserted in the Moran first-order contiguity coefficient with appropriate calculation of its mean and standard deviation. This enables us to construct an approximately $N(0,1)$ distributed test statistic [cf Bartels and Hordijk (1977) for a description and a justification of the appropriateness of this procedure]. Binary weights have been used for the calculation of this statistic. For the migration flow from r to r' a weight 1 is given to

the flows from r'' to r' where r'' is first-order contiguous to r,

the flows from r to r''' where r''' is first-order contiguous to r'.

For migration to the north the test statistic equals $1 \cdot 28$ and for migration from the north we obtain a value of $1 \cdot 30$. Hence for the optimal specification the null hypothesis of no spatial autocorrelation cannot be rejected with 95% reliability.

Since we had intended to obtain migration relationships appropriate for prediction purposes, our results in tables 2 and 3 seem to imply that the attempt to find such relationships has been successful. For migration to and from the north we estimated 'optimal' specifications that account for roughly 90% of the variance in the migration data. The maximum number of indpendent variables is four, which property is attractive for a prediction of future migration flows. All coefficient estimates do differ significantly from zero, and have signs that could be expected a priori. The standard assumptions on the disturbances cannot be rejected for our optimal specification, using several specific test statistics. For both types of migration flows, the distance variable seems to be an important explanatory factor (as far as the t value is used as an indicator). Its coefficient differs, however, and is smaller (in absolute value) for the flows to the north. This might indicate that people from the north perceive distance as a more important bottleneck for migration than people elsewhere in the country. For migrants to the north, the labour force and housing variables help to explain the variance, whereas for other migrants the housing variable is replaced by the indicator of natural environment and an unemployment indicator. To what extent these findings indeed reflect differences in decisionmaking at the microlevel cannot be judged from these results. This would require a confrontation with data on a more disaggregated level. Since we aim to include migration relations in a more comprehensive labour market model, it can be remarked that an attractive feature of our relations is their explicit incorporation of regional labour market variables (employment and unemployment).

For an appropriate prediction of interprovincial migration flows a next step has to be an investigation of the pattern of variation in parameter values in time, since the independent variables will be either constant or changing only very gradually. This investigation would bring us beyond the scope of the present paper, however.

7 Concluding remarks

In this paper we considered the question of how to obtain an attractive functional form of a migration relation. We chose a statistical–empirical point of departure by using a generalised functional form approach with the ultimate choice of the specification depending on statistical estimation results. The procedure has been illustrated by means of two data sets relating to interprovincial migration in the Netherlands. The empirical results indicate that for both data sets the loglinear specification is to be preferred above the linear one, since it resulted as a good second-best solution. As an optimum solution, for both migration equations a Box and Cox tranformation with transformation parameter close to $0 \cdot 2$ has been found. The generalised power transformations as used in this paper hence provide an attractive procedure to choose an appropriate functional form. Instead of generalising the results for the particular data sets being studied here, it is recommended to apply the procedure to each new data set in order to detect peculiarities of the data.

Since, in general, theoretical frameworks are very weak constructs in economics, a single reliance on traditional functional forms based on such constructs is not appropriate. More empirical experiments with different specifications are required. The choice can then be based on statistical criteria. If one adopts this approach, several extensions of the present paper can easily be indicated, for example a comparison of the power transformation with other transformation functions.

Acknowledgements. This research was financed by the Federation of Northern Economic Institutes (FNEI) as a part of a project to construct a regional labour market model for the northern part of the Netherlands.

References
Bartels C P A, 1979 "Operational statistical methods for analysing spatial data" *Exploratory and Explanatory Statistical Analysis of Spatial Data* Eds C P A Bartels, R H Katellapper (Nijhoff, Leiden)
Bartels C P A, Hordijk L, 1977 "On the power of the generalized Moran contiguity coefficient in testing for spatial autocorrelation among regression disturbances" *Regional Science and Urban Economics* **7** 83-101
Bartlett M S, 1947 "The use of transformations" *Biometrics* **3** 39-52
Box G E P, Cox D R, 1964 "An analysis of transformations" *Journal of the Royal Statistical Society, Series B* **26** 211-243
Bradu D, Mundlak Y, 1970 "Estimation in lognormal linear models" *Journal of the American Statistical Association* **65** 198-211
Drewe P, Rodgers H, 1973 "Step towards action-oriented migration research: a progress report" *Regional and Urban Economics* **3** 315-325
Goldberger A S, 1968 "The interpretation and estimation of Cobb-Douglas functions" *Econometrica* **35** 464-472
Greenwood M J, 1975 "Research on internal migration in the United States: a survey" *Journal of Economic Literature* **13** 397-433
Hoyle M H, 1973 "Transformations. An introduction and a bibliography" *International Statistical Review* **41** 203-223
Kane E J, 1968 *Economic Statistics and Econometrics. An Introduction to Quantitative Economics* (Harper and Row, London)
Kendall M G, Stuart A, 1973 *The Advanced Theory of Statistics* (Griffin, London)
Klaassen L H, Drewe P, 1973 *Migration Policy in Europe—A Comparative Study* (Lexington Books, DC Heath, Lexington, Mass)
Schlesselman J, 1971 "Power families: a note on the Box and Cox transformation" *Journal of the Royal Statistical Society, Series B* **33** 307-311

Somermeyer W H, 1971 "Multi-polar human flow models" *Papers of the Regional Science Association* **26** 131–144

Taylor P J, 1971 "Distance transformation and distance decay functions" *Geographical Analysis* **3** 221–238

Tukey J W, 1957 "On the comparative anatomy of transformations" *The Annals of Mathematical Statistics* **28** 602–632

Weeden R, 1973 *Interregional Migration Models and Their Application to Great-Britain* (Cambridge University Press, London)

Willis K G, 1972 "The influence of spatial structure and socio-economic factors on migration rates. A case-study: Tyneside 1961–1966" *Regional Studies* **6** 69–82

Wood J I, 1974 "An extension of the analysis of transformations of Box and Cox" *Applied Statistics* **23** 278–283

Zarembka P, 1968 "Functional form in the demand for money" *Journal of the American Statistical Association* **63** 502–511

Zarembka P, 1974 "Transformation of variables in econometrics" in *Frontiers in Econometrics* Ed. P Zarembka (Academic Press, New York) pp 81–104

Labour Market Dynamics: A Stochastic Analysis of Labour Turnover by Occupation

D PALMER, D GLEAVE
Centre for Environmental Studies, London

1 Introduction

The labour market is a dynamic system in which mobility is constrained by two factors—geographic location and occupational classification (job type). Regional science analysts have become increasingly interested in the processes which result in migratory activity rather than the activity itself. Consequently it has become usual to focus upon employment-motivated migration (or its absence) as a means of analysing the restructuring of the space economy. It is our contention that most research on labour migration has been extremely imbalanced in its approach in a number of respects, the most significant of which is that labour migration itself is only one by-product of the employment matchmaking process. This argument is outlined more fully elsewhere (see Gleave and Palmer, 1977). Most analyses have ignored constraints which reduce labour migration, such as housing ties, and therefore failed to recognise that occupational mobility often occurs when workers wish to make a career progression or move into a job from being unemployed. Occupational mobility could be regarded as an alternative to geographic mobility. Our project is concerned with understanding all mobility processes which affect the behaviour of the labour market.

Too much attention has been focused upon the supply of labour, too little on the supply of jobs; too much attention has been placed upon the unemployed worker as compared with those moving between jobs. This paper attempts to rectify this balance by concentrating specifically upon the problem of occupational turnover.

A previous paper (Gleave and Palmer, 1977) conceptualised the labour market as consisting of various stocks and flows which interact to determine the matching of labour and jobs. These relationships may be easily introduced into an accounting framework for statistical analysis, subject to the satisfactory definition of labour-market boundaries and an occupational taxonomy. Occupational turnover is one important mechanism whereby the restructuring of the supply of labour is determined. Using data from the 1971 Census (OPCS, 1971), we have applied various dynamic models in order to predict the occupational structure of the supply of labour at the national level. Since the labour market is comprised of many individuals, learning new skills and changing jobs or location for a variety of reasons, a deterministic approach is not applicable. A probabilistic or stochastic methodology must be applied instead.

We apply two stochastic models to predicting changes which are attributable to occupational turnover. These models, consisting of a Markov chain and a modified Markov model with feedback properties, have been used to analyse migration behaviour. Each one is implemented on the basis of two alternative assumptions concerning the population at risk within each of the occupation classes.

The remainder of this paper initially summarises basic theory of Markov chains. The 'closed' system models, ignoring the effects of entrants or retirements from the economic system, are then outlined. An 'open' model is developed whereby retirements from occupations are permitted and entrants into the occupation groups, based on a variety of speculative assumptions, are allowed. The results of these models, incorporating the entry–turnover–retirement process, are then reported and analysed.

As a concomitant to this labour supply analysis, shift–share methodology has been used to consider trends in the demand for labour. In particular, changes which may be due to the restructuring of occupations within industry groups, or to the relative growth and decline of various industry groups, are identified.

Finally, the implications of these results for manpower are considered and how they relate to labour-market mobility in particular.

2 Markov models

We have suggested above that without a comprehensive understanding of our system of interest a stochastic rather than a deterministic estimate of future levels of employment should be made. A stochastic process is one in which changes of state, related by the laws of probability, succeed one another at random or detailed intervals. At any point in time the system may exist in only one of a finite number of mutually exclusive and exhaustive states. The combination of time and states raises four possibilities:
a. Markov models discrete both in time and in behaviour space;
b. Markov models discrete in space but continuous in time;
c. Markov models discrete in time but continuous in space;
d. Markov models continuous both in time and in space.

The points in time may be equally spaced, such as calendar spacing, or may be dependent upon the behaviour of the system in which the process is embedded, such as the time lapse between job changes. This dichotomy is discussed in more detail below.

A stochastic process is a Markov chain if it has the property that the conditional probability of any future event, given any past event and the present state of the system, is independent of that past event and depends only on the present state of the process—that is

$$p(X_{t+1} = j \,|\, X_0 = h_0,\, ...,\, X_{t-1} = h_{t-1},\, X_t = i)$$

$$= p(X_{t+1} = j \,|\, X_t = i)\,,$$

for $t = 0, 1, ..., T$, and every sequence $h_0, ..., h_{t-1}, i, j$. Where $h_0, ..., h_{t-1}, i$, and j define the system states. The conditional probabilistics $p(X_{t+1} = j | X_t = i)$ are one-step transitions which are stationary if, for each i and j,

$$p(X_{t+1} = j | X_t = i) = p(X_1 = j | X_0 = i) , \qquad \text{for } t = 0, 1, ..., T .$$

A stochastic process is defined to be a finite-state Markov chain with discrete time and space if it has the following four characteristics (Hillier and Lieberman, 1974):
1. a finite number of states;
2. the Markovian property of independent probabilities;
3. stationary transition probabilities;
4. a set of initial probabilities, $P(X_0 = i)$ for all i.
The n-step transition matrix can be calculated directly from the one-step transition matrix such that

$$\mathbf{P}^{(n)} = \mathbf{P} \times \mathbf{P} \times \mathbf{P} \times ... \times \mathbf{P} = \mathbf{P}^n .$$

Occupational mobility within the labour market possesses the first and the fourth of these characteristics but some doubts may arise concerning the second and the third. The second characteristic requires that any future state of the system be independent of past states. However, the interaction of labour supply and labour demand in an imperfect market may be affected by past transactions. This heuristic element of labour-market dynamics is most probably associated with new entrants to the labour market and therefore is unlikely to affect transitions between states in the closed system. Nonetheless, the closed system is something of a metaphysical concept, for different individuals are continuously processed through the labour market as new entrants join and retirees quit. The characteristic of stationary transition probabilities is similarly affected by the labour throughput of the system. For example, in the case of the geographic mobility of labour it has been shown that destination-choice probabilities vary with age (Gleave, 1976). More serious, it has been demonstrated that the propensity to change state varies with age (Lowry, 1966) and with duration of residence (Land, 1969; Myers et al, 1973). A number of solutions have been proposed to resolve this problem. Bartholomew (1973) and Gleave and Cordey-Hayes (1977) have proposed an extension of the state space in order to identify stationary transition parameters. However, if this state-space extension involves the incorporation of a time dimension, such as duration of residence, it may be more appropriate to consider the process of change to be semi-Markovian (see Ginsberg, 1967). The assumptions concerning the embedded transition matrix range from the elementary to the complex. Blumen et al (1955) assumed two classes of actors: movers and stayers. The former group behaved as a simple Markov chain with fixed time between moves and stationary transition matrices. The latter group simply did not move. Hyman (1976) also dichotomised actors into two classes; those with a high propensity to be mobile and those with a low propensity to be mobile. He also considered the probability of movement between classes.

The more generalised semi-Markov process resolves the problems of stationarity and point-in-time mobility by considering the distribution of time between moves and by extending the number of classes in the system to ensure stationarity (and for that matter homogeneity). The process of occupational mobility possesses many of the characteristics of the process of geographic mobility (see Gleave and Palmer, 1977), and therefore the problem of stationarity and the distribution of times between moves requires further discussion.

Consider the distribution of workers amongst a discrete and exhaustive class of occupations at two points in time t_0 and t_1. The two states may be adjacent states in a sequence or they may not be adjacent. In order to determine the stationary, embedded, transition matrix it is necessary to know the distribution of time between moves. The state of our system of interest at time t_1 will be defined by a composite set of transitions, for a proportion of actors will have made no transitions, a different proportion will have made a single transition, and so on. To simplify the analysis, we assume that actors who have not changed classes have in fact made a single transition and remained in the same class. The apparent transition matrix of moves between time t_0 and t_λ is defined as

$$T_\lambda = a_1 T + a_2 T^2 + a_3 T^3 + \ldots + a_n T^n ;$$

T is the embedded transition matrix, and $a_1, \ldots, a_n$ are the proportion of actors moving once, twice, ..., n times between t_0 and t_λ. The distribution of actors moving once, twice, ..., n times may take the form of a Poisson distribution, so that

$$a_i = \lambda^i \exp\left(-\frac{\lambda}{i!}\right),$$

where λ is the mean distribution time between moves.

If this distribution is known, it is possible to identify the embedded transition matrix. If it is not known, the time interval t_0 to t_λ should be defined so that the parameter a_i takes a high value. In those circumstances the apparent transition matrix approximates the embedded matrix and the process may be treated as a simple Markov chain. A simple example will illustrate the point.

The embedded transition matrix of a simple stochastic process is known and takes the form

$$T = \begin{vmatrix} 0{\cdot}4 & 0{\cdot}3 & 0{\cdot}3 \\ 0{\cdot}2 & 0{\cdot}5 & 0{\cdot}3 \\ 0{\cdot}3 & 0{\cdot}2 & 0{\cdot}5 \end{vmatrix} .$$

However, the observed transition matrix between t_0 and t_λ takes a different form depending upon the distribution of times between moves. Assume in case (1) that the distribution is such that half the actors move once and half move twice. In a second case, case (2), assume three quarters of the actors move once and a quarter move twice. Then the observed transition matrices will take the form

$$T_\lambda^{(1)} = 0 \cdot 5\,T + 0 \cdot 5\,T^2 ,$$

$$T_\lambda^{(2)} = 0 \cdot 75\,T + 0 \cdot 25\,T^2 .$$

$$T_\lambda^{(1)} = \begin{vmatrix} 0\cdot355 & 0\cdot315 & 0\cdot330 \\ 0\cdot235 & 0\cdot435 & 0\cdot330 \\ 0\cdot305 & 0\cdot245 & 0\cdot450 \end{vmatrix} .$$

$$T_\lambda^{(2)} = \begin{vmatrix} 0\cdot3775 & 0\cdot3075 & 0\cdot3150 \\ 0\cdot2175 & 0\cdot4675 & 0\cdot3150 \\ 0\cdot3025 & 0\cdot2225 & 0\cdot4750 \end{vmatrix} .$$

That is to say, as $a_1 \to 1 \cdot 0$, $T_\lambda \to T$ if a decreases monotonically.

In order to treat the process of occupational mobility as a simple Markov chain, we determined a transition matrix T_λ from observations of moves over a one-year period. Since these transitions represented the only available data from the 1970–1971 Census, it was not possible to determine the form of the distribution of times between moves, but it seems unlikely that a significant proportion of actors exhibited multiple transitions.

3 The occupational mobility model

The model used in this exercise generated four separate estimates of future employment by occupation and was developed in two stages. The first stage involved generating a multiple Markov model for a closed system of actors and was based on the unrealistic assumption that no actors either entered or left the labour market during the period of simulation. The second stage was concerned with modifying the model so that entrants to the system and retirements from the system were permitted. It is the output from the two-stage integrated model which is reported below.

The four separate estimates were produced to allow for different types of transition between states. Two estimates assumed that the population behaved as stayers or movers, and two assumed that all the population moved. Similarly, two models assumed that the numbers moving between states depended upon the population in the origin state, whereas two models assumed that the transitions depended upon the numbers both in the origin and in the destination states. The four types of estimate are summarised as

	Mover/stayer assumption	Mover assumption
Origin determined transitions	Markov estimate, assumption 1	Markov estimate, assumption 2
Origin/destination determined transitions	modified Markov estimate, assumption 1	modified Markov estimate, assumption 2

The transition parameters which determined the numbers changing state were therefore affected by the two assumptions and the two process types outlined. The predictor equations of the numbers in state i at time t are now outlined.

In the case of the Markov estimate under assumption 1, we assume that only the mobile population determine the transitions. The mobile population were those who were observed to change class during 1970–1971 and included some movers who were in the same class at the end of the period. This apparent paradox occurred because occupations were defined at two levels. The top tier level were the occupation orders and defined the states i, j etc, whereas the second tier level defined specific occupations within the top tier classes. A person who remained in the same state but was recorded as a mover was a person who had changed his second tier occupation but not his occupation order. Persons who changed their jobs but not their second tier occupation were, for the purpose of this analysis, deemed to be stayers. The proportions of the population who were movers and the proportion who were stayers were

$$\frac{M_{i*}}{P_i} \quad \text{and} \quad \frac{P_i - M_{i*}}{P_i} \, .$$

The conditional probability of being a mover from state i and arriving in state j was given by

$$p_{ij}^{M1} = \frac{M_{ij}}{M_{i*}} \, ,$$

and hence the numbers moving from class i to class j were

$$M_{ij}^{M1} = P_i \frac{M_{i*}}{P_i} \frac{M_{ij}}{M_{i*}} \, ,$$

where M_{ij}^{M1} are the number moving from i to j according to the Markov equations under assumption 1, M_{i*} are the total number moving out of class i, and P_i is the population of class i. This equation is generalised to give the population of class i at time t:

$$P_i^t = (P_i^0 - M_{i*}^0) + \sum_j \frac{M_{ji}^0}{M_{j*}^0} (P_j^{t-1} - P_j^0 + M_{j*}^0)$$

in which the first term enumerates the number of stayers in class i from the previous period and the second term calculates the persons moving from all j classes (including i) into class i.

The Markov model under assumption 2 defines the probability of changing classes over unit time as

$$p_{ij}^{M2} = \frac{M_{ij}}{P_i}, \qquad \text{for } j \neq i,$$

$$p_{ii}^{M2} = \frac{(P_i - M_{i*} + M_{ii})}{P_i}.$$

Hence the numbers moving from class i to class j were

$$M_{ij}^{M2} = P_i \frac{M_{ij}}{P_i}, \qquad \text{for } j \neq i.$$

During the first increment of time, this provides an estimate which is equal to the numbers moving according to assumption 1. This equation may also be generalised to give the population in class i at time t.

$$P_i^t = \frac{(P_i^0 - M_{i*}^0 + M_{ii}^0)P_i^{t-1}}{P_i^0} + \sum_{j \neq i} \frac{M_{ji}^0 P_j^{t-1}}{P_j^0}.$$

The use of the modified Markov models is more akin to a gravity-model approach, for they assume that the flow between classes is a function of an 'attraction' term and an interaction term. In this analysis the attraction term was defined as the product of the origin and destination populations. The interaction term was incorporated in the transition parameters. This term effectively measured the behaviour distance between occupations (see Gleave and Palmer, 1977). The modified Markov approach was developed to offset the simple Markov property of fossilising the destination effect as it operated at time t_0, which allocates migrants between competing destinations on a proportional basis which remains constant (Gleave, 1975). This property of the Markov chain should not be incorporated if the flow of migrants between classes is a gravity process. It was therefore necessary to develop a concept of field strength between pairs of occupations; this was defined as

$$f_{ij} = \frac{M_{ij}}{W_i W_j},$$

where f_{ij} represents the field strength from i to j, and W_i and W_j are appropriate population measures. The population measures were defined as the mover population according to assumption 1 and the total population according to assumption 2. In the case of each occupation a constant of proportionality, which varied through time, ensured that all mobile workers were allocated to a new occupation.

The population in class i at time t according to the modified Markov equations under assumption 1 was

$$P_i^t = (P_i^0 - M_{i*}^0) + \sum_j \left\{ M_{j*}^{t-1} \frac{M_{ji}^0}{M_{i*}^0} \middle/ \sum_i M_{i*}^{t-1} \frac{M_{ji}^0}{M_{i*}^0} \right\}$$

Again, the first term relates to the stayers and the second term to the movers. The movers at time $t-1$ can be defined in terms of the populations at time $t-1$ and 0 and the movers at time 0. The above equation becomes

$$P_i^t = (P_i^0 - M_{i*}^0)$$

$$+ \sum_j \left\{ (P_j^{t-1} - P_j^0 + M_{jj}^0)(P_i^{t-1} - P_i^0 + M_{ii}^0) \frac{M_{ji}^0}{M_{i*}^0} \middle/ \sum_k (P_k^{t-1} - P_k^0 + M_{kk}^0) \frac{M_{jk}^0}{M_{k*}^0} \right\}.$$

In the case of the modified Markov equations under assumption 2, the population in state i at time t was given by

$$P_i^t = \sum_j \left\{ P_j^{t-1} P_i^{t-1} \frac{M_{ji}^0}{P_i^0} \middle/ \sum_k P_k^{t-1} \frac{M_{jk}^0}{P_k^0} \right\} ,$$

where

$$M_{ii}^0 = P_i^0 - M_{i*}^0 + M_{ii}^0 .$$

These four estimator equations were then modified to take account of entrants to and retirements from the labour-market system.

The methodology applied to account for retirements from the labour-market system was restricted by the absence of adequate data. Although we were in possession of occupation data disaggregated by age, this could only have been incorporated dynamically into our model had we either known precisely how occupational transitions varied with age or assumed that occupational mobility was zero in the case of older cohorts. The second assumption may have been reasonable, in which case the numbers retiring would have been the numbers in each occupational cohort aged 60–65 during the first quinquennium, aged 55–60 during the second quinquennium, and so on. In fact we were unable to test any hypothesis relating occupational mobility and age. The assumption built into the model, which is only reasonable for short-run projections, considered that mobility behaviour preserved the initial distribution of occupational employment by age. The numbers who retired in succeeding five-year cohorts were expressed as the proportions in each occupation group aged 60–65 in 1971, aged 55–60 in 1971, etc. Although this method was far from ideal it did produce a pattern of dispersal in which relatively large numbers were retired from occupations with a high average age, and relatively small numbers were retired from occupations with a low average age. A future version of the model will fully disaggregate employment by age (as well as by occupation) so that a more rigorous accounting of retirements by occupation will be facilitated.

Entrants to the system were allocated in two ways. Firstly, they were allocated to the labour market in the same proportions as those aged 15–19 and 20–24. This method required us to calculate the proportion of a cohort aged 15–19 who entered the labour market whilst aged 15–19, and the proportion who entered whilst aged 20–24. Next the conditional probabilities were calculated according to the distributions amongst occupations of those aged 15–19 in 1971 and the distributions amongst occupations of those aged 20–24 in 1971. The second method of allocating entrants to the labour market assumed that they were sensitive to labour demand. They were allocated according to the occupational distribution of vacancies in 1971.

4 Results

The open-system models were implemented under various assumptions concerning the allocation of entrants and retirees as indicated earlier. However, using the population forecasts from the Office of Population Censuses and Surveys (OPCS) to define the total number of entrants to the labour force created a methodological problem. Our analysis has been particularly concerned with occupational turnover, but the level of this mobility is low when compared to the numbers who are expected to join the economically active population over the next few years. This 'bulge' is due to the 'baby boom' of the early 1960s which will rapidly increase the number of school and college leavers who are seeking employment from 1975 to 1985. The effect of this phenomenon was to cause a 'population growth effect' in our projections, whereby all occupations were growing rapidly owing to the number of new entrants to the labour force. In order to overcome this, the total of entrants was standardised according to the 1971 age distribution so the results identify the turnover process without the effects of future population growth.

This section will not report upon the trajectories projected for all twenty-five occupation orders, but will consider a subset in some detail. In general the most credible output was given by the Markov model, since the modified Markov model, with its cumulative approach, often exaggerates the trends occurring in the Markov model. The modified Markov model is useful for identifying occupation groups which, for example, capture in-movers from orders which themselves are growing rapidly, and expels workers to groups which are declining slowly. In such cases the modified Markov model may indicate a growth pattern, whereas the normal Markov model predicts a decline.

Looking at the output specifically, we shall first consider the approach whereby entrants were allocated on the basis of the 1971 age distributions for the 15–19 and 20–24 age cohorts. Occupation-order 2 (miners and quarrymen) exhibits a declining trajectory as one would expect given the age distribution (over 50% of all miners were aged over 44 years in 1971).

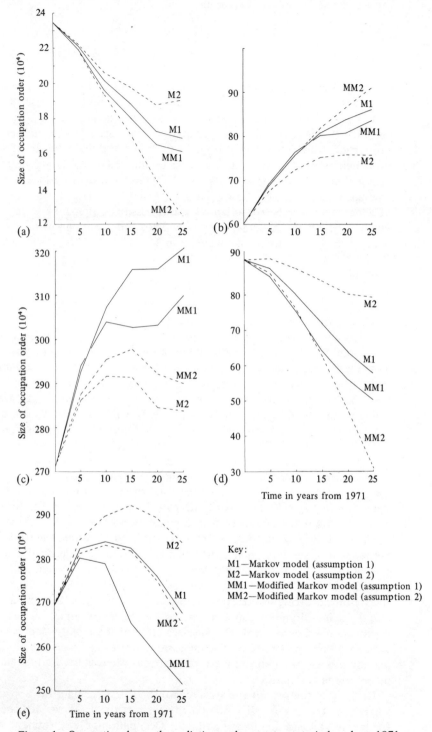

Figure 1. Occupational growth predictions, where entry rate is based on 1971 age distribution for 15–19 and 20–24 age cohorts, for occupational orders (a) 2: miners and quarrymen; (b) 6: electrical and electronics workers; (c) 7: engineers; (d) 24: administrators and managers; (e) 25: professional and technical workers.

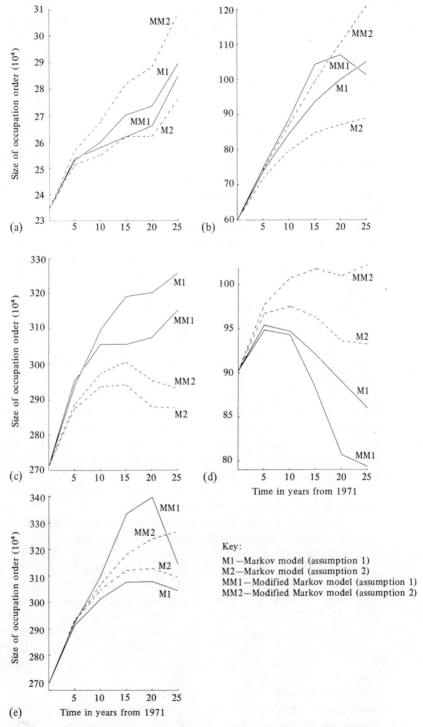

Figure 2. Occupational growth predictions, where entry rate is based on demand for labour, for the occupational orders (a) 2: miners and quarrymen; (b) 6: electrical and electronics workers; (c) 7: engineers; (d) 24: administrators and managers; (e) 25: professional and technical workers.

The reduction in the rate of expansion or increase in the number of miners [see figure 1(a)] is owing to a reduction in the numbers retiring.

The electrical and electronics workers occupation group comprises a very young population. With an entry rate into the group based on the 1971 age distribution and low retirement rates, the growth trajectories show rapid increases [figure 1(b)]. A closed Markov model excluding the entry and retirement processes would not give a growth path since, based on the statistics of the transitions of 1970–1971, this occupation order experienced a net decline.

Another occupation order of particular importance to the British economy is that of engineers (occupation-order 7). It is interesting to note that all projections exhibit very similar trends, starting with refined growth that peaks before a decline starts (under assumption 2) or continuing to grow at a slower rate [see figure 1(c)]. The industry employs many school-leavers and the later decline may be attributed to the progressive increase in retirements.

Considering two service occupations (orders 24 and 25), it is interesting to see the different trends exhibited. Administrators and managers are seen to be declining in all four forecasts. This is because of the low number of entrants in the 15–24 age-cohorts—most managers, for instance, acquire their skills and responsibilities at a particular stage of the life cycle. Furthermore the 1970–1971 transition rates were unusual in indicating a net decline owing to occupational mobility. A decline in the order projected by the modified Markov model (under assumption 2) is unlikely to occur [figure 1(d)]. Another occupation identified as being part of the primary labour market (see Gleave and Palmer, 1977) is that for professional and technical workers. All projections indicate a fairly rapid growth initially, reaching a peak and then a rapid decline [figure 1(e)]. This behaviour is again because of the age structure, which is biased towards the younger cohorts. As time progresses the proportion who retire steadily increases, thus inducing a decline.

Figure 2 reports the results for the same occupation groups but based upon the entry hypothesis regarding the effect of the demand for labour upon new entrants. The vacancy notification rates for occupation groups at the time of the census were used to define these entry rates. A very different picture emerges when compared to the earlier results. Occupation-order 2 is now seen to be growing steadily rather than declining [figure 2(a)]. Thus it appears that the demand for miners may have been growing even before the oil crisis.

The numbers of electrical and electronics workers can be seen to be growing at a slightly faster rate than before, although the growth trajectories exhibit the same basic trends [figure 2(b)]. The decline in the modified Markov model (under assumption 1) may indicate the start of a fluctuating trajectory. Occupation-order 7 (engineers) exhibits a pattern remarkably similar to that from the previous entry assumption [figure 2(c)].

The similarity of both sets of results may derive from the behaviour of employers in reporting vacancies. Both occupation groups hire younger people for apprenticeships, etc, so the entry rates based upon their distribution or on vacancies is unlikely to alter significantly.

A significant change may be seen in the case of administrators and managers [figure 2(d)]. The effect of the retirement proportions is noticeable and the initial growth stems from the demand for those skills in 1971. Occupation-order 25 (professional and technical workers), however, exhibits similar trends [figure 2(e)]. The growth rates, far higher than in the first projections, indicate the importance of the vacancies being notified.

Finally, it is important to point out that the models applied are fairly crude, based as they are on a one-year transition matrix which could give a biased indication of mobility trends. A model incorporating the age-specific occupation transition rates, with an allowance for variations in the male–female ratios, would be more realistic. The two approaches for allocating entrants are not the only alternatives. Perhaps a methodology that takes account of the long-term trends in the occupational demands for labour would be more relevant. Thus these projections should not be considered as definite predictions but rather as experiments upon which the regional scientist can develop.

5 Shift and share methods
The examination of occupational mobility by Markov analysis provides only one method of calculating employment projections by occupation. An alternative approach involves the use of the shift and share technique. Like Markov analysis, the shift and share technique is devoid of a substantive theoretical content. It does not provide the opportunity for making projections based upon a well-defined causal process incorporating relevant explanatory variables. It is usually employed as a measurement model to assess the types of change occurring within a disaggregated economic or demographic system and not to make predictions of future changes. Nonetheless it does make certain assumptions about how and why occupational employment changes vary, and in so doing is an appropriate technique for predicting future change. Unlike Markov analysis it does not require data input which directly measures the occupational mobility of persons in the labour market, and consequently requires no 'second stage' development of the type outlined in section 3. Labour supply is regarded as being exogenous in shift and share analysis, which is not concerned with the histories of employees in particular employment groups. The usage of shift and share methods for prediction purposes is best facilitated by effecting two or more analyses of employment change. This will be justified below. The data requirements are three or more matrices of employment disaggregated by occupation and by industry.

The time intervals between the observations should be equally spaced and the classifications by occupation and industry must remain stationary. The methodology of shift and share analysis is well established and has been outlined in many papers (see, for example, Ashby, 1970; Barras et al, 1977; Brown, 1972; Buck, 1970; Gleave, 1971; Paris, 1970; Stilwell, 1969).

Basically the technique assumes that changes in employment by occupation can be attributed to three factors. First, there is the growth of the economic system, which will usually be accompanied by an oscillatory component associated with trade-cycle fluctuations. Second, there is a component associated with the differential growth of industries and the initial distribution of employment by occupation amongst these industries. Last, there is a residual component which measures the extent to which occupations are substituting each other within the various industries. In a sense shift and share analysis, although not being concerned with the occupational mobility of workers, recognises, from the perspective of labour demand, three processes which are contributing to the changing match of labour and jobs. It does not explain why industries are growing differentially, neither does it explain why particular occupational substitutions are occurring. It is a measurement model which enumerates employment change as a function of these three general processes.

A shift and share analysis was carried out on data disaggregated by occupation and industry for the years 1961, 1966, and 1971. For projection purposes it is necessary either,
a) to estimate future values of system growth, proportional shift (the second component), and differential growth (the third component), or
b) to impute the system growth and proportional shift from exogenous estimates of industrial growth, and to estimate future values of differential growth.

Our analyses found that the relationship between the proportional and differential components was very tenuous (although the two shifts were positively correlated). Therefore it is not possible to estimate the future values of the shift components from exogenous information alone. Instead, we found that the values of the proportional shift and the differential shift were best predicted for most occupations by the use of the historic values of the components themselves. It is for this reason that two or more analyses should be performed. This finding is not in itself surprising, because it merely reflects the long-run processes of growth and decline of the various industry groups. Secondly it measures the long-run process of interoccupational substitution. Our preliminary results suggest that most industries are generating occupational changes through the use of more technology-oriented labour, more management and associated clerical workers, and more unskilled labour. Reductions are occurring in occupation groups associated with older craft skills. There were some occupations which were very volatile in terms of the values of their shift components, particularly those associated with the construction industry. In general the long-run consistency of *relative* industrial growth rates and occupational substitution suggested that the use of one-year occupation transition probabilities in the Markov models was fairly sound.

The components of occupational change were not extrapolated to provide alternative employment projections, but the components of change are given in table 1 so that the occupational growth occurring between 1961–1971, which we expect to continue for some time, can be compared with the results of the Markovian models.

Table 1. Shift–share components of occupational change due to industrial change.

Occupation order		Component shift		Total shift
		proportional	differential	
1	Farmers, foresters, fishermen	−15247	−4137	−19384
2	Miners and quarrymen	−21910	−3864	−25773
3	Gas, coke, and chemical makers	−790	−185	−975
4	Glass and ceramics makers	−807	−1357	−2164
5	Furnace, forge etc workers	−2315	−5345	−7660
6	Electrical, electronic workers	−1213	7408	6195
7	Engineering etc workers nec	−7563	11820	4257
8	Woodworkers	−49	−3302	−3351
9	Leather workers	−2307	−2921	−5227
10	Textile workers	−9821	−3959	−13781
11	Clothing workers	−7574	−1834	−9409
12	Food, drink, tobacco workers	−669	−560	−1229
13	Paper and printing workers	−218	−2544	−2762
14	Makers of other products	1468	−3004	−1536
15	Construction workers	1495	−5584	−4089
16	Painters and decorators	699	−7143	−6444
17	Drivers of stationary engines etc	−2334	967	−1367
18	Labourers nec	−2064	−12865	−14929
19	Transport etc workers	−7068	−5237	−12305
20	Warehousemen, storekeepers etc	−2622	−2863	−5485
21	Clerical workers	14092	21589	35681
22	Sales workers	−6363	−1188	−7552
23	Service, sport, recreation workers	28430	12444	40874
24	Administrators and managers	621	23784	24405
25	Professional, technical etc workers	41845	20304	62149
26	Armed forces	2700	−12037	−9337
27	Inadequately described occupations	−416	−18384	−18800

6 Conclusions

In this paper, we have developed a simple methodology for making projections of future employment by occupation. Furthermore, we have suggested an alternative method for making similar projections. The two methods have been based on a limited number of simple assumptions about the nature and behaviour of labour supply and labour demand, and which incorporate no substantive theory about the labour-market system.

Consequently they do not provide the policymaker with findings which allow him to specify policies for steering levels of labour supply to prespecified goals. In order to provide such information it is our belief that a more fundamental understanding of labour-market processes is required. There is, nonetheless, a rationale for developing simple models of the type which we have outlined. Firstly, they enable the policymaker to evaluate options, and monitor policies which have been applied, on the basis of existing knowledge. The Markovian model is constructed on the assumption of stationary transition parameters. The policymaker is able to affect these parameters in a variety of ways, by job retraining schemes for example, which redirect the trajectory of the system—hopefully towards the specified goals. Systems characteristics such as voluntary retirement, or even youth unemployment, could be evaluated for their impact on employment by occupation. Here we have provided a method for testing policies whilst a firmer understanding of the mechanics of the labour market is sought. Secondly, Markovian methods and shift and share analysis provide us both with measurements and with findings that provide the opportunity for proposing new hypotheses. In this context the transition parameters used for the modified Markov projections provide empirical measures of the attraction and interaction effects between occupations. A suitable measure of 'distance' between occupations (see Gleave and Palmer, 1977) permits the opportunity of factorising out interaction effects and suggesting which causal variables determine the propensity to quit occupations and which determine the values of occupational attraction. Our research findings based on the shift and share approach, which is more firmly related to labour-demand considerations, suggest that the long-run processes of industrial growth, decline, and capital substitution for labour, should be further studied as independent processes which, in the short run, can be assumed to possess stationary characteristics.

The application and development of simple labour-market models is therefore useful both from a policy monitoring perspective and in order to assist in the development of hypotheses. Only when a better understanding of the detailed mechanisms and processes of the labour market has been gained by a rigorous verification of research findings will it be productive to build and operate large-scale models. In the meantime employment policy must to some extent be speculative given existing knowledge about the labour market.

References
Ashby L D, 1970 "Changes in regional industrial structure: a comment" *Urban Studies* 7(3) 298–304
Barras R, Broadbent A, Booth D, Jaffe M, Palmer D, 1977 "Operational techniques for structure planning" unpublished Final Report, Centre for Environmental Studies, London
Bartholomew D J, 1973 *Stochastic Models for Social Processes* (John Wiley, Chichester, Sussex)

Blumen I, Kogan M, McCarthy P, 1955 *The Industrial Mobility of Labour as a Probability Process* (Cornell University Press, Ithaca, New York)

Brown A J, 1972 *The Framework of Regional Economics in the UK* (Cambridge University Press, London)

Buck T W, 1970 "Shift and share analysis—a guide to regional policy?" *Regional Studies* 4(4) 445-450

Ginsberg R, 1967 "Two papers on the use and interpretation of probability models: with applications to the analysis of migration" WP-73, Centre for Environmental Studies, London

Gleave D, 1971 "A shift and share analysis of the industrial economy 1961-1966" Department of Geography Seminar Papers number 20, University of Newcastle, Newcastle upon Tyne

Gleave D, 1975 "The utility and compatibility of simple migration models" IIASA RR 75-10, International Institute of Applied Systems Analysis, Laxenburg

Gleave D, 1976 "Macroscopic representation of causal factors in long-range migration" paper presented to the Quantitative Methods Section of the Institute of British Geographers, University of Sheffield (available from Centre for Environmental Studies, London)

Gleave D, Cordey-Hayes M, 1977 "Migration dynamics and labour market turnover" *Progress in Planning* 8 (Part 1) (Pergamon Press, Oxford)

Gleave D, Palmer D, 1977 "Labour mobility and the dynamics of labour market turnover" paper presented to the 17th European Congress of the Regional Science Association, Krakow, Poland. WN-460, Centre for Environmental Studies, London

Hillier F S, Lieberman G J, 1974 *Introduction to Operations Research* Series in Industrial Engineering and Management Science (Holden-Day, San Francisco)

Hyman G, 1976 "Cumulative inertia and the problem of heterogeneity in the analysis of geographic mobility" RP-11, Centre for Environmental Studies, London

Land K, 1969 "Duration of residence and prospective migration" *Demography* 4 293-309

Lowry I S, 1966 *Migration and Metropolitan Growth: Two Analytical Models* (Chandler, San Francisco)

Myers G C, McGinnis R, Masnick G, 1973 "The duration of residence approach to a dynamic stochastic model of internal migration: a test of the axiom of cumulative inertia" *Eugenics Quarterly* 14(2) 121-126

OPCS, 1971, Census Tables, Economic Activity Tables Part III, Table 22 (Office of Population Censuses and Surveys, London)

Paris J D, 1970 "Regional structural analysis of population changes" *Regional Studies* 4(4) 425-443

Stilwell F J B, 1969 "Regional growth and structural adaptation" *Urban Studies* 6(2) 162-178

Attitude and Social Meaning—A Proper Study for Regional Scientists

MARY BENWELL
Cranfield Institute of Technology

1 Explanation—a personal perspective

Whether or not the atmosphere of 'quiet disquiet' that has been attributed to recent discussions among regional scientists (Bennett et al, 1976) can be said to be symptomatic of the experience referred to by Kuhn (1962) as a scientific revolution leading to a paradigm shift, is quite beyond the scope of the present paper. It is, however, pertinent to the subsequent discussion to begin by providing a personal perspective on the direction in which development within regional science is likely to take place. From the fringe, recent outputs seem to suggest that the varied body of scholars who would apply to themselves the label 'spatial scientist' are now facing a series of decisions addressed to the question of how far the a priori modelling paradigm which has so far provided unification and distinctiveness should continue to form a unique focus, or to what extent alternative approaches, not necessarily compatible with existing practice, should be actively pursued as absolute alternatives (for example Carney et al, 1976). Insofar as a greater incorporation of methods of explanation from the social sciences are concerned, this can be characterised in terms of a choice between decisions to engage more actively in the exploration of theoretical approaches from disciplines such as sociology and politics, which operate according to rather different paradigms, and decisions to concentrate on a further integration of theory mainly from those disciplines such as economics and psychology, which operate according to the same paradigm as much of the existing literature of regional science, with similar logical–methodological rules.

The answer to this question will depend on the view taken by those within the subject area of precisely what it is that constitutes their distinctive contribution to knowledge; whether this resides within a particular closely defined method, or whether it is represented by a more general statement of the phenomena under study—the nature of the area of interest.

For the purpose of this paper, regional science is characterised as deriving unity from its methodology. Accordingly, research employing theory from the social sciences in order to increase levels of explanation is thought most likely to be directed so that it parallels closely or feeds directly into the existing body of knowledge within regional science. The author is here aligning directly with calls for greater attention to explanation (Cordey-Hayes, 1976) and at the same time accepting that such explanation must derive from a variety of social science perspectives. For the patterns and processes studied within regional science are the outcome of decisions, attitudes, and actions and cannot therefore be understood purely as 'objectified processes' (Habermas, 1972). However, the view is taken that the process of developing explanation must ideally be incremental to existing practice.

In proposing that certain methods from social psychology deserve more attention, the view adopted here is one of man as a 'significant intervening variable' within the existing paradigm of regional science. Thus, although a case is put forward for more attention to attitude and social meaning as of causal significance independent of objectified physical context, the method proposed is one which should offer a means for a possible refinement of existing modelling procedures through an understanding of the meaning attached by individuals to activities and places.

The paper will proceed by examining both the rationale for, and the perceived failings of, certain attempts to evolve a behavioural approach within regional science before moving to a discussion of Fishbein theory. This theory from social psychology is presented as a framework capable of overcoming certain problems encountered so far in attempts to adopt a psychological perspective within spatial studies. The potential contribution of the framework is then illustrated through a proposed research strategy.

2 Perception and space

To suggest that the spatial sciences should concern themselves with cognitive processes is, of course, hardly new. The traditions of behavioural geography have long involved a seeking for a better understanding of perception and attitude. There is now a considerable body of literature on the subject, to which Gould and Downs, have been prominent contributors (for example Gould, 1966; Downs, 1970; Downs and Stea, 1973a; Gould and White, 1975). But, as Cullen (1976) recently noted, such studies have so far tended to explain little and to generate no testable hypotheses. No obvious future directions have so far been charted and the work remains fragmentary.

To adopt a psychological perspective in the study of human spatial behaviour is to focus on the individual as a reflective significant initiator of action, whose stimulus does not derive in any objectively determinable or simple sense from the physical or social environment. The history of the appropriateness of such an approach can be derived from Kant, who acknowledged the existence of two quite different conceptions of space:
(1) that of the Newtonians—the concept of space as a real entity, with an existence independent of mind and matter;
(2) that of space as an idea—springing from the mental pattern of association between perceived objects (Kant, 1770 *Critique of Practical Reason*, cited in Beck, 1960).
The recent history of the notion that subjective space or place may provide a useful construct for understanding behaviour can be traced to the work of Tolman (1948), who introduced the idea that animals and

E

man both use a personal organising framework for their knowledge of space, and that this can be conceptualised as a cognitive map.

The mental map has now become a standard theoretical construct in human geography. For the most part, such studies have been concerned to discover the components of the individual's mental map and to depict these maps (see Gould, 1966; Gould and White, 1975; Pocock, 1976). In a recent examination of mental maps, Pacione summarised quite well the rationale for such work:

"Cognitive maps ... comprehensively influence man's locational decisions and spatial behaviour" (Pacione, 1976, page 282).

The nature of that influence has not been made explicit in many perception studies. In those instances where the relationship between cognitive process as exemplified through the mental map has been studied in conjunction with behaviour, a learning theory framework has been applied in combination with explanatory mechanisms related to activity space and action space (for example Horton and Reynolds, 1971; Moore and Brown, 1970; Mercer, 1971). In such studies, awareness of and attitude towards place is seen as a product of the learning process or the external reinforcement history of the individual or the household (Briggs, 1973). Interest is thereby focused on attitude formation in the hope that this process provides a key to prediction. In all of these studies there is an absence of any attempt to adopt a theoretical stance which explicitly links attitude to future behaviour. Indeed, the range of psychological theory evidenced in these studies points to a particularly restricted borrowing. Almost all of these studies borrow at a general level from behaviourist psychology (Skinner, 1953) adopting, for the most part, a straightforward but nonexplicit cause–effect paradigm as their aid to explanation. [It is ironic to reflect that the organisation of knowledge in this area and the perspectives adopted may have become a microcosm of the environmental determinist origins of human geography itself (Harvey, 1969).]

This paradigm, and this style of analysis, does of course have attractions. It offers the promise that, if behaviour is explicable as a response to a set of external attractions and constraints, then we have only to view the cognitive process as some kind of black box which determines systematic patterns of association between external phenomena and events and subsequent behaviour. Understanding cognitive structure amounts, then, to the identification and definition of relationships between inputs and outputs of the cognitive structure. This enables us conceptually to move from the purely physical cause–effect paradigm,

$$\beta = f(E) , \tag{1}$$

employed in a physical systems analogy, to the simple cognitively processed version;

$$\beta = f(E,R), \tag{2}$$

where

β is behaviour,

E is environmental factors,

R is the individual's reinforcement history.

But this remains a very general statement; it provides no directive on the nature of that function and thus no firm link to behaviour. There is an additional difficulty in that from this formulation there is no ready capacity for aggregation from the individual. These are fundamental weaknesses, and a severe limitation in applicability of the 'mental map' approach to cognitive structure within behavioural geography. They are seen here as key reasons why few testable hypotheses or powerful explanations of behaviour have emerged from such studies—a criticism already made by Cullen (1976).

3 Perception and the case of consumer behaviour

To demonstrate the problem outlined in general terms above, it may be helpful to consider in more detail the evidence related to one particular group of studies—shopping behaviour and shopping centre choice. The case for adopting an attitudinal approach to shopping behaviour has been thoroughly expounded elsewhere (for example Hudson, 1976) and will be well-known. It is possible to cite, for the UK, a range of studies in which an attempt has been made to operationalise an attitude model (Downs, 1970; Davies, 1973; Rigby, 1975; Hudson, 1976). In all of these studies there is an implicit objective of attempting to identify what are conceived of as 'key decision variables'. The identification of such variables would, according to the logic of the approach, ultimately make possible the incorporation into retail models of a more valid term for attraction—valid in that it conforms to the considerations used by the individual in making the decision to use a particular centre or location, and for which the standard existing indices can only form proxies. Such studies are, then, undertaken in search of explanation of the use of locations and the assumption made is that predictive capacity will be improved through identification of key elements in the decision process. These, through their susceptibility to empirical identification, are seen as a possible alternative to the use of microeconomic theory.

Unfortunately, none of the studies employing psychological variables have so far provided any improvement on the standard physical proxies. Rigby (1975) has compared the performance of a simple gravity model using a perception-based attraction index (based on empirically derived attributes and weightings) with the same model using retail floorspace as the attractor. He concludes that it seems likely that no substantial

improvement in model formulation will result from the use of a psychological approach, but remains hopeful that such studies may afford an
increase in the degree of explanation achieved. Hudson (1976) also
accepts the conceptual validity of the approach, but admits to considerable
problems of translation of the concepts into an operational form. Hudson's
work was concerned with the testing of probabilistic models of shopping
centre choice, in which the most likely choice is described as a function
of the combined weighting on a group of variables which represent those
attributes previously established empirically as crucial to the individual's
discrimination between centres. Both Rigby and Hudson accept, as
Downs (1970) had done earlier, that the explanation of shopping
movements must rest on a recognition that such movements are the
outcome of processes which must be conceptualised in terms more complex
than distance minimisation or a balancing of distance reduction against
objectively definable characteristics of destinations, particularly where low
levels of aggregation are used.

The apparent incapacity of this kind of research to identify in more
definitive terms, through the generation of testable explanatory propositions,
the way in which perception studies should be directed, might be taken as
a signal for the demise of the perception or attribute approach as being
inoperable, despite the compelling rationale for the initiation of such
studies. But such a verdict would, it is argued, be premature since the
failure adequately to operationalise this approach could be said to derive
from a failure to appraise rigorously enough the theoretical implications
of what has been attempted, rather than from some intrinsic incompatibility
of technique. The main point which this paper seeks to establish is that
the construct that has been used in the studies outlined above, and in a
number of others, is an incomplete formulation of the constructs 'attitude'
or 'cognitive process' as understood in social psychology. Researchers
have tended to devote attention only to the attributes of destinations,
whether subsequently treated by ranking (Hudson, 1976), rating (Rigby,
1975), or in some combinational formula (Downs, 1970). There is no
theoretical basis in social psychology for suggesting that any index or
formula so derived will have any specific directive influence on behaviour,
whether alone or in combination with objectively derived constraints and
attractors. No psychologist would, therefore, be surprised at the lack of
potential for development observable in such studies.

If it is accepted that, despite the difficulties so far encountered in the
development of methods of explanation derived from psychology, it is
appropriate to attempt to incorporate a view of human behaviour which
acknowledges determinants internal to the individual, then it seems that a
new way of incorporating this view must be sought. What will be required
is a theoretical base which is capable of providing an integrative framework
within which attitude to place/space and its relationship to behaviour can
be specified and tested. Ideally, such a framework would be capable of

operationalisation for empirical testing. Susceptibility to mathematical formulation may also be seen as an advantage, but this should be a secondary rather than a primary requirement.

4 Fishbein theory—an applicable framework

4.1 The theory

Fishbein theory (Ajzen and Fishbein, 1975) fulfils all of the conditions outlined above. The theory has been developed by psychologists through a series of models, starting from a model of cognitive structure which is then built into an expectancy value or predictive form. The formulations thus provide links from cognitive structure to behaviour (see figure 1). It should not be claimed that the theory is new to the spatial sciences for Downs, for example, did cite some early work of Fishbein (Downs and Stea, 1973b) in a collection of papers on attitude and environment. (He appears not to have considered it worthy of further attention within spatial studies.)

The cognitive structure employed in Fishbein theory conceives of a complex set of interrelated components which together constitute the construct referred to widely in the nonspecialist literature as 'attitude' or 'perception'. Within the Fishbein framework, beliefs, attitudes, intentions (and also behaviours in the expectancy-value version) are distinct variables, with different determinants, but with stable and systematic relationships between them. It is important to note the differences between these components.

A *belief* is a probability judgement linking some object or concept to some quality or attribute[1]. The content of the belief is defined by the aspect and attribute in question and the strength of the belief is defined as the individual's subjective probability that the object–attribute relationship exists or is true.

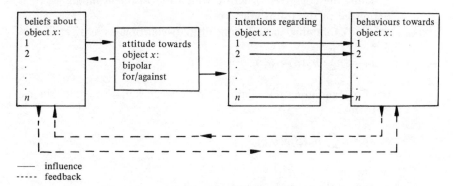

---- influence
----- feedback

Figure 1. Schematic representation of Fishbein's cognitive structure and its link with behaviour (after Otway and Fishbein, 1976).

[1] This is a generic use of object and attribute to refer to any discriminable aspect of an individual's world, for example, that shop A (object) is cheap (attribute).

Attitude or more correctly *affect* is an evaluative judgement on a bipolar scale. It is essentially subjective and an expression of favourable or unfavourable feelings towards the object.

Intention is a probability judgement linking the individual to some specific action, that is, the individual's belief that he will perform some behaviour. The intention will have a strength that is defined by the individual's subjective probability that he will engage in that behaviour.

Behaviour is the observable action.

Figure 1 summarises the relationship in Fishbein theory between beliefs, attitudes, intentions, and behaviours. The term 'attitude' as used in the general literature must be deemed to constitute the whole of this complex hypothetic construct. A person's 'attitude' towards any object, situation or place will thus be a function of his beliefs about that object weighted by his evaluations of associated attributes. It is important to recognise that attitude will be determined not by any one specific belief but by a set of salient beliefs (those key beliefs which the individual applies to the object/situation in question). A person's attitude towards an object is likely to be determined by a relatively small number of salient beliefs—a number between five and nine (Miller, 1956; Mandler, 1967). Salience will tend to vary from time to time, as it will depend to a varying extent upon the context in which the attitude object is brought into focus (Kaplan and Fishbein, 1969). Once an attitude has been formed towards an object, a person is predisposed to perform a pattern of behaviour with respect to that object. It must, however, be recognised that the attitude predisposes a person to engage in a set of behaviours that, when taken together, are consistent with the attitude—it does *not* predispose (or therefore offer a predictive capacity for) particular behaviour in the micro sense.

Thus, the cognitive structure which the Fishbein model assumes is expressed in the following terms:

(a) For examining the relationship between objects and attributes

$$a_o = \sum_{x=1}^{m} b_x(o)\, e(\alpha_x) . \tag{3}$$

(b) For examining the relationship between behaviours and their expected outcomes

$$a_\beta = \sum_{x=1}^{n} b_x(\beta) e(\omega_x) \tag{4}$$

where

a_o is the attitude towards object o,

$b_x(o)$ is the strength of belief x relating object o to attribute α_x,

$e(\alpha_x)$ is the evaluation of attribute α_x,

m is the number of beliefs about object o,

a_β is the attitude towards behaviour β,

$b_x(\beta)$ is the strength of belief relating behaviour β to outcome ω_x,

$e(\omega_x)$ is the evaluation of outcome ω_x,

n is the number of beliefs about outcomes of behaviour β.

These models represent the cognitive structure built up by the individual through his history of transactions with the external world. The structure consists of cognitive entities ('objects') linked by beliefs about attributes of these entities and weighted by evaluation of those attributes.

A predictive model can be developed from this cognitive theory and is explained in more detail by Thomas (1975). This model bases behavioural intention on two factors: (1) The personal feelings or affect towards the behaviour in question as derived from equation (3) or equation (4) above, and (2) external pressures of a normative kind. These pressures can be expressed in the form of beliefs about the expectations of reference groups, significant referent individuals, or institutions. Within the predictive model, components (1) and (2) are kept as separate terms, although they are not qualitatively different. This, as Thomas explains, is in keeping with the traditions of social psychology. The resultant model for the prediction of behavioural intention is thus:

$$\beta \approx i_\beta = a_\beta w_I + s_\beta w_2 , \tag{5}$$

where

β is the behaviour in question,

i_β is the intention to engage in that behaviour,

a_β is the attitude towards performance of that behaviour,

s_β is the generalised social norm with respect to that behaviour,

w_1 and w_2 are empirically determined weights.

The theoretical base from which the models derive has supported a large number of empirical studies. The cognitive structure it assumes is far more complex than that implied by any of the work carried out so far in space perception. Although the mathematics involved in any of the forms of study engaged in so far involving these models [equations (3), (4), or (5)] is simple, possibly naive, the models have been shown to be of operational value. The constructs employed in this theory are integrated in a way which makes it a very flexible tool; it can be used for both evaluative and predictive purposes, and it provides a basis for rigorous study of the dynamics of attitude change (Wyer, 1970).

4.2 Applications

Although these models have not so far been applied to any aspect of locational choice, they have provided a base from which a considerable range of empirical studies have been conducted across a variety of volitional behaviours. For instance, for the relationship between attitude towards an object and the beliefs held about it [equation (3)] Fishbein (1963) demonstrated the link with a correlation of $r = 0 \cdot 80$ in a study of attitudes towards negroes. In a more recent study of attitude towards electoral candidates, Fishbein and Coombs (1974) obtained correlations of $r = 0.69$ and $r = 0.87$. Likewise the relationship between attitude towards, and beliefs about, the outcome of a particular behaviour [equation (4)] have been demonstrated with a correlation of $r = 0.73$ (Jaccard and Davidson, 1972). The part of Fishbein theory which is most likely to be of interest within regional science is the behaviour prediction model [equation (5)]. Although it is a more recent development within the theory, this too has a growing support from empirical studies in that here also high levels of correlation have been identified. Jaccard and Davidson (1972), for instance, in a study of intention to use the contraceptive pill, obtained a multiple correlation of $R = 0.84$. In market research (where there has been much interest in the theory), Wilson et al (1975) obtained a value of $R = 0.67$ in a study of intention to buy a given brand of toothpaste. Thomas (1976), in a recent application of a modified version of the expectancy-value model for the prediction of transport mode use, obtained a value of $R = 0.73$ for the prediction of transport mode for midweek shopping at a regional centre from a suburban origin.

It can be demonstrated, then, that the cognitive structure that the theory assumes, and the theoretic links to behaviour, are susceptible to empirical verification and that the studies carried out to date have confirmed the applicability of the framework to a wide range of volitional behaviour.

Although there is not the scope within the present paper to give a really detailed account of particular studies, it is relevant here to focus briefly on two particular capacities which the Fishbein methodology offers for improving understanding of behaviour. The first of these is the capacity to provide a complex statement of attitude which can, where appropriate, be summed to give one attitude score, which can then be employed as a basis for disaggregation of a population. But at the same time this summed attitude score can be examined in its molecular form to allow for examination of differences among a population in the scoring on individual salient beliefs. Otway and Fishbein (1976) in an ongoing research project, have recently employed this facility in an attempt to improve understanding of the totality of social response to nuclear technology. This is of interest at the overall attitude (molar) level for, as has been outlined, summed 'attitude' as derived from equation (3) can be expected to provide a clear picture of the general pattern of behaviours that individuals will perform. This particular study also identified key differences in determinant beliefs about nuclear power between the two 'attitude groups' among respondents, those of positive and of negative overall attitude. It was found that the groups did not differ significantly in their beliefs about risk-related attributes but that it was possible, from the objective measures obtained, to identify major differences arising from opposite beliefs about benefits. The main factors distinguishing between what Otway and Fishbein (1976) identify as the 'risk' and 'risk averse' groups were the beliefs that people are exposed to nuclear risks involuntarily. This research has enabled a more rigorous and detailed appraisal of the differences in perception that had been generally supposed to give rise to social conflict. By understanding the way in which differential characterisation of the technology arises, it becomes possible to ask relevant questions about how far changes in the technology may effect a response in the cognitive structures underlying the overall response of particular subgroups. At this level, the Fishbein method is being employed to examine attributes in a way that can be thought of as a parallel with certain existing studies of place. Harrison and Sarre (1971) for example have used personal construct theory to attempt to measure the image of the urban environment held by individuals. Salient beliefs and personal constructs have much in common. The main advantage of the Fishbein method for this kind of work derives from its ability to guide the formulation of expected behaviours through the links developed in equations (4) and (5).

One of the more recent studies which has included a test of the predictive version of the models, is that undertaken by Thomas (1976) with respect to transport-mode choice behaviour. The 'attitude' approach in transport research has had a rather similar history to that of the attitude approach to location studies. Here too, early work has been much concerned with the use of scorings on transport system attributes as a means of disaggregating populations (segmenting them, in the market-research term), on the assumption that this would enable key attitudes to be identified. Thomas (1976) provides a discussion of the way in which this style of research, by ignoring the question of salience, fails to operationalise appropriate theoretical concepts and is based on an inexplicit view of the attitude–behaviour link.

Thomas's work on the use of the bus for off-peak shopping had two main aims:
(1) to test the expectancy-value model in its summed form [equation (5)],
(2) to examine the content and stability of the belief systems, while testing the model in its molecular form [equation (4)].

The relationship between predictor variables and overt behaviour gave values of $R = 0 \cdot 734$ for 'using the bus' and $R = 0 \cdot 720$ for 'not using the bus'. The relationship between the attitude variables and intention for the two acts over the aggregated sample of all women gave multiple correlations of $R = 0 \cdot 768$ and $R = 0 \cdot 725$ for the two behaviours (Thomas et al, 1977).

In an examination of the structure and stability of belief systems about transport modes, it was found that the beliefs held reflected closely the alternatives each individual perceived as relevant to her. One important finding was the improvement in prediction which resulted when evaluations of use/nonuse and the difference between them were used in the prediction equation. Overall, although significant correlations were found between attitude, intention, and behaviour, these were lower than in other studies (28% of variance accounted for in comparison with ~50% elsewhere). Thomas concluded that, because of the routinised nature of much travel, attitude may in this instance be more influenced by behavioural commitment (a feedback loop from behaviour to attitude). It is interesting to relate this comment to the notions inherent in the activity-system approach to transport demand (Horton, 1972).

4.3 General applicability within regional science

These examples, although not directly of interest within regional science, have been quoted in support of the claim that the Fishbein methodology is extremely flexible and worthy of closer evaluation within a spatial context. It appears to have the following combined advantages not so far met in total by any existing approach to attitude within regional sciences:
(a) It assumes a complex structure of the construct 'attitude' which is rigorously related to a theory which is widely accepted within social psychology. This is in distinct contrast to the use of overall affect, common in perception studies, whose simple structure tends to be implicit rather than explicit. Such a simple structural view of attitude has no widely accepted theoretical base within psychology, since it subsumes, or ignores, other components of attitude structure.
(b) The elements within the models in all of their forms [equations (2), (4), and (5)] are highly operational and have been widely used in a variety of empirical studies (Thomas, 1976; Otway and Fishbein, 1976; Fishbein and Coombs, 1974; Jaccard and Davidson, 1972).
(c) The models have considerable flexibility of application. If a term for place, movement, or activity is substituted for the term object or behaviour in equations (3), (4), or (5), it can be seen that it becomes possible to use the models to build an understanding of the meaning and construction placed by the individual on locations and activities.
(d) The models are integrative in that they build from a theory of attitude structure into a predictive mode. They thus provide a framework into which studies can be linked at a variety of scales and levels of explanation from descriptive evaluation of place/activity/space to the prediction of behaviour.
(e) The molecular structure of the models makes it possible to derive a variety of bases for disaggregation at different levels (for example, through common weightings on salient beliefs, similarities in degree of personal or normative (external) control of behaviour, differences in the degree of correlation between attitude and behaviour). This choice can be made during analysis and offers great flexibility for insights into a data set.

The major disadvantage of the Fishbein method is its requirement for extensive primary data. The methods prescribed by all of the models call for a multistage in-depth survey. At the design stage, an initial survey is required to elicit salient beliefs which are common to the cognitive framework of a whole population or subgroups of that population. The modal salient beliefs are then used for a second-stage survey on the full survey population, at which stage the weightings on the salient beliefs, evaluation of them, and behavioural intention are established. At this stage any other data specified by the researcher will also be collected. This requirement will be specified through the research design, but is likely to include demographic and locational data for any research designed within regional science. Where the predictive version of the model is being tested or used as a tool, there is then a need for data on the subsequent performance of the particular behaviour under examination. This stage may be carried out through a self-completion data-collection technique, but it is likely to require one or more follow-up contacts by the research staff. The technique is thus particularly costly in data-collection terms and, like all social surveys, it is dependent on the cooperation of the survey population. This could be seen as a source of weakness or potential lack of rigour. These disadvantages are, of course, common to all attitude research, and do not apply only to the Fishbein method.

5 A strategy for an integrated research programme

One reason why Fishbein theory may be of immediate interest as a tool in regional science is its obvious applicability in association with existing techniques of study. This is less true of, for example, methods of sociological explanation, whose application may be expected to require a longer timescale.

Since shopping models are already, as outlined earlier, a focus of interest for psychological studies (Downs, 1970; Hudson, 1976, etc) they offer an obvious starting point in that relevant problem areas have already been identified. It is thus possible to identify several phases in an overall strategy for research using the Fishbein method (see table 1). Because of the cost of data, it is helpful to design individual projects with a longer-term strategy in mind.

Phase 1. An early phase would be the examination of cognitive structure [equation (3)] as it relates to the shopping activity. The key objective at this stage would be an examination of the beliefs and belief strengths held by populations from a selected number of origins about certain named centres available to them. It will, of course, be important to classify shopping activity and to control for the fact that it is not one definitive activity. The use of named centres would enable the researcher to examine the extent to which objective characteristics relate to the weightings on the subjective conceptions. It is likely that research on process may be required within this phase of the work. The output from this work should also provide a means of identification of several (objective and subjective) criteria for disaggregation of the population, useable for calibration purposes at phase 2.

Phase 2. The next phase of the research would use the models at equations (4) and (5), incorporating means of relating to phase 1 findings. Research now focuses on the relationship between attitude, behavioural intention, and behaviour. At this stage research must be designed with the deterrence term in the spatial model as a constant either across subgroups or for the full population. The objective of this phase would be to test the possibility of identifying subjectively derived terms for attractors in place of existing proxies. This would be achieved through the examination of the relationship between subjective and objective measures of destinations and the formulation of a logic about the processes involved in consumer behaviour. At this phase, calibration of the shopping model would incorporate a test of usefulness of different groupings identified at phase 1.

So far the outlined research attempts, via a different method, to test the same notions as those presented by Rigby (1975) and Hudson (1976). The Fishbein framework now enables a further stage to be specified, which would build on the research outlined above.

Phase 3. This phase would be a more general testing of the relationships established or suggested at phases 1 and 2, in order to evaluate the level

Table 1. General description of a strategy for the evaluation of Fishbein theory in relation to shopping models.

Phase	Fishbein model to be used	Research question to be answered
1	$a_o = \sum_{x=1}^{m} b_x(o)e(\alpha_x)$	What is the cognitive structure of given shopping centres for a particular activity? (with the use of a population from one origin) How do beliefs, their strengths, and their evaluations vary across the population? How do subjective and objective descriptors of destinations compare?
2	$a_\beta = \sum_{x=1}^{n} b_x(\beta)e(\omega_x)$ and $\beta \approx i_\beta = a_\beta w_1 + s_\beta w_2$	What is the relationship between individual weightings on modal beliefs, evaluations, etc and behavioural intention? What subgroups are identifiable? How do these match output from phase 1?
3	All these versions	How generalisable are the findings from phases 1 and 2? Are *operational* new variables indicated? Do newly identified subgroups improve goodness-of-fit? How far can new variables be used without a full Fishbein survey?

of generalisation attainable. At this point, the researcher attempts to move from a microlevel to a macrolevel by testing, without a full Fishbein survey, the validity of the attraction measures and the population aggregations already identified in the micro studies at phases 1 and 2. Here certain crucial questions have to be answered:

(a) How far do the nonspatial attributes highlighted by this approach correspond, contradict, or reinforce the traditionally employed spatial variables?

(b) Is sensitivity and goodness-of-fit improved by the adoption of the new variables?

(c) To what extent does the research enable us to specify, for any study area, better attractor variables which apply at a nomothetic level?

(d) Do the groupings established on the basis of differential attitudes, beliefs, or perceptions suggest useful guidelines for an improved method of aggregation/disaggregation of population through the use of variables or weightings from data which are widely available?

It is upon the answers to the last two questions that the regional scientist is most likely to judge the relevance and applicability of the approach. If the answer to questions (a) and (b) is affirmative, then the responses to questions (c) and (d) will define whether a completely new method, or merely refinement of existing practice, is indicated.

6 Conclusions

Regional science has been depicted as a field of scientific endeavour which may in Kuhn's (1962) terms be in the throes of a scientific revolution, the point at which paradigm shift occurs. Although some of the pressures are external (through a change of specification of style and level of explanation required by decisionmakers applying the subject) certain of the reasons for this may be internal (a partial failure to comply with the 'puzzle-solving' rules of the paradigm adopted). It has been suggested that a richer level of explanation, and one which is more readily applicable to operational problemsolving may be found through a more active acceptance within regional science of man as a reflective initiator of action, whose motivations constitute a proper area of study. To this end, a particular applicable method from social psychology has been outlined and a general research strategy set out.

Although there is nothing particularly novel in the aspiration, the method suggested appears to offer an important breakthrough in that it provides both the sound theoretical base and the integrative conceptual framework which, it is here argued, have been lacking in existing studies of attitude to place and space perception.

The potential applicability of this methodology has been only briefly sketched. It is inevitably influenced by the author's own research interests and there are good reasons to propose that the methodology could be applied not only to the attraction but also to the deterrence terms in the gravity-based models of spatial behaviour. The scope and flexibility of the framework are likely to allow application to a whole range of activities and scales of study, both static and dynamic.

All that is sought at this stage is conviction on the part of a small number of researchers that the method briefly described above is applicable, and that the pursuit of knowledge within this framework has relevance in areas which are currently construed as problems.

References
Ajzen I, Fishbein M, 1975 *Belief, Attitude, Intention and Behaviour: An Introduction to Theory and Research* (Addison-Wesley, Cambridge, Mass)
Beck L W, 1960 *A Commentary on Kant's 'Critique of Practical Reason'* (University of Chicago Press, Chicago, Ill.)
Bennett R, Thrift N, Wrigley N, 1976 "Report on Proceedings of the Joint IBG/RSA Conference, May 1976" *Area* 8(4) 243–245
Briggs R, 1973 "Urban cognitive distance" in *Image and Environment* Eds R Downs, D Stea (Edward Arnold, London) pp 361–388
Carney J, Hudson R, Ive G, Lewis J, 1976 "Regional underdevelopment in late capitalism: a study of the Northeast of England" in *London Papers in Regional Science 6. Theory and Practice in Regional Science* Ed. I Masser (Pion, London) pp 11–29
Cordey-Hayes M, 1976 "A structural approach to dynamic modelling" paper delivered to Joint IBG/RSA Conference, May, University College London
Cullen I G, 1976 "Human geography, regional science, and the study of individual behaviour" *Environment and Planning A* 8(4) 397–410
Davies R L, 1973 "Patterns and profiles of consumer behaviour" RP-10, Department of Town and Country Planning, University of Newcastle upon Tyne, England
Downs R, 1970 "The cognitive structure of an urban shopping area" *Environment and Behavior* 2 13–39
Downs R, Stea D, 1973a *Image and Environment* (Edward Arnold, London)
Downs R, Stea D, 1973b "Cognitive maps and spatial behaviour: process and products" in *Image and Environment* Eds R Downs, D Stea (Edward Arnold, London)
Fishbein M, 1963 "An investigation of the relationship between beliefs about an object and attitude to that object" *Human Relations* 16 233–240
Fishbein M, Coombs F S, 1974 "Basis for decision: an analysis of voting behaviour" *Journal of Applied Social Psychology* 4 95–124
Gould P R, 1966 "On mental maps" *Michigan Inter-University Conference on Mathematical Geography* 9 1–54
Gould P, White P R, 1975 *Mental Maps* (Penguin, Harmondsworth, Middx)
Habermas J, 1972 *Knowledge and Human Interests* (Heinemann, London)
Harrison J A, Sarre P, 1971 "Personal construct theory in the measurement of environmental images" *Environment and Behavior* 3 351–374
Harvey D, 1969 *Explanation in Geography* (Edward Arnold, London)
Horton F E, 1972 "Behavioural models in transportation planning" *ASCE Transportation Engineering Journal* 98 411
Horton F E, Reynolds D R, 1971 "Effects of urban spatial structure on individual behaviour" *Economic Geography* 47 36–48
Hudson R, 1976 "Linking studies of the individual with models of aggregate behaviour: an empirical example" *Transactions, Institute of British Geographers* 1(2) (new series) 159–173

Jaccard J J, Davidson A R, 1972 "Towards an understanding of family planning behaviour: an initial investigation" *Journal of Applied Social Psychology* **2** 228–235

Kaplan H J, Fishbein M, 1969 "The source of beliefs, their saliency and prediction of attitude" *Journal of Social Psychology* **78** 63–74

Kuhn T S, 1962 *The Structure of Scientific Revolutions* (University of Chicago Press, Chicago, Ill.)

Mandler G, 1967 "Verbal learning" in *New Direction in Psychology* volume 3, Ed. T M Newcomb (Holt, New York) pp 1–50

Mercer D, 1971 "Discretionary travel behaviour and the urban mental map" *Australian Geographical Studies* **9**(2) 133–143

Miller G A, 1956 "The magical number seven; plus or minus two: some limits of our capacity for processing information" *Psychological Review* **63** 81–97

Moore E G, Brown L A, 1970 "The intra-urban migration process: a perspective" *Geografiska Annaler Series B* **52** 1–13

Otway H J, Fishbein M, 1976 "The determinants of attitude formation: an application to nuclear power" RM-76-80, Institute for Applied Systems Analysis, Laxenburg, Austria

Pacione M, 1976 "Shape and structure in cognitive maps of Britain" *Regional Studies* **10**(3) 275–284

Pocock D C D, 1976 "Characteristics of mental maps" *Transactions, Institute of British Geographers* **1**(4) (new series) 493–512

Rigby D, 1975 "Consumers perceptions of shopping centres" Transactions, Seminar M, Annual Meeting PTRC (PTRC, London)

Skinner B F, 1953 *Science and Human Behavior* (Macmillan, New York)

Thomas K, 1975 "A test of the predictive accuracy of a modified expectancy value model and an examination of evaluative and cognitive variables in the use of a suburban bus service" Technical Report, Centre for Transport Studies, Cranfield Institute of Technology, Cranfield, Beds, England

Thomas K, 1976 "A reinterpretation of the 'attitude' approach to transport-mode choice and an exploratory empirical test" *Environment and Planning A* **8**(7) 793–810

Thomas K, Bull H C, Clark J M C, 1977 "Attitude measurement in the forecasting of off-peak travel behaviour" in *Urban Transportation Planning* Eds M A Dalvi, P W Bonsall, P J Hills (Abacus Press, London)

Tolman E C, 1948 "Cognitive maps in rats and men" *Psychological Review* **55** 189–208

Wilson D T, Matthews H L, Harvey J W, 1975 "An empirical test of the Fishbein behavioural intention model" *Journal of Consumer Research* **1** 39–48

Wyer R S, 1970 "The prediction of evaluations of social role occupants as a function of the favourableness, relevance and probability associated with attributes of those occupations" *Sociometry* **33** 79–96

Approaches to Multiple-objective Decisionmaking with Ranked Criteria

A D PEARMAN
University of Leeds

1 Introduction

In recent years an increasing number of papers has been appearing in the regional science literature, concerned with both the theory and the practice of multiple-criteria decisionmaking. French and Dutch authors in particular have made significant contributions. The majority of early formal work in multiple-criteria decisionmaking appears to have emanated from the United States and to be attributable to psychologists and management scientists. However, many of the techniques derived are far from being restricted in their application to single subjects, and many other potential areas of application exist. For example, public policy decisions, including the large number which are of interest to regional scientists, frequently involve the consideration of a wide range of consequences which affect many different groups of people in different places and in different ways. It is not surprising, therefore, that regional scientists should be fully involved in the development of a coherent and applicable body of knowledge concerned with multiple-criteria decisionmaking.

Section 2 of this paper contains a brief review of the wide range of formal techniques available to assist in multiple-criteria decisionmaking problems. It emphasises that there is no single technique which is unambiguously superior to all others. The most appropriate method, or indeed combination of methods, will vary from problem to problem. The need is to develop a strategy for presenting all those potential courses of action which might reasonably be regarded as attractive without obscuring what is at best likely to be a complex decision by the presence of many less desirable possibilities.

Section 3 then goes on to introduce a new formal technique for comparing different courses of action. Its principal recommendations are simplicity of application, the use of an ordinal rather than a cardinal scale for assessing the relative importance of different criteria, and comparison based on the performance of each alternative policy relative to the performance of all other possibilities for each individual criterion. Section 4 gives a brief numerical example and section 5 concludes the paper with an assessment of the current state of multiple-criteria decisionmaking, particularly from the point of view of practising regional scientists.

2 Formal techniques for assisting with multiple-criteria decisionmaking

Many questions of public policy, including a great number of interest to regional scientists, have to be answered in the face of two major problems.

These are first, uncertainty and, second, the difficulty if not impossibility of unambiguously mapping the multidimensional descriptions of the consequences of alternative policies onto a single ordinal scale. The use of formal methods rather than a purely subjective ranking of alternatives cannot totally dissipate the difficulties caused by these two factors. It does, however, have some value. Formalisation can help clarify both what is being aimed at and the relative importance of conflicting goals. Furthermore communication with other decisionmakers and with members of the public is facilitated if some framework for presenting and comparing the consequences of different courses of action exists.

Even if it may ultimately be possible to develop a single strategy for handling simultaneously the twin problems of uncertainty and multiple criteria, current practice is nowhere near this point. This section therefore concentrates on the formal assessment of preferences in the presence of multiple criteria. It ignores the problem of uncertainty. What will be presented is a brief outline of a series of different approaches to handling deterministic multiple-criteria problems. No one of the techniques is superior to all others. Each has its own weaknesses, which it is important to recognise in deciding what method, or combination of methods, is most likely to aid the solution of any given problem.

The best-known methods for reducing multiple consequences to a single dimension are of course straightforward financial appraisal and cost–benefit analysis. In the former case, market prices are used to evaluate the different consequences of a course of action. In the latter, account is taken of consequences which may not have a market and for which shadow prices have to be estimated. The criticisms of cost–benefit analysis and related techniques are well documented, see for example Nijkamp (1975, pages 89–91) for a brief summary. They need not be recounted here. Essentially, however, the problem is that in reducing the multiple-dimensional consequences of an act to a single-dimensional evaluation, information is inevitably lost. If there is no doubt about the rates at which decisionmakers are prepared to trade off different consequences against each other at all different levels of attainment of those consequences, then reduction to a single dimension should cause no great problem. If, however, as is very likely, this is not the case, then two major techniques of multiple-criteria analysis immediately gain importance. One of these is the comparison and ranking of strategies on the basis of more than one dimension of decision. The other is the reduction of the dimensionality of the problem by fixing acceptable weights to the different consequences of strategies and the exploration of the implications of some tolerance in the precise values of those weights. In almost all cases of any complexity the second will be an essential component of any evaluation strategy. What will vary is the manner in which the weights are decided upon and the extent to which strategy comparison takes place before weights are used to reduce the original problem to a single dimension.

Thus, when the notation of Keeney and Raiffa (1976) is used, the typical situation is to be faced with a set of feasible policy choices (acts), A, with individual members, a. [In this paper, acts, strategies, and courses of action will be used interchangeably, unlike, for example, Fishburn (1964).] With each $a \in A$ is associated an n-tuple, $X = (X_1, ..., X_n)$ of evaluators of each act, a. This n-tuple maps the act, a, into n-dimensional consequence space. X may be regarded as a vector of attributes. Although some (relatively weak) methods will be discussed for ranking different X vectors while they are still in vector form, the principal concern will be with techniques for collapsing the $X_1, ..., X_n$ into a scalar index of value by using a function defined on consequence space such that

$$v(X_1, ..., X_n) \geqslant v(X_1', ..., X_n') \Leftrightarrow (X_1, ..., X_n) > (X_1', ..., X_n')$$

or, equivalently, $a > a'$. (The symbol $>$ represents weak preference. Throughout this section it is assumed that high levels of the value function are preferable, that is, that 'highest' is synonymous with 'best'.) Both the parameters of the value function and the sensitivity of policy choice to changes of parameter values will be important.

MacCrimmon (1973) provides a valuable survey of multiple-criteria decisionmaking models, identifying four major categories, (1) weighting methods; (2) sequential-elimination methods; (3) mathematical programming methods, and (4) spatial-proximity methods.

(1) *Weighting methods.* These methods construct the scalar index of value, $v(X_1, ..., X_n)$, by associating a weight with each attribute, aggregating the weighted individual measures, and selecting the alternative with the highest-weighted sum. At one point or another, a weighting method is central to the evaluation procedure of most practical multiple-criteria decisionmaking models. The main difference between methods lies in the techniques used for establishing the weights. For example, if numerical values can be associated with each consequence and a numerical evaluation exists for past decisions of a similar nature, then linear regression techniques can be used. The regression coefficients found by regarding the level of each consequence as an explanatory variable for the overall decision score are used as weights to establish the ranking of future possible actions. The regression approach, of course, requires that an adequate number of past decisions has occurred to estimate the regression equation and that such decisions have been undertaken on a desirable and consistent basis. If this is not the case, the regression model has little value as a normative decisionmaking aid. In many matters of regional public policy, one or more of these requirements may well not hold.

Alternatively weights may be established by direct analysis of the decision-maker's response to a series of hypothetical questions. Contradictions in decisionmaking are likely to be highlighted by such an approach and these have to be overcome by forcing the decisionmaker to reconcile such inconsistencies. This can be a time-consuming process. The weights ultimately elicited may well be a good summary of the decisionmaker's attitude to hypothetical choices, but there will always be an element of doubt that his behaviour in handling real choices may be, for example, more cautious.

A very simplistic, but on occasion useful, weighting scheme uses ideas from the field of decisionmaking under uncertainty, *viz* maximin and maximax. In the maximax case, for each possible strategy, a weight of one is given to the consequence recording the highest score for that strategy. A maximax choice then selects that strategy which has the maximum maximum level of achievement in terms of all the consequences considered. Maximin strategy choice is defined analogously. The use of this kind of approach to weighting is discussed further in section 3.

(2) *Sequential-elimination methods.* These techniques should perhaps be seen as filtering methods rather than ways of identifying a single optimal act. They can be used to rank acts still described in their basic vector form. For example, one common approach is to use constraints or standards to reject unacceptable solutions. If the imposition of one set of standards fails to reduce the set of feasible solutions sufficiently, further constraints may be added. No trade-offs between consequences are possible, however. Alternatively the decisionmaker may look for dominance between different acts; see for example van Delft and Nijkamp (1976) and section 4 of this paper. The existence of a single dominating strategy, however, will be relatively rare. Lexicographic elimination is another possibility, whereby a strategy unambiguously superior on the basis of the first criterion is regarded as optimal. If, however, several strategies are ranked equally by the first criterion, a second criterion is brought into play and applied in the same way, and so on until only a single strategy remains. Again, the basic objection to this approach is the failure to recognise potential trade-offs between criterion scores.

(3) *Mathematical programming methods.* The application of mathematical programming is more a matter of design, rather than strategy choice. Provided all consequences are controllable within a region defined by appropriate constraints, then strategy choice/design may be based on the value of an objective function with weights reflecting the relative importance of the various consequences. Optimal point(s) within the feasible region identify the desirable strategy. A variation on this basic theme is design based on goal programming, where the aim becomes to minimise the weighted aggregate deviation from certain prescribed standards. Alternatively, if the decisionmaker is unable to specify an objective function precisely, or if the constraint set is too complex, interactive programming methods can facilitate the identification of promising strategies, although the ultimate choice between alternatives still remains to be decided.

(4) *Spatial-proximity methods.* These methods tend to rely on geometric representation or intuition and to be problem-specific in their application.

The indifference curve map of economic theory is a well-known example. Another approach is to use multidimensional scaling to choose the alternative which is closest in some sense to a point in multidimensional space corresponding to the decisionmaker's ideal set of consequences. Generally, the potential of these methods for solving public policy questions in a regional context seems rather small, though an exception is the multi-dimensional scalogram analysis of Hill and Tzamir (1972).

Of the four groups of techniques identified by MacCrimmon and discussed above, weighting methods are by far the most important. Sequential elimination and proximity analysis have limited application and mathematical programming methods, even when appropriate, will usually require a set of criterion weights in order to formulate an objective function. The remainder of this paper therefore will be concerned with weighting methods, but in particular with one group which was not discussed by MacCrimmon, but which has attracted a good deal of interest among regional scientists. This group contains techniques which are rather less definite about the weights that can be derived and applied. As such, they involve a step towards the incorporation of qualitative, rather than just quantitative information about the relative importance of different consequences. The best-known is concordance analysis, which appears first to have been developed in association with the ELECTRE multiple-criteria decisionmaking algorithm developed at SEMA in the 1960s (see Guigou, 1971). A number of extensions of the basic technique also exist (for example Nijkamp, 1975; van Delft and Nijkamp, 1976). At root, however, it is concerned with the pairwise assessment of all possible strategies on the basis of all criteria. A concordance index for each strategy pair (n, n') is computed by first adding together the number of occasions when strategy n is weakly preferred to strategy n' according to each criterion, each occasion being weighted by the importance of the criterion concerned. The concordance index is then formed by dividing this quantity by the sum of all criterion weights. The incorporation of the preference relation means that the ranking of weights is important, as well as the weights themselves. A discordance index may also be formed, with those criteria where weak preference does not exist taken into account. Strategy choice is then based on a comparison of the two $n \times n$ matrices, respectively of concordance and discordance indices. The principal tools of comparison are externally set standards for the difference between the corresponding concordance and discordance indices and, in the final stages of the analysis, a search for dominance.

A further step towards qualitative analysis has been taken by Paelinck (1976). Developing Jaquet-Lagrèze's technique of successive permutations, he assumes that both criterion weights and the level of achievement of the criteria themselves can only be measured on an ordinal scale. Ultimately, some form of quantification is necessary to give a ranking of strategies, but this is postponed until as late as possible. As will be seen in section 3, the CHOOSE algorithm he develops has certain important aspects in common with the technique to be explained in the present paper.

3 Maximin–maximax weighted evaluation

The implication of the previous section is that, although a limited amount of ranking of acts may be possible on the basis of the full n-tuples $(X_1, ..., X_n)$ of consequences, the question of reducing the dimension of the comparison cannot in practice be postponed for long. Further, at the stage of dimension reduction, loss of information is inevitable. Two matters are therefore important. One is that the weights used to collapse multiple dimensions into a single dimension are well conceived in the context of the problem in hand. Some techniques for achieving this were outlined in the previous section. Second, no matter how well conceived the weighting scheme used, it is natural to wish to explore the sensitivity of solutions to some variation in the weights selected. The ready incorporation of sensitivity analysis is thus also important.

The ranking of criteria, rather than the establishment of exact weights, is a sensible way of incorporating a view of the relative importance of different consequences without at the same time imputing too much reliability to the means by which the decisionmaker's attitudes to the consequences were established. This approach has been employed usefully by the French and Dutch authors quoted earlier. It is the approach which is adopted here also.

Concordance analysis and Paelinck's CHOOSE algorithm can require calculations which are potentially complex and/or time-consuming. The technique to be presented in this section is much simpler, but the price paid is that the range of problems to which it is applicable is narrower. It is, in fact, a generalisation of the maximin–maximax weighting scheme described in section 2. Maximin analysis in its pure form will be appropriate when, for technical or political reasons, an act will be assessed in terms of 'the weakest link in the chain'. That is, evaluation will depend on its performance in the dimension in which it performs most poorly. Maximax can be applied when the system under examination is sufficiently flexible in its operation that, after its implementation, it may be used in such a way as to exploit the particularly outstanding level of achievement of the consequence for which it was chosen. For example, in public policy choice it may well be desirable to favour acts which are relatively unlikely to encourage opposition by certain lobbying groups. Maximin choice will select policies which avoid unduly poor performances in terms of any single criterion and so will reduce the probability of causing major offence to any influence groups.

In its basic form, however, maximin–maximax analysis is open to three significant objections:
1 it assumes that the scales on which the different attributes are measured are directly comparable;

2 it ignores all consequences of each act except the very worst in the
   maximin case or the very best in maximax;
3 it ignores any relative importance that the decisionmaker may wish to
   place on different attributes.

Consider, initially, the first objection. Frequently a plausible objective
on the part of the decisionmaker will be to avoid strategies for which any
criterion score is significantly lower than that achieved by other strategies
for that criterion. Such an attitude may be incorporated, and the problem
of comparability handled by first standardising each set of criterion scores
across all available strategies by subtracting the mean score for that
criterion, and then dividing by its standard deviation. This is close in
spirit to the normalisation used in concordance analysis; see for example
Nijkamp (1975, page 95) and the appendix to this paper. Alternatively,
if comparability is not a problem but it is still desired to avoid poor relative
performances, a regret matrix may be computed in the normal way and,
for example, a minimax weighted regret strategy sought.

Objections 2 and 3 above may now be handled in the following way.
Consider the maximin case, since maximax follows by direct analogy.
Suppose, instead of giving a weight of one to the worst (standardised)
outcome of each strategy and one of zero to all others, that, taking into
account the standardisation that has taken place, the decisionmaker weights
relative achievement according to the different criteria ($j = 1, ..., n$) with
nonnegative weights w_j, where, without loss of generality, it is assumed
that $\sum_{j=1}^{n} w_j = 1$. Further, assume that these weights are not known
quantities, but merely reflect a ranking of the importance of the criteria,
$w_1 \geqslant w_2 \geqslant ... \geqslant w_n$. It may now be shown that it is possible to calculate
extreme values of the sum of the weighted individual criteria values, which
are consistent with the decisionmaker's ranking. By comparing minima
across strategies (in the maximin case) an optimal strategy may be selected.

For simplicity, consider the problem of determining the extreme
weighted evaluations, W, for a single strategy, with criterion scores S_j
($j = 1, ..., n$), where S_j is the standardised score of the strategy for
criterion j, as defined in the appendix. By adopting the approach of
Cannon and Kmietowicz (1974) and Kmietowicz and Pearman (1976) in
the context of decisionmaking under uncertainty, the problem may be
formalised as a pair of linear programming problems:

$$\text{maximise or minimise } W = \sum_{j=1}^{n} w_j S_j ,$$

subject to

$$\sum_{j=1}^{n} w_j = 1 , \tag{1}$$

$$w_j - w_{j+1} \geqslant 0 \qquad [j = 1, ..., (n-1)] , \tag{2}$$

$$w_j \geqslant 0 \qquad (j = 1, ..., n) . \tag{3}$$

The problem may be simplified greatly by the application of the following transformations:

$$v_j = w_j - w_{j+1} \qquad [j = 1, ..., (n-1)] ,$$

$$Y_j = \sum_{k=1}^{j} S_k \qquad (j = 1, ..., n) ;$$

$v_n = w_n$ (since $w_{n+1} = 0$) and so the original constraints (1) and (2) collapse into just one functional constraint, (1'), and n nonnegativity constraints, (3'). Further, since $w_j = \sum_{k=j}^{n} v_k$, and given that constraint (3') holds, then the nonnegativity constraints (3) are also obeyed. Therefore, the original problem may be reexpressed:

maximise or minimise $W = \sum_{j=1}^{n} v_j Y_j$,

subject to

$$\sum_{j=1}^{n} jv_j = 1 , \tag{1'}$$

$$v_j \geqslant 0 \qquad (j = 1, ..., n) . \tag{3'}$$

A linear programming problem of this type, with only one functional constraint, will have an optimal solution with just one of the decision variables, v_j, positive and all other v_j zero. From (1'), if only one v_j is nonzero, its value must be $1/j$. Thus the objective function will be maximised when Y_j/j is maximised, and minimised when Y_j/j is minimised. To identify maximum and minimum values of W, all that is necessary is to calculate all partial sums $W_j = (1/j) \sum_{k=1}^{j} S_k$ and locate the extreme values. Strategy choice is then simply a matter of comparing weighted minima across strategies and selecting that policy with the maximum minimum score. A numerical example will be given in the next section.

Two forms of extension of the basic results are possible, both concerned with assessing the sensitivity of the extreme weighted evaluations just determined. In its basic form, the technique uses only one extreme weighting per strategy to evaluate that strategy. It does not give any information about how the weighted evaluation will vary if an actual weighting, still consistent with the given ranking of criteria, but not the extreme possibility, were in fact employed. In practice therefore a decisionmaker might give some additional value to a strategy whose evaluation was relatively insensitive to a departure from the extreme set of weights actually used for the strategy's evaluation. It could be regarded as more 'reliable' than strategies with similar extreme weighted scores, but of greater sensitivity. Such a strategy would then be relatively secure against the argument that the weighted extreme was based on a weighting 0.5,

0·5, 0, 0 whereas, in some critic's judgement, the correct weighting should be 0·4, 0·3, 0·15, 0·15.

An index of strategy sensitivity to consistent but nonextreme weightings is the maximum weighted squared deviation about a weighted evaluation which can be attained. This indicator is derived by analogy with the variance index of deviation about a mean, since $\sum_{j=1}^{n} w_j = 1$. The lower is this maximum, the more reliable the strategy may be held to be.

The maximum weighted squared deviation indicator can be computed by a series of simple arithmetic steps. As is shown in a different context in Kmietowicz and Pearman (1976), all that is required is to compute a series of partial sums,

$$\frac{1}{j} \sum_{k=1}^{j} S_k^2 - \left(\frac{1}{j} \sum_{k=1}^{j} S_k\right)^2 , \qquad j = 1, ..., n .$$

The maximum such partial sum gives the value of the required indicator. Depending on the value judgements of the decisionmaker, sensitivity measured in this way may be traded off against the extreme W figure obtained from the linear programming analysis.

A second approach to sensitivity testing is to examine changes in the W index as a result of changes in the ranking of criteria or of the introduction of new criteria. This question has been examined from the point of view of decisionmaking under uncertainty in Pearman and Kmietowicz (1976). If a major perturbation in the ranking of criteria occurs, then it is probably simplest to recompute all the partial sums from scratch. If, however, the ranking change consists only of the inversion of two criteria, say those previously ranked g and h, where $1 \leqslant g \leqslant h \leqslant n$, then the following holds. If the previous extreme weighted evaluations occurred for the j^*th partial average where $j^* \geqslant h$ or $j^* < g$ then no change will take place. Otherwise, new partial sums, $W_j' = W_j + 1/j(S_h - S_g)$ must be calculated for $j = g, ..., (h-1)$. All these new partial averages will have to be compared with those unaffected by the inversion in order to locate the new extrema.

If a new criterion is introduced, ranked in the gth position, then again it is not necessary to perform an entire calculation of partial sums again. Partial sums $W_1, ..., W_{n-1}$ will be unchanged. All subsequent partial sums will change as follows:

$$W_k' = W_k + \frac{1}{k}(S_N - S_k) \qquad k = g, ..., n ,$$

$$W_{n+1}' = \frac{1}{n+1}(S_1 + ... + S_{g-1} + S_N + S_g + ... + S_n) ,$$

where S_N is the standardised score of this strategy on the new criterion. Other sensitivity analyses, for example for changes in the S_i, are possible.

These are explained in Pearman and Kmietowicz (1976). They are not quite as straightforward as those presented here, but are by no means complex.

The extreme weighted evaluation technique just discussed is close in its operation to certain stages of Paelinck's CHOOSE algorithm. Essentially, he computes a set of ranking scores for each of the $m!$ permutations of preferences over the m strategies available and for each of the n criteria. For m and n that are at all large, this is a considerable computational task. He then calculates extreme weighted values of the ranking scores, and finally looks for a dominating permutation of strategies. The weighting scheme used, $w_1 \geqslant w_2 \geqslant ... \geqslant w_n$, is the same as in this paper, but the proof of the identification of the extreme weighted values is rather less direct. There are other significant differences between the CHOOSE algorithm and the method presented here, but these arise essentially out of differences in the assumptions made about the nature of the information available to assess strategies.

Overall, what this section has done is to introduce a new formal method of multiple-criteria decisionmaking for the common case where fixed weights for the different criteria are not available, but only a ranking. Compared with other methods, it is very straightforward in its theory and its application. This should render it both comprehensible and usable by nonspecialists. The price which is paid is the relatively narrow range of 'weakest link' or 'strongest link' problems to which it is applicable. However, this range is still quite wide, even just within the context of regional science problems.

4 A numerical example

In this section, a brief numerical example is given. It is based on one in van Delft and Nijkamp (1976, pages 51–55), which involved five possible plans assessed on the basis of ten different criteria. The plans refer to different development schemes for a new industrial area near Rotterdam. The criteria are such as value added per hectare, demand for labour, environmental quality, proportion of foreign labourers employed, etc. The normalised plan impact matrix they give on page 54 has been transformed to a standardised plan impact matrix, as shown here in table 1, using the relationship between normalised and standardised scores developed in the appendix. Further, four rankings of criteria, A, B, C, and D have been considered. These are consistent with the preference scores 2, 3, 4, and 5 on page 55 of van Delft and Nijkamp (1976). Where equal preference scores were originally given, an arbitrary ranking has been imposed, although, with the technique developed here, the possibility of some equal weighting is not excluded. The four rankings are shown in table 2.

The first step is to compute all partial sums and thus find the extreme weighted evaluations for each plan. These calculations are shown fully for ranking A in table 3, and in summary form for the remaining rankings in table 4. The main conclusion which can be reached in this example, with either maximin or maximax strategy choice, is that plan 2 clearly dominates all others over quite a wide range of weight rankings. This is in line with the conclusion of van Delft and Nijkamp, who used a concordance analysis coupled with an analysis of dominance.

Given the performance of plan 2, it is unlikely that any sensitivity information would be required in this case. However, for purposes of illustration, table 5 shows, for the first ranking only, the calculation of the maximum weighted squared deviation measure described earlier, and table 6 shows the effect of reversing the third and fifth ranked criteria, again in ranking A, so that the order of criteria is 4, 8, 6, 10, 5, ... The maximum

Table 1. The standardised plan impact matrix.

Criterion	Plan number				
	1	2	3	4	5
1	−0·516	−0·476	0·262	0·665	0·065
2	0·641	0·165	0·165	−0·663	−0·307
3	−0·457	−0·418	0·026	0·781	0·067
4	−0·909	0·600	0·199	−0·011	0·122
5	−0·527	0·791	−0·011	−0·183	−0·069
6	−0·923	0·231	0·103	0·359	0·231
7	0·597	0·357	−0·021	−0·673	−0·261
8	0·673	−0·007	−0·040	0·027	−0·653
9	0·332	0·409	−0·260	−0·279	−0·202
10	0·061	0·832	−0·528	−0·557	0·192

Table 2. The four rankings examined.

Criterion	Ranking				Criterion	Ranking			
	A	B	C	D		A	B	C	D
1	7	2	5	6	6	5	6	6	5
2	10	9	3	4	7	9	8	1	1
3	6	7	8	9	8	2	3	10	8
4	1	4	2	2	9	8	10	7	7
5	3	5	4	3	10	4	1	9	10

Table 3. Partial sum calculations for ranking A. The minimum value for each plan is shown in italic type and the maximum value in bold type.

Plan	j									
	1	2	3	4	5	6	7	8	9	10
1	*−0·91*	−0·12	−0·25	−0·18	−0·33	−0·35	−0·37	−0·28	−0·19	**−0·10**
2	**0·60**	0·30	0·46	0·55	0·49	0·34	*0·22*	0·22	0·26	0·25
3	**0·20**	0·08	0·05	*−0·10*	−0·06	−0·04	0·00	−0·03	−0·03	−0·01
4	−0·01	0·01	−0·06	*−0·18*	−0·07	0·07	**0·15**	0·10	0·01	−0·05
5	**0·12**	*−0·27*	−0·20	−0·10	−0·08	−0·02	−0·01	−0·03	−0·06	−0·08

variance measure tends to support the claim of plan 3 to be the second best option available. However, as table 6 shows, should there be a change of opinion about the ranking such as to reverse the third- and fifth-ranked criteria, then the position of plan 3 is much less secure as runner up, and it might well be desirable to consider the claims of plan 4.

Table 4. Extreme weighted evaluations for rankings B, C, and D.

	Ranking		
	B	C	D
Plan 1			
minimum	−0·37	−0·27	−0·28
maximum	0·07	0·59	0·59
Plan 2			
minimum	0·12	0·21	0·18
maximum	0·83	0·48	0·48
Plan 3			
minimum	−0·53	−0·02	−0·02
maximum	0·02	0·12	0·12
Plan 4			
minimum	−0·56	−0·67	−0·67
maximum	0·15	0·00	0·00
Plan 5			
minimum	−0·13	−0·26	−0·26
maximum	0·19	−0·04	−0·04

Table 5. Partial squared deviation calculations for ranking A.

Plan	j										Maximum
	1	2	3	4	5	6	7	8	9	10	
1	0·00	0·63	0·46	0·36	0·37	0·32	0·28	0·30	0·34	0·37	0·63
2	0·00	0·09	0·12	0·12	0·11	0·20	0·26	0·24	0·20	0·18	0·26
3	0·00	0·02	0·01	0·07	0·06	0·05	0·06	0·06	0·05	0·05	0·07
4	0·00	0·00	0·01	0·05	0·09	0·18	0·20	0·19	0·23	0·25	0·25
5	0·00	0·15	0·11	0·11	0·10	0·09	0·08	0·07	0·07	0·07	0·15

Table 6. Effect of changed ranking on the extreme weighted evaluation.

Plan	Old minimum	New minimum	Old maximum	New maximum
1	−[a]	−	−	−
2	−	−	−	−
3	−0·10	−0·06	−	−
4	−0·18	−0·07	−	−
5	−	−	−	−

[a] No change as a result of new ranking.

5 Summary and conclusions

The techniques discussed in sections 2 and 3 are all concerned with multiple-criteria decisionmaking. Their existence suggests that decision problems of this kind are frequently being encountered, and their heterogeneity implies that application to real problems is unlikely to be straightforward. Many problems in regional science are undoubtedly of a multiple-criteria type, and so regional science as a discipline must be aware both of the techniques themselves and of the potential difficulties in their application.

Most acts, however trivial, have multiple consequences, but exploration of the processes which ensue between initial recognition of a set of feasible alternatives and the (partial) ranking which is implied in strategy choice, is still at an early stage. In many instances decisions will be sufficiently simple, or one attribute so overwhelmingly important, that to indulge in the complexity of formal multiple-criteria analysis will be quite unnecessary. This will not always be the case, however. Furthermore, in practice, in these more complex cases it is unlikely to be feasible to quantify reliably all the trade-offs that the consideration of widely different strategies may require. There is likely always to be a need for comparing and reconciling imprecise rankings of criteria, qualitative assessments, and political judgements. The major difficulty to be faced then is how far it is possible for formal methods to assist in making these difficult decisions before excessive formality begins to stand in the way of good decisionmaking.

In problems of this kind, a judgement must be made about the extent to which it is safe to make decisions in terms of a single criterion or of an established weighting of criteria. The alternative is to retain a more open mind, carrying forward a series of possibilities to the next stage in the decision process. The growth in the study of multiple-criteria decision-making is a recognition of the fact that trade-offs between the consequences of different decisions are not always as well understood as some mathematical modelling sequences imply. Ultimately, any complete decision process modelled formally must make a commitment to a single unambiguous method of comparing the importance of different kinds of consequences in different strategies. But such a firm commitment to a single technique of decision may not always be wise. The multiple-criteria approach is basically a plea for caution in choosing weights, for making explicit the effects of different weightings and, if necessary, for final choice in terms of expert or political judgement.

At one extreme, regional scientists are frequently concerned with major public policy choices and this leads naturally to an interest, both descriptive and normative, in how multiple criteria are reconciled in this kind of large-scale decisionmaking. This is the kind of decisionmaking with which this paper has implicitly been concerned. However, it should be borne in mind that multiple-criteria decisions also take place at another stage which, too, is of great importance in the analysis of public policy. This is at the level of the individual's decisions, the modelling of which is often a major behavioural input right at the start of the process which culminates in policy choice.

The possibility of decisions at this early stage being viewed in the same kind of multiple-criteria light as is implied by the analysis of the final policy choice stage is disturbing. The behavioural models, which are often dependent on optimisation or simulation in terms of a single variable or of a fixed weighted sum of variables, are quite complex as they are. Although consistency may suggest that the existence of multiple criteria should be recognised throughout all stages of an analysis, practicality does not. The fact that behavioural models are often concerned with the actions of large groups of individuals provides some justification for concentrating on only the most commonly adopted criteria and for using a set of weights which ignore individual quirks. But these are relative rather than absolute arguments, and there do appear to be good reasons in some circumstances for recognition of multiple criteria, even at early stages of analysis.

A recent paper by Grey (1977) has highlighted this point. His main concern was with the generalised-cost measure frequently used, for example, in transport models. He puts forward two principal arguments against generalised cost, which is typically a weighted sum of the main disutilities of travel—monetary cost, travel time, waiting time, etc. The first is simply a criticism of the techniques employed to establish the weights and of the actual numerical values used. The second, however, is more far-reaching. The argument is essentially that it is dangerous to model (travel) behaviour by using a single generalised-cost index as the explanatory variable. Among other problems, it is likely to induce relationships between travel demand and basic cost components which do not have theoretical or empirical justification. Also, it implies a degree of substitutability between the attributes of a journey which is misleading.

Grey favours the modelling of travel demand directly in terms of attributes rather than indirectly via a generalised-cost index. This does not, however, deal with the problem of estimating the relationships or of their reliability for predictive purposes if used significantly outside the range of observations from which they were calibrated. If novel approaches to travel problems are to be evaluated then a more searching investigation is required than the use of a single model, followed by sensitivity testing. It could well be that substitution rates between attributes taken to levels which are extreme by current standards are markedly different from those implied by calibration based on existing experience. It is in circumstances such as these that the application of the multiple-criteria philosophy will prove worthwhile. Implementing it in practice, of course, cannot be expected to be straightforward. Probably the most that can be asked is to endeavour, on the basis of *a priori* reasoning or otherwise, to segment the attributes believed to influence behaviour in such a way that groups with predictable intragroup substitutability are formed and held separate from each other where intergroup substitutability is understood with less confidence. This is the type of approach suggested by the search for preferential independence discussed in Keeney and Raiffa (1976). It would then be advisable, and hopefully practicable, to look carefully at the implied intergroup trade-offs, and to consider fully the implications of trade-offs markedly different from those presently observed. If significant variation in policy choice occurs when weights are varied, and if agreement cannot be reached on an appropriate weighting, then strategies which are flexible in implementation, such as bus lanes, may be preferable to less flexible alternatives, for example, light tramways. The problem of amalgamating decisions under uncertainty and multiple-criteria decisions arises again.

The extent to which it is feasible or necessary to approach the full range of regional modelling components from the multiple-criteria point of view is a matter which deserves fuller consideration. For the present, however, there is little doubt that policy choice at the final stages can often benefit from this type of approach. The new technique put forward in this paper represents an extension of existing methods. Although limited in the types of choice to which it can be applied, its simplicity makes it potentially valuable for presenting a series of solutions to final decisionmakers, on the basis of a clear ranking of criteria and in such a way that the effects of changes in the basis of the original calculations can readily be made and their effects demonstrated. The departure which this technique and others related to it suggest from current common practice is not an absolute one. It lies in the relatively greater concentration it gives to the presentation of sets of good solutions rather than of a single optimal outcome, and in its emphasis on the tentative understanding which exists of the trade-offs between many important consequences. It encourages those concerned with decisions to face firmly awkward, qualitative concepts, which might otherwise wrongly be excluded from consideration. It promotes the exploration of the implications of changes in rankings, etc. It is this exploratory aspect as much as anything which is the main potential contribution of multiple-criteria decisionmaking.

References

Cannon C M, Kmietowicz Z W, 1974 "Decision theory and incomplete knowledge" *Journal of Management Studies* **11** 224–232

Delft A van, Nijkamp P, 1976 "A multiobjective decision model for regional development, environmental quality control and industrial land use" *Papers of the Regional Science Association* **36** 35–57

Fishburn P C, 1964 *Decision and Value Theory* (John Wiley, New York)

Grey A, 1977 "The generalised cost dilemma" *Proceedings of the 1977 PTRC Summer Annual Meeting, Seminar G* (PTRC, London)

Guigou J L, 1971 "On French location models for production units" *Regional and Urban Economics* **1** 107–138, 189–316

Hill M, Tzamir Y, 1972 "Multidimensional evaluation of regional plans serving multiple objectives" *Papers of the Regional Science Association* **29** 139–165

Keeney R L, Raiffa H, 1976 *Decisions with Multiple Objectives: Preferences and Value Tradeoffs* (John Wiley, New York)

Kmietowicz Z W, Pearman A D, 1976 "Decision theory and incomplete knowledge: maximum variance" *Journal of Management Studies* 13 164–174

MacCrimmon K R, 1973 "An overview of multiple objective decision making" in *Multiple Criteria Decision Making* Eds J L Cochrane, M Zeleny (University of South Carolina Press, Columbia) pp 18–44

Nijkamp P, 1975 "A multicriteria analysis for project evaluation: economic–ecological evaluation of a land reclamation project" *Papers of the Regional Science Association* 35 87–111

Paelinck J H P, 1976 "Qualitative multiple criteria analysis, environmental protection and multiregional development" *Papers of the Regional Science Association* 36 59–74

Pearman A D, Kmietowicz Z W, 1976 "Decision theory and incomplete knowledge: sensitivity analysis" DP-40, School of Economic Studies, University of Leeds

APPENDIX

Standardised criterion scores and normalised criterion scores are closely related. Consider a set of m acts which, for a given criterion, record scores $X_1, ..., X_m$. These criterion scores may be standardised according to definition (A1) or normalised according to definition (A2).

$$S_i = (X_i - \overline{X})\left[\sum_{k=1}^{m}(X_k - \overline{X})^2\right]^{-\frac{1}{2}}, \qquad i = 1, ..., m , \tag{A1}$$

$$N_i = X_i\left(\sum_{k=1}^{m} X_k^2\right)^{-\frac{1}{2}}, \qquad i = 1, ..., m , \tag{A2}$$

where

$$\overline{X} = \frac{1}{m}\sum_{i=1}^{m} X_i . \tag{A3}$$

From equation (A2)

$$X_i = N_i\left(\sum_{k=1}^{m} X_k^2\right)^{\frac{1}{2}} . \tag{A4}$$

Combining equation (A3) and (A4) gives

$$\begin{aligned}
\overline{X} &= \frac{1}{m}\sum_{i=1}^{m} N_i\left(\sum_{k=1}^{m} X_k^2\right)^{\frac{1}{2}} = \frac{1}{m}\left(\sum_{k=1}^{m} X_k^2\right)^{\frac{1}{2}}\sum_{i=1}^{m} N_i \\
&= \frac{1}{m}\left(\sum_{k=1}^{m} X_k^2\right)^{\frac{1}{2}} m\overline{N} \qquad \left(\text{since } \overline{N} = \frac{1}{m}\sum_{i=1}^{m} N_i\right) \\
&= \overline{N}\left(\sum_{k=1}^{m} X_k^2\right)^{\frac{1}{2}} .
\end{aligned} \tag{A5}$$

Therefore

$$S_i^2 = \frac{X_i^2 - 2\overline{X}X_i + \overline{X}^2}{\displaystyle\sum_{k=1}^{m} X_k^2 - 2\overline{X}\sum_{k=1}^{m} X_k + m\overline{X}^2} = \frac{X_i^2 - 2\overline{X}X_i + \overline{X}^2}{\displaystyle\sum_{k=1}^{m} X_k^2 - m\overline{X}^2}$$

Substituting from equations (A4) and (A5) gives

$$S_i^2 = \frac{N_i \displaystyle\sum_{k=1}^{m} X_k^2 - 2\overline{N}\left(\sum_{k=1}^{m} X_k^2\right)^{\!\!\frac{1}{2}} N_i\left(\sum_{k=1}^{m} X_k^2\right)^{\!\!\frac{1}{2}} + \overline{N}^2 \sum_{k=1}^{m} X_k^2}{\displaystyle\sum_{k=1}^{m} X_k^2 - m\overline{N}^2 \sum_{k=1}^{m} X_k^2}$$

$$= \frac{N_i^2 - 2\overline{N}N_i + \overline{N}^2}{1 - m\overline{N}^2} = \frac{(N_i - \overline{N})^2}{1 - m\overline{N}^2} \ .$$

Therefore

$$S_i = \frac{N_i - \overline{N}}{(1 - m\overline{N}^2)^{\frac{1}{2}}} \tag{A6}$$

From the point of view of the maximin–maximax weighted-evaluation technique described in this paper, since S_i is derived from N_i by subtracting one constant and dividing by another constant—but, it should be noted, different constants for different criteria—there is no guarantee that the ranking of different acts will remain the same if scores are switched from standardised to normalised, or vice versa.

Conflicting Social Priorities and Compromise Social Decisions

P NIJKAMP, P RIETVELD
Free University, Amsterdam

1 Introduction

Generally, policymakers and planners have to base their decisions on a multiplicity of criteria. In addition to a careful examination of the set of feasible solutions, they have to evaluate the impacts of all alternatives. The existence of several alternatives and of several decision criteria frequently obviates a straightforward evaluation procedure, particularly when a certain decision situation is new for the decisionmaker (DM). These difficulties often stem from the fact that the DM is confronted with limited information and uncertainty about the set of feasible alternatives and the evaluation strategies to be employed.

These difficulties imply that a DM runs the risk of taking nonoptimal decisions on alternative solutions, when he has to take into account several attributes. In general, a multiplicity of attributes is the rule rather than the exception in decision situations, and the following examples may illustrate the importance of these:
—a job-seeker takes into consideration many aspects of a job, such as salary, place of work, career prospects, and so forth;
—a city council confronted with the decision about infrastructural investments will take account of the various aspects of these investments such as accessibility, costs, social benefits, etc;
—a planning committee composed of different interest groups will have different priorities with regard to the elements of plans to be decided on.

These types of decision problems are receiving increasing attention from researchers in various fields such as physical planning, economics, operations research, psychology, organization theory, and geography. In all these disciplines researchers are trying to develop techniques aimed at providing the DM with instruments to tackle the complex problems related to a multiplicity of objectives or criteria.

In this paper some of the results obtained to date will be presented. Special attention is paid to the selection of nondominated solutions and to alternative ways of characterizing them (section 2), *inter alia* by introducing some measures for the degree of conflict among objectives. Section 3 is devoted to the presentation of several multiobjective methods, each characterized by a certain information need about the priorities of the DM. In section 4, we deal with a particular decision method, namely an interactive method based on a structured communication process, between a DM and an analyst, about possibilities and desirabilities.

F

In this context the relationships between minimum standards, shadow prices, and weights will be analyzed. In section 5, a numerical illustration of the concepts and methods developed in the preceding sections will be given by means of a relatively simple transportation model concerning home-to-work trips. The final section presents some conclusions and suggestions for further research.

It should be stressed that in the context of this paper several aspects of modelling decision problems will not be included. For example, we shall neglect the whole process of formulating general objectives, the specification of measurable criteria, the identification of instruments, and the calculation of the relationships between objectives and instruments. It will be assumed that all these model-building stages have been accomplished successfully. A discussion of these elements can be found among others in Roy (1976), and delphi-techniques may prove to be useful [see, for example, Dalkey et al (1972), Linstone and Turoff (1975), and Skutsch and Schofer (1973)]. Uncertainty of data will not be discussed: valuable approaches to the handling of this problem are found in Goicoechea et al (1976) and Wilhelm (1975), among others.

2 Efficient points
2.1 The payoff matrix
Efficient points play a crucial role in multiattribute and multiobjective decision problems. In this section some important aspects of efficient points will be described in more detail.

Assume the following elements of a decision problem:
a set of I instruments x, $x = (x_1, ..., x_I)$, $x \in \mathbb{R}^I$;
a convex set K of feasible values of the instruments, $K \subset \mathbb{R}^I$;
a set of J scalar valued concave objective functions ω, $\omega = (\omega_1, ..., \omega_J)$,
    each mapping $x \in \mathbb{R}^I$ to $\omega_j \in \mathbb{R}^1$.

Notice that no assumption has been made about the relative importance attached by the DM to the objective functions. Consequently conventional economic analysis cannot be applied, because no general utility scheme has been given. The basic question then arises how an analyst should proceed in this situation to provide all relevant information about the feasible solutions to the DM. In the degenerate case, when only one objective (say j) has to be considered, the answer to the question is straightforward—the analyst has only to solve the mathematical programming problem[1]:

$$\left.\begin{array}{l} \text{maximize } \omega_j(x), \quad \text{for a certain } j, \\ \text{subject to } x \in K. \end{array}\right\} \tag{1}$$

[1] For the ease of presentation it has been assumed in sections 2-4 that all objectives have to be maximized.

In this case the only relevant information for the DM is the optimal set of instruments $\overset{*}{x}_j$ and the corresponding value of the objective $\omega_j(\overset{*}{x}_j)$.

It is clear that this approach fails as soon as two or more objectives are considered, because normally diverse objectives are conflicting. In other words, a successive solution of objective (1) for $j = 1, ..., J$ leads to a series of different optimal solution vectors, $\overset{*}{x}_1, ..., \overset{*}{x}_J$. The conflicting nature of the decision problem can be illustrated by means of the payoff matrix $\mathbf{P}$, of which the J successive columns show the effects of the J instrument vectors, x_j, on the objectives:

$$\mathbf{P} = [\omega(\overset{*}{x}_1), ..., \omega(\overset{*}{x}_J)] . \tag{2}$$

For example, the element $p_{jj'}$ indicates the value of the jth objective resulting when the j'th objective is maximized. Let $\overset{*}{\omega}$ be the main diagonal of $\mathbf{P}$. Then $\overset{*}{\omega}$ contains the maximum attainable values of the J respective objectives.

The information contained in matrix $\mathbf{P}$ can be used to define a certain measure of conflict among objectives. It is intuitively clear that the conflict between objectives j and j' is greater as the difference between a certain $\overset{*}{\omega}_j$ and a certain $p_{jj'}$ is larger. This idea can be formalized as follows: let $\overline{\omega}$ be the vector of minimum attainable values for each of the J objectives, that is

$$\overline{\omega}_j = \min_{j'}(p_{jj'}) . \tag{3}$$

Then $\mathbf{P}$ can be normalized as follows:

$$\mathbf{P_N} = (\mathbf{P} - \overline{\omega}\iota') \cdot (\overset{\wedge}{\overset{*}{\omega} - \overline{\omega}})^{-1} , \tag{4}$$

where ι indicates a vector with unit elements, and the symbol $\wedge$ indicates a diagonal matrix. It can safely be assumed that $\overset{*}{\omega}_j \neq \overline{\omega}_j$ for any j, because otherwise the jth objective would be irrelevant for the decision problem. Clearly all elements of $\mathbf{P_N}$ are nonnegative and smaller than or equal to 1. The main diagonal contains unit elements. Any row of $\mathbf{P_N}$ contains at least a zero element. Obviously, the conflict among the objectives will be greater as $\mathbf{P_N}$ approaches the identity matrix $\mathbf{I}$. Therefore a meaningful aggregate measure for conflict is,

$$\gamma_1 = 1 - \frac{\iota'(\mathbf{P_N} - \mathbf{I})\iota}{J^2 - 2J} , \qquad J \geqslant 3 , \tag{5}$$

where the denominator indicates the maximum attainable value of the sum of the elements of $(\mathbf{P_N} - \mathbf{I})$ [$2J$ elements of $(\mathbf{P_N} - \mathbf{I})$ will be equal to zero]. It is clear that:

$$0 \leqslant \gamma_1 \leqslant 1 . \tag{6}$$

A value of γ_1 close to 1 indicates a high degree of conflict; a value of γ_1 close to 0 indicates the opposite case.

2.2 Efficient solutions

So far we have concentrated only on some extreme solutions of the
decision problem as reflected by matrix **P**. However, it is also useful to
provide information about intermediate solutions reflecting certain
compromises among objectives. In respect of this, the well-known concept
of an efficient solution will be introduced, viz: a vector $x \in K$ is an
efficient solution if no other feasible solution $x^0 \in K$ exists such that

$$\left.\begin{array}{ll} \omega_j(x^0) \geqslant \omega_j(x) , & j = 1, ..., J \\ \text{and} \\ \omega_j(x^0) \neq \omega_j(x) & \text{for at least one } j . \end{array}\right\} \tag{7}$$

Theoretically speaking, one should restrict attention to this class of
feasible solutions [cf Fandel and Wilhelm (1976)], although in practice
many inefficient decisions seem to be made [cf Leibenstein (1976)].

There are basically two different approaches to identify efficient points,
namely by means of *weights* and of *side-conditions* in the mathematical
programming model (1).

The first method requires the concept of *proper* efficiency [which is
included in the efficiency concept defined in conditions (7)] to prevent
some anomalies in nonlinear cases [for an exposition see, for example,
Geoffrion (1968)]. Kuhn and Tucker (1951) have proved:

Theorem 1.
x^p *is properly efficient with respect to K and* ω *if and only if there exists
a vector of weights* λ ($\lambda \geqslant 0$, $\iota'\lambda = 1$) *such that* x^p *is optimal for the
programming problem*:

$$\left.\begin{array}{l} \text{maximize } \lambda'\omega(x) , \\ \text{subject to } x \in K . \end{array}\right\} \tag{8}$$

This theorem enables the analyst to identify the set of proper efficient
solutions by solving problem (8) by varying the values of λ repetitively
and systematically. Another important implication of theorem 1 is that
once a certain properly efficient solution has been selected, this solution
can be interpreted in terms of a certain combination of weights λ.

The second method has been thoroughly elaborated by Haimes and
Hall (1974). It is based on the next theorem.

Theorem 2
x^p *is efficient with respect to K and* ω *if and only if there exists a vector
of constraint values* ϵ ($\epsilon \geqslant 0$, $\epsilon_j = 0$ *for an arbitrary j*) *so that* x^p *is
optimal for the programming problem*:

$$\left.\begin{array}{ll} \text{maximize } \omega_j(x) , \\ \text{subject to } x \in K , & \omega \geqslant \overline{\omega}+\epsilon . \end{array}\right\} \tag{9}$$

Thus by varying the side-conditions it is, in principle, possible to identify all efficient solutions by means of problem (9). An advantage of (9) as compared with problem (8) is that, by means of (9), one is also able to capture problems with nonconvex sets K [Bowman (1976) presents another method of attack on nonconvex situations].

Theorem 2 has not been formulated like theorem 1 in terms of weights, but it is possible to interpret it in this way, given the values of the shadow prices of the side-conditions $\omega \geqslant \overline{\omega} + \epsilon$ [Cohon and Marks (1973), Haimes and Hall (1974), and Miller and Byers (1973) utilized this possibility in their studies of water resource systems]. Haimes and Hall (1974) also attempted to fit tradeoff functions describing the relationship between the constraint values $\epsilon_{j'}$ (for a certain j') and the values of the corresponding dual variables.

Obviously, however, both methods generally share the drawback that so much information about efficient solutions will be provided that normally the DM will not be able to digest it. An exception in some cases may be the *linear* multiobjective programming problem, which will be dealt with later.

2.3 Compromise solutions
The abovementioned ways of providing relevant information to a DM include the provision of some extreme solutions (section 2.1) as well as a certain number of arbitrarily chosen efficient solutions (section 2.2). The present subsection will be devoted to some less arbitrary choice procedures for identifying solutions which reflect a compromise between the various objectives, so that a simultaneous consideration of the objectives is guaranteed.

It should be noted that an operationalization of the vague concept of 'compromise' is not unambiguous. In the context of the present paper the following suggestions are made.

(a) Find the solution x^a which dominates the greatest number of feasible solutions, that is, solve

$$\left. \begin{aligned} &\text{maximize} \prod_{j=1}^{J} [\omega_j(x) - \overline{\omega}_j] \,, \\ &\text{subject to } x \in K \,. \end{aligned} \right\} \tag{10}$$

(b) Find the solution x^b which is dominated by the smallest number of alternatives in the cube defined by the opposite corner-points $\overset{*}{\omega}$ and $\overline{\omega}$, that is, solve

$$\left. \begin{aligned} &\text{minimize} \prod_{j=1}^{J} [\overset{*}{\omega}_j - \omega_j(x)] \,, \\ &\text{subject to } x \in K \,. \end{aligned} \right\} \tag{11}$$

(c) Find the solution x^c which has a minimum distance with respect to the ideal solution $\hat{\omega}$. This idea requires normalization [see equation (4)] of the objective functions, and an appropriate choice of a distance metric. A frequently used form is the Minkovsky metric,

$$d = \left[\sum_{j=1}^{J} (\hat{\omega}_j - \overline{\omega}_j)^p \right]^{1/p} , \qquad p \geqslant 1 , \qquad (12)$$

which can be interpreted as a measure of distance [cf Beckenbach and Bellman (1961); see also van Delft and Nijkamp (1977b), and Nijkamp and Rietveld (1977)]. For example, if $p = 1$ and $p = 2$, the following successive programming problems are obtained:

$$\left. \begin{array}{l} \text{minimise } \iota'(\hat{\omega} - \overline{\omega})^{-1}[\hat{\omega} - \omega(x)] , \\[2mm] \text{subject to } x \in K \end{array} \right\} \qquad (13)$$

and

$$\left. \begin{array}{l} \text{minimize } [\hat{\omega} - \omega(x)]'(\hat{\omega} - \overline{\omega})^{-2}[\hat{\omega} - \omega(x)] , \\[2mm] \text{subject to } x \in K . \end{array} \right\} \qquad (14)$$

For $p \to \infty$, only the objective function with the dimension showing the largest difference appears to be important. Then the corresponding programming problem is

$$\left. \begin{array}{l} \text{minimize } \max_j \left[\dfrac{\hat{\omega}_j - \omega_j(x)}{\hat{\omega}_j - \overline{\omega}_j} \right] , \\[4mm] \text{subject to } x \in K . \end{array} \right\} \qquad (15)$$

(d) Find the solution x^d which is as far as possible from the minimum solution $\overline{\omega}$:

$$\left. \begin{array}{l} \text{maximize } \left\{ \sum_j \left[\dfrac{\omega_j(x) - \overline{\omega}_j}{\hat{\omega}_j - \overline{\omega}_j} \right]^p \right\}^{1/p} , \qquad p \geqslant 1 \\[4mm] \text{subject to } x \in K . \end{array} \right\} \qquad (16)$$

(e) Find the solution x^e which is optimal with respect to a set of weights λ reflecting a compromise in some way. There are various ways to attain such a compromise vector, λ. If, for example, all objectives are given the same weight, the programming problem will be (taking into account the different scales of measurement)

$$\left. \begin{array}{l} \text{maximize } \left[\dfrac{1}{J} \iota'(\hat{\omega} - \overline{\omega})^{-1} \right] \omega(x) , \\[4mm] \text{subject to } x \in K . \end{array} \right\} \qquad (17)$$

Another way to find a compromise vector λ is to derive the weights according to which all extreme solutions of the **P** matrix are valued equally [cf Fandel (1972), Nijkamp and Rietveld (1976a; 1976b), and Nijkamp (1977)]:

$$\mathbf{P}'\lambda = c\iota, \qquad \iota'\lambda = 1. \tag{18}$$

λ can clearly be conceived of as a combination of compromise weights, as equation (18) expresses no special interest for any of the J extreme solutions. The solution of (18) is

$$\lambda = \frac{(\mathbf{P}')^{-1}\iota}{\iota'(\mathbf{P}')^{-1}\iota}, \qquad c = \frac{1}{\iota'(\mathbf{P}')^{-1}\iota}, \tag{19}$$

provided $\mathbf{P}$ is nonsingular.

A drawback of this method is that there is no guarantee that $\lambda \geqslant 0$, so that in this case theorem 1 cannot be used to generate a compromise efficient solution. Nijkamp and Rietveld (1976b) propose a game-theoretic approach to derive a vector of weights, similar to equation (19), in order to avoid this problem. This can also be applied for a singular $\mathbf{P}$.

Figure 1 presents a picture illustrating the various compromise measures in the case of two dimensions (ignoring, for the moment, the scaling problem).

At first glance, the five approaches presented above are all reasonable ways of reflecting the idea of compromise solutions. It can be proved rather easily, for example, that x^a, ..., x^e (related to ω^a, ..., ω^e, respectively) are efficient solutions [see, for example, Huang (1972), who proves that x^c for $p = 2$ is efficient]. A closer examination, however, teaches that not all measures can be maintained. The solution x^b, for example, appears to be an extreme solution, as the objective function specified in operation (11) appears to attain its minimum value (zero) when $\overset{*}{\omega}_j = \omega_j(x)$ for a certain j. The same holds true for x^d in certain cases, as, for $p > 1$, the criterion used in operation (16) may prefer extreme solutions to more centrally located efficient points. For $p = 1$ this statement does not hold true. It is interesting, however, that for

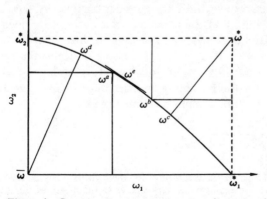

Figure 1. Compromise concepts in a two-dimensional decision problem.

$p = 1$ the solution of operation (16) is identical to the solution of problem (13) as well as that of problem (17).

From the remaining approaches, (a) has the advantage that it implies a multiplicative decision criterion, so that no scaling procedure has to be applied [which always implies a certain arbitrariness; cf Miller and Starr (1960)]. The approach described in equation (18) also avoids this scaling procedure and has the additional advantage of being the only approach in which the decision criterion has been based on more information than just $\overset{*}{\omega}$ and $\overline{\omega}$.

2.4 Measures of conflict

An interesting feature of each of the three remaining approaches is that they give rise to the formulation of a corresponding conflict measure:

$$\gamma_2 = \left[1 - \frac{\prod_j [\omega_j(x^a) - \overline{\omega}_j]}{\prod_j (\overset{*}{\omega}_j - \overline{\omega}_j)} \right] \left[1 - \left(\frac{1}{J}\right)^J \right]^{-1} , \tag{20}$$

$$\gamma_3 = \left\{ \sum_j \left[\frac{\overset{*}{\omega}_j - \omega_j(x^c)}{\overset{*}{\omega}_j - \overline{\omega}_j} \right]^p \middle/ J \left(\frac{J-1}{J}\right)^p \right\}^{1/p} , \quad p \geqslant 1 , \tag{21}$$

$$\gamma_3 = \max_j \left[\frac{\overset{*}{\omega}_j - \omega_j(x^c)}{\overset{*}{\omega}_j - \overline{\omega}_j} \right] \middle/ \left(\frac{J-1}{J}\right) , \quad p \to \infty , \tag{22}$$

$$\gamma_4 = \frac{\lambda'[\overset{*}{\omega} - \omega(x^e)]}{\min_j \gamma'[\overset{*}{\omega} - \omega(\overset{*}{x}_j)]} . \tag{23}$$

The measures have been defined in such a way that their range is the interval [0,1]. Notice, that when λ, as defined in problem (10), is substituted into equation (23), it will yield the same value for the denominator for any j.

Each measure provides some information on a compromise solution with regard to the ideal solution. One might wonder if it is possible to define additional measures which do not consider one ($\gamma_2, \gamma_3, \gamma_4$), or some ($\gamma_1$), efficient points, but all efficient points. Such a measure might be the analogue of the Gini coefficient as a measure of inequality in the field of income distributions[2]. If $J = 2$, this measure indicates the fraction of the triangle $\overset{*}{\omega}_1, \overset{*}{\omega}_2, \overset{*}{\omega}$ which is not feasible (cf figure 1). So, if a functional expression for the possibility frontier [$\omega_2 = f(\omega_1)$] could be found, this measure of conflict could be formalized as

$$\gamma_5 = \int_{\overline{\omega}_1}^{\overset{*}{\omega}_1} f(\omega_1) \, d\omega_1 \middle/ \frac{2}{(\overset{*}{\omega}_1 - \overline{\omega}_1)(\overset{*}{\omega}_2 - \overline{\omega}_2)} . \tag{24}$$

[2] There are more similarities between measures for these fields. The measures for the compromise solutions, for example, are very similar to the measures for the average of an income distribution.

The five γ-measures will be numerically illustrated in section 5. It is worthwhile to note that they can be used to describe the conflict among all J objectives as well as among various subsets of objectives. Thus it seems possible to identify the most crucial conflict elements of the decision problem.

2.5 Identification of efficient solutions in the linear case

Thus far the only assumptions about K and ω have been that the former is convex and the latter concave. If linearity is assumed, some useful specific results can be attained. Therefore we pose that

$$\left. \begin{array}{l} K = \{x \,|\, Ax \leqslant b,\, x \geqslant 0\}, \\[2mm] \omega(x) = Cx, \end{array} \right\} \tag{25}$$

where A is an $N \times I$ matrix, b an N vector, and C a $J \times I$ matrix.

This formulation allows a concise description of the set of efficient solutions, as each efficient solution can be written as the convex combination of a finite number of efficient corner solutions [cf Zeleny, 1974). See for example figure 2, where four such corner solutions have been represented. The crucial point now is how to identify these corner solutions, and a number of researchers have been developing algorithms for this purpose: Philip (1972), Gal and Nedoma (1972), Evans and Steuer (1973), Zeleny (1974; 1976), and Steuer (1976).

It is possible at the moment to derive the set S of corner solutions $\{\overset{+}{x}_1, ..., \overset{+}{x}_L\}$ for not too large problems. The two objective functions have been represented by the interrupted lines through $\overset{+}{x}_1$ and $\overset{+}{x}_4$.

Figure 2 shows two essential features of such linear programming problems:

(a) there are many different values for λ in problem (8) that lead to the same corner solution;

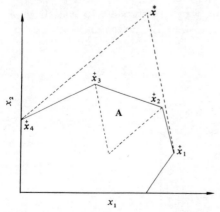

Figure 2. Corner solutions in a two-dimensional case.

(b) there are many minimum standards, $\omega^{\min}$, that lead to efficient points characterized by only one certain value for λ in problem (8). For example, all minimum standards in A result in efficient points on the line between the 2nd and the 3rd corner point.

Sengupta et al (1973) and Kornbluth (1974) have concentrated on the first feature in order to provide information to the DM about the efficient solutions. In this way it is possible to indicate how insensitive certain corner solutions are for variations of the weights vector λ.

In this paper some attention will be devoted to the second feature. Suppose that all m faces of a problem have been identified (cf Zeleny, 1974).

$$\left.\begin{array}{ll} \{\overset{+}{x}_{1_1}, ..., \overset{+}{x}_{1_s}\} & : \text{face } 1 \\ \quad \cdot & \quad \cdot \\ \quad \cdot & \quad \cdot \\ \quad \cdot & \quad \cdot \\ \{\overset{+}{x}_{m_1}, ..., \overset{+}{x}_{ms}\} & : \text{face } m \end{array}\right\}. \tag{26}$$

Figure 2, for example, shows three faces: $\{\overset{+}{x}_1, \overset{+}{x}_2\}$, $\{\overset{+}{x}_2, \overset{+}{x}_3\}$, and $\{\overset{+}{x}_3, \overset{+}{x}_4\}$. Each face m can be characterized by a certain weight vector λ_m and a constant c_m so that

$$\left.\begin{array}{l} \lambda'_m C\{\overset{+}{x}_{m_1}, ..., \overset{+}{x}_{ms}\} = c_m \iota', \\ \iota' \lambda_m = 1. \end{array}\right\} \tag{27}$$

An interesting question now is how to find the set T_m of minimum standards $\omega_m^{\min}$, so that all efficient solutions of

$$\left.\begin{array}{l} \text{maximize } Cx, \\ \text{subject to } Ax \leqslant b, \qquad x \geqslant 0, \qquad Cx \geqslant \omega_m^{\min}, \end{array}\right\} \tag{28}$$

will be elements of face m. If T_m can be identified, it is possible to indicate how insensitive certain weight vectors are for variations of the minimum standards. In order to find T_m, define $\overset{+}{\omega}_l$ as

$$\overset{+}{\omega}_l = C\overset{+}{x}_l. \tag{29}$$

Now project the face $\{\overset{+}{\omega}_{m_1}, ..., \overset{+}{\omega}_{ms}\}$ onto the J basic planes respectively, that is

$$\left.\begin{array}{ll} \text{plane} & \text{projection of face} \\ \omega_1 = \overline{\omega}_1 & : \{\overset{+}{\omega}^1_{m_1}, ..., \overset{+}{\omega}^1_{ms}\} \\ \quad \cdot \quad \cdot & \quad \cdot \quad \cdot \\ \quad \cdot \quad \cdot & \quad \cdot \quad \cdot \\ \quad \cdot \quad \cdot & \quad \cdot \quad \cdot \\ \omega_J = \overline{\omega}_J & : \{\overset{+}{\omega}^J_{m_1}, ..., \overset{+}{\omega}^J_{ms}\} \end{array}\right\}. \tag{30}$$

So, the jth element of each $\overset{+}{\omega}{}^{j}_{ms}$ is equal to $\bar{\omega}_j$; the other elements are equal to the corresponding elements of $\overset{+}{\omega}_{ms}$.

T_m can then be written as the following convex polyhedron:

$$
\left.
\begin{aligned}
T_m = \{\omega_m^{\min} \mid \, \exists \; n_1, ..., n_J, \; \iota' n_j &= 1 \;,\; n_j \geqslant 0 \text{ for } j = 1, ..., J, \text{ so that} \\
\omega_m^{\min} = (\overset{+}{\omega}_{m_1}, ..., \overset{+}{\omega}_{m_s}, \overset{+1}{\omega}_{m_1}, ..., \overset{+1}{\omega}_{m_s}) & n_1 \\[-0.2em]
\cdot \qquad\qquad \cdot & \\
\cdot \qquad\qquad \cdot & \\
\cdot \qquad\qquad \cdot & \\
\omega_m^{\min} = (\overset{+}{\omega}_{m_1}, ..., \overset{+}{\omega}_{m_s}, \overset{+J}{\omega}_{m_1}, ..., \overset{+J}{\omega}_{m_s}) & n_J \}.
\end{aligned}
\right\}
\tag{31}
$$

Thus T_m can be conceived of as the intersection of J different polyhedra with corner points $(\overset{+}{\omega}_{m_1}, ..., \overset{+}{\omega}_{m_s}, \overset{+j}{\omega}_{m_1}, ..., \overset{+j}{\omega}_{m_s})$.

It is a very interesting feature of polyhedron (31) that it describes in fact a vector maximization problem like problem (28). So, in order to identify the corner points of T_m, one has to apply the algorithms mentioned earlier. In this way a two-step method has been devised, the first step implying the identification of corner solutions $\overset{+}{x}_1$, and the second step the identification of corner solutions for $\omega_m^{\min}$.

A short inspection tells us that T_m will never be empty because the elements of face m itself will always satisfy the requirements of equation (31). It is not certain, however, whether T_m contains other faces in addition to face m. Consider, for example, the case when the jth element of λ_m is negative. Because $\overset{+j}{\omega}_{jms} \leqslant \overset{+}{\omega}_{jms}$ and $\overset{+j}{\omega}_{kms} = \overset{+}{\omega}_{kms}$ for $j \neq k$, it follows that

$$
\lambda'_m \overset{+}{\omega}_{ms} \leqslant \lambda'_m \overset{+j}{\omega}_{ms} .
\tag{32}
$$

Combination of relation (32) and the jth equality of equations (31) yields

$$
\lambda'_m \omega_m^{\min} \geqslant c_m .
\tag{33}
$$

For a positive element of λ_m, however, the same form of reasoning results in

$$
\lambda'_m \omega_m^{\min} \leqslant c_m .
\tag{34}
$$

The only values of $\omega_m^{\min}$ satisfying both relations (33) and (34) are the values corresponding to face m.

The conclusion may therefore be drawn that, as soon as one element of λ_m is negative, the relevant part of T_m will be empty. The assumption that a certain weight is negative is not far-fetched at all. Section 5 shows a numerical example (with $J = 3$) where eight of the fourteen faces share this characteristic. An exception should be made for the two-dimensional case, where it can be shown straightforwardly that a negative weight and efficient corner solutions are incompatible.

The foregoing conclusion is completely in line with the fact that the interior points of face m are not efficient when the corresponding vector

λ_m contains nonpositive elements (cf Zeleny, 1974). Starting from an interior point, it is always possible to find a point on the edge of the face so that at least one objective has been improved and no objective has become worse off. If, for example, $\lambda_{1m} < 0$, and $\lambda_{2m} > 0$ for any interior point $\omega' = (\omega_1, ..., \omega_J)$ satisfying $\lambda'_m \omega = c_m$, other points in this hyperplane exist like $(\omega_1 + a/-\lambda_{1m}, \omega_2 + a/\lambda_{2m}, \omega_3, ..., \omega_J)$ with better or equal performances for all objectives (provided $a > 0$). So, on this face, ω_1 and ω_2 are nonconflicting objectives, as these objectives can be improved simultaneously.

This (at first glance counter-intuitive) result is important for the practice of multiple-objective decisionmaking, since it may, for example, provide a possibility of checking the consistency of the DM's behaviour. It also provides an additional argument in favour of concentrating the analysis mainly on corner solutions, thus giving decision problems a discrete nature in order to constrain the amount of information produced on behalf of the decisionmakers.

3 Decision methods

The previous section has shown that there are many ways of providing information about efficient solutions. In many cases it will be unlikely, however, that the DM will be able to make his final choice on this basis, because the quantity and quality of the information provided should satisfy at least two requirements. First, it should be so extensive that it contains a sufficiently complete picture of the decision problem. Second, it should be so limited that the DM will be able to digest it. It is exceptional when these two requirements can be met in one step and therefore it is recommendable for the analyst to transfer the information in two or more steps.

This approach has the advantage that the DM gets more actively involved in the information procedure, because he has the opportunity to give his impressions about the information provided. The present section will be devoted to a number of proposals of how to structure the communication process between analyst and DM. Two main approaches can be distinguished, depending on the question as to whether the DM may express his preferences (a) only once or (b) repeatedly.

When a DM expresses his preferences only once, he should present a considerable amount of information if he wants the analyst to find a unique solution of the decision problem. In fact, he has to explicate a utility function with J objectives as its arguments. Various examples of this approach can be given. Roy (1971), for example, assumes that the DM has been able to explicate the weights attached to the various objectives. Another possibility is that the utility structure is assumed to be lexicographic (Fishburn, 1974); in this case the DM has to arrange the objectives in order of importance. In addition to this, he has to specify satiation levels for each objective. The treatment of this type of problem would imply the successive solution of a number of mathematical programming problems, starting with the most important objective. For the maximization of each subsequent objective an extra constraint on foregoing objectives is added, so that the foregoing objective certainly reaches its satiation level. The procedure ends when an objective is found which cannot reach this level because of the restrictions imposed on the foregoing objectives. A similar hierarchical procedure can be found in van Delft and Nijkamp (1977a).

A related approach is goal programming [see, among others, Charnes and Cooper (1961)]. Here the DM has to express only the desired level for each objective. The optimal solution is the feasible solution which is as close as possible to the desired levels. A mathematical program such as problem (14) is the result.

An obvious drawback of these methods is that the DM must perform the difficult task of expressing his preferences while he has incomplete information about the feasibility ranges of the problem.

It is therefore worth calling attention to some interactive methods, each of which offers possibilities of a feedback to the DM. These methods share two common elements, namely
(a) the analyst presents a provisional solution to the DM; and
(b) the DM expresses his opinion about this solution.

As has been discussed in section 2.4, provisional (or compromise) solutions can be found in various ways. Distance metrics, for example, have been used by Benayoun et al (1971), Fichefet (1974), and Nijkamp and Rietveld (1977). Compromise weights have been applied by Fandel (1972), Monarchi et al (1973), Nijkamp and Rietveld (1976a), and Zionts and Wallenius (1976). Belenson and Kapur (1973) and again Fichefet (1974) used compromise weights derived from game-theoretic approaches.

In addition to the provisional solution, a number of other possible and meaningful solutions may be presented in order to provide a frame of reference for the DM. Most authors quoted above present the payoff matrix (2). Zionts and Wallenius (1976) propose the calculation, in the linear case, of all adjacent corner solutions.

As to the reaction of the DM, most authors propose that he be asked which of the objectives in the provisional solution is definitely unsatisfactory. In addition, the DM may be permitted to specify minimum achievement levels for other objectives, indicating how far he allows reductions in these objectives in order to improve the unsatisfactory objectives. Monarchi et al (1973) let the analyst ask the DM to fix a desired value for a certain objective. Zionts and Wallenius (1976) advocate another approach: they do not want to compare the performance of each of the objectives of the provisional solution, but they do want to compare the provisional solution with each of the adjacent corner solutions. For each solution, the DM has to indicate whether he prefers it to the provisional solution or not.

The answer given by the DM can easily be integrated into mathematical programming models in the form of extra constraints, so that the next provisional solution reflects the DM's preferences in a more satisfactory way. In some cases (such as Monarchi et al, 1973) it may appear that the added constraints make the feasible area empty—if so the DM should be asked to revise his reaction. All methods share the property that they lead to a converging communication between analyst and DM. Difficulties may of course arise when a DM wants to abandon constraints, formulated in former steps. No convergence can then be proved.

All methods discussed above deal with efficient points only. Geoffrion et al (1972) present a method in which the provisional solution is not necessarily efficient. They propose the DM be asked to express directly the weights attached to the objectives. Here we find another difference, because the above mentioned methods only deal implicitly with weights. This is an advantage, because DM's appear to have great difficulties in specifying weights explicitly (cf Wallenius, 1975).

4 An interactive decision method
This section is devoted to the presentation of a certain variant of interactive multiple-objective decisionmaking. Special attention will be paid to the relationships among constraints, shadow prices, and weights.

The core of the procedure can be delineated as follows:

stage 1   The analyst solves J mathematical programming problems in order to find $\mathbf{P}$, $\overset{*}{\omega}$, and $\overline{\omega}$. He calculates the compromise solution (13). This solution is presented to the DM.

stage 2   The DM mentions the objectives with an unsatisfactory performance. If all objectives are satisfactory, the procedure can be finished. If all objectives are unsatisfactory, the problem does not allow an acceptable solution.

          If only some objectives are unsatisfactory, the analyst has to add constraints to the mathematical program, indicating that the performance of those objectives concerned should be improved. Then go back to *stage 1*.

Of course, the improvement of the unsatisfactory objectives can only be realized at the cost of worse performances for some of the other objectives. Fandel (1972) shows that this kind of procedure leads to a converging process.

The information processed in *stage 1* is an essential element of the procedure. The analyst may provide additional facts in order to offer the DM more meaningful information about the problem. A number of possibilities for that purpose have already been discussed in section 2. One special subject, viz the relationship between the shadow prices of the constraints added and the weights of the utility function assumed, still has to be discussed.

Theorem 1 tells us that any efficient solution can be considered the optimum solution for a linear utility function with a certain combination of weights. Therefore the procedure described above may be thought of as a way to help the DM select a certain solution as well as to approximate his implicit preferences. It may be illuminating for the DM to see how, during each step of the procedure, the addition of constraints has repercussions for the weights. Consider for example the following J mathematical programs, performed during *stage 1* of each step.

$$\text{maximize } \epsilon_j Cx, \qquad j = 1, ..., J, \\ \text{subject to } Ax \leqslant b, \qquad x \geqslant 0, \qquad Cx \geqslant \omega^{\min}. \tag{35}$$

ϵ_j is a basic vector with $J-1$ zero elements and a unit element at position j. $\omega^{\min}$ contains the minimum levels, specified during preceding steps. The optimal solutions of programs (35) are $\overset{\circ}{x}_1, ..., \overset{\circ}{x}_J$, respectively.

One may wonder now which weight vectors μ_j in

$$\text{maximize } \mu_j' Cx, \\ \text{subject to } Ax \leqslant b, \qquad x \geqslant 0, \tag{36}$$

would lead to the same optimal solutions. The answer to this question may be given when the corresponding dual problems are formulated:

$$\text{minimise } (b' \vdots \omega^{\min'}) \binom{y}{r}, \\ \text{subject to } (A' \vdots -C') \binom{y}{r} \geqslant C' \epsilon_j, \qquad y, r \geqslant 0; \tag{37}$$

and

$$\text{minimize } b'y \\ \text{subject to } A'y \geqslant C' \epsilon_j, \qquad y \geqslant 0. \tag{38}$$

As objective (35) has an optimal solution, the duality theorem [see, for example, Zionts (1974)] states that problem (37) also has an optimal solution, say $\overset{\circ}{y}_j, \overset{\circ}{r}_j$. In addition, it states that

$$\epsilon_j' C \overset{\circ}{x}_j = (b' \vdots \omega^{\min'}) \binom{\overset{\circ}{y}_j}{\overset{\circ}{r}_j}. \tag{39}$$

Consider now the other pair of programming problems, (36) and (38). Note that $\overset{\circ}{x}_j$ is a feasible solution of (36) and that $\overset{\circ}{y}_j$ is feasible in (38), if at least we set

$$\mu_j = \epsilon_j + \overset{\circ}{r}_j. \tag{40}$$

If we can prove that $\overset{\circ}{x}_j$ and $\overset{\circ}{y}_j$ are optimal solutions of problems (36) and (38) respectively, we may conclude that equation (40) is the appropriate expression for μ_j. Calculate therefore for $\overset{\circ}{x}_j$ and $\overset{\circ}{y}_j$ the difference d of the outcomes of the objective functions of problems (36) and (38):

$$d = \mu_j' C\overset{\circ}{x}_j - b'\overset{\circ}{y}_j . \tag{41}$$

The combination of expressions (39)–(41) results in

$$d = \overset{\circ}{r}_j' (C\overset{\circ}{x}_j - \omega^{min}) , \tag{42}$$

and, given the primal–dual relationships, we may conclude that $d = 0$, which means that $\overset{\circ}{x}_j$ and $\overset{\circ}{y}_j$ are the optimal solutions searched for and hence that equation (40) is indeed the intended expression for μ_j.

This result looks rather specific because of the special form of the weightvector ϵ_j and the linear structure of program (35). It will be clear, however, that for every weightvector a result similar to equation (40) can be obtained. In addition it can be proved in a straightforward way that, for the nonlinear case, equation (40) is in complete accordance with the Kuhn–Tucker necessary conditions for an optimum.

One should interpret the findings thus far carefully. Note that it is not certain that $\overset{\circ}{x}_j$ is the only optimal solution corresponding to μ_j—there may be more optimal solutions. Nor is it certain that only one value for μ_j can be found, as program (35) may be degenerate. In that case the additional restrictions have been formulated in such a way that there are more active restrictions than basic variables (see, for example, figure 2). The result is that different basic solutions can be chosen, each leading to another value for $\overset{\circ}{r}_j$, and hence for μ_j.

The conclusion is that, although the values of μ_j may be ambiguous to a certain extent, they may contain useful information for the DM. The converging weights $(\mu_1, ..., \mu_J)$ present, during each step of the interaction, an interesting picture of the convergence of the solutions $(\overset{\circ}{x}_1, ..., \overset{\circ}{x}_J)$.

5 A transportation model
The concepts and methods developed above are now applied to a transportation and modal choice model, dealing with home-to-work trips. Thus far, transportation models have been applied mainly to single-objective cases, such as the minimization of transport costs or the maximization of entropy [cf Nijkamp (1975)]. Barr and Smillie (1972) and Leinbach (1976), however, argued that in fact more objectives have to be considered, especially in order to be able to discriminate between multiple optimal solutions.

Therefore a multiple-objective transportation model has been formulated. The objectives are the minimization of three kinds of costs ($j = 1, 2, 3$): ($j = 1, 2, 3$):
1. total private transport cost (measured in units of money);
2. total damage to the urban environment (measured in units of urban environmental quality); and
3. total damage to the natural environment (measured in units of natural environmental quality).

This model will be applied to a hypothetical closed region with six different locations ($k = 1, ..., 6$) and two modes of transport, namely car and train ($m = 1, 2$). Some locations show labour shortages, others show surpluses. For the total region the balance of labour indicates a certain amount of unemployment. Some locations are directly connected. The set S^m, with elements (k, l), indicates the pairs of locations between which a direct connection exists with respect to transport mode m. The costs (category j) of transport by means of mode m between the directly connected locations k and l for one person will be denoted by $c_{k,l}^{m,j}$. Let $x_{k,l}^m$ denote the number of persons travelling by mode m from k to $l^{(3)}$.

For the general case with J cost categories and M modes of transport, the objectives of the programming problem are:

$$\text{minimize } \omega_1 = \sum_m \sum_{k,l \in S^m} c_{k,l}^{m,1} x_{k,l}^m ,$$

$$\left.\begin{array}{c} \cdot \\ \cdot \\ \cdot \end{array}\right\} \tag{43}$$

$$\text{minimize } \omega_J = \sum_m \sum_{k,l \in S^m} c_{k,l}^{m,J} x_{k,l}^m .$$

The constraints of the problem are of various kinds:
(1) capacity constraints,

$$x_{k,l}^m \leqslant \bar{x}_{k,l}^m \qquad \forall m , \ \forall (k,l) \in S^m ; \tag{44}$$

(2) constraints related to the situation on the labour market in each location,

$$\sum_m \sum_{k,n \in S^m} x_{k,n}^m - \sum_m \sum_{n,k \in S^m} x_{n,k}^m - u_n + v_n = s_n \qquad \forall n , \tag{45}$$

where u_n, v_n, and s_n represent unemployment, vacancies, and net local labour demand of location n, respectively;
(3) a constraint indicating the number of vacancies allowed in the whole region,

$$\sum_n v_n \leqslant V ; \tag{46}$$

(4) nonnegativity constraints,

$$\left.\begin{array}{ll} x_{k,l}^m \geqslant 0 & \forall m, \ (k,l) \in S^m , \\[6pt] u_n, v_n \geqslant 0 & \forall n . \end{array}\right\} \tag{47}$$

We now turn to the description of the data of the transportation network. The network has been depicted in figure 3.

$^{(3)}$ Notice that it has not been assumed that k and l are the starting and end points, respectively, of the trips. (k, l) may be only a part of the route followed by the commuters.

The network consists of six nodes, nine connections by car and two by train; capacity constraints have been specified for two connections. The situation on the labour market has been described in table 1.

The total region shows a certain excess labour supply. One of the interesting characteristics of a multiple-objective transportation model is that the localization of the unemployment at one of the excess-supply nodes (1, 2, 3, 6) depends on the weights attached to the various transportation cost categories. These costs per person can be found in table 2 for both modes of transport. In addition to this, table 2 presents the capacity constraints $\bar{x}^m_{k,l}$ mentioned before.

It has been assumed that the connections are symmetric, so that

$$\left.\begin{array}{l} c^{m,j}_{k,l} = c^{m,j}_{l,k}\ , \\[2mm] \bar{x}^m_{k,l} = \bar{x}^m_{l,k}\ , \end{array}\qquad m = (1,2)\ \ \forall(k,l) \in S^m\ ,\quad j = (1,2,3)\ . \right\}\qquad (48)$$

Capacity constraints have been included in the model for only two of the connections by car. The capacity constraint on transport by train means that only 14000 persons can travel by train from a certain location to a subsequent one during their trip from home to work. Finally, it has been assumed that no vacancies exist in the region ($V = 0$).

The programming problem (43)–(47) is a linear one. This is to a certain extent unrealistic, because it is then impossible to deal with a problem like congestion in a satisfactory way. Given the purpose of the

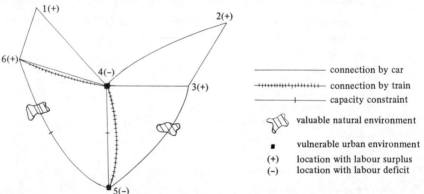

Figure 3. A transportation network.

Table 1. Labour demand and supply.

Location	1	2	3	4	5	6	Σ
Employment[a]	1500	2500	5000	20000	65000	5000	99000
Labour supply[a]	5000	3000	10000	15000	50000	17000	100000
Net labour demand[a]	−3500	−500	−5000	5000	15000	−12000	−1000

[a] All figures indicate numbers of persons.

model, however, namely to illustrate the possibilities of a multiple-objective transportation model, this approach may be satisfactory. In addition to its simplicity, it has the advantage that some of the concepts from section 2.5 can be applied.

In accordance with the approach of section 2, we first concentrate on the set of efficient solutions. These appear to comprise fifteen efficient corner solutions, which can be found in table 3.

The use of the routes (1, 6) and (2, 3) for home-to-work trips appears to be inefficient. It also appears that the distribution of the unemployment among the locations depends upon the priorities attached to the various cost categories. For example, high priorities to avoid the environmental costs lead to a concentration of unemployment in location 2, whereas a priority to avoid private transport costs results in a more equal distribution of unemployment.

Table 2. Transportation costs per person and capacity constraints.

mode (m)	1									2	
path (k,l)	(1,4)	(1,6)	(2,3)	(2,4)	(3,4)	(3,5)	(4,5)	(4,6)	(5,6)	(4,5)	(4,6)
$c_{k,l}^{m,1}$ a	23	14	16	30	18	34	25	21	30	27	24
$c_{k,l}^{m,2}$ a	10	9	5	9	11	14	18	14	16	7	6
$c_{k,l}^{m,3}$ a	20	15	10	13	12	35	8	9	40	3	3
$\bar{x}_{k,l}^m$ (number of persons)	-	-	-	-	-	-	7000	-	10000	14000	

a Measured in the units mentioned above under the definition of costs.

Table 3. Efficient corner solutions.

Number of corner	ω_1	ω_2	ω_3	$x_{1,4}^1$	$x_{2,4}^1$	$x_{3,4}^1$	$x_{3,5}^1$	$x_{4,5}^1$	$x_{6,4}^1$	$x_{6,5}^1$	$x_{4,5}^2$	$x_{6,4}^2$	u_1	u_2
	in thousands of the appropriate units			measured in hundreds of persons										
1	817·5	368·5	274·5	25	5	50	-	10	120	-	140	-	10	-
2	716·5	253·5	433·5	25	5	-	50	-	-	40	60	80	10	-
3	826·5	395·5	265·5	25	5	50	-	100	30	-	50	90	10	-
4	776·5	305·5	345·5	25	5	-	50	-	80	-	100	40	10	-
5	808·5	353·5	289·5	25	5	40	10	-	120	-	140	-	10	-
6	629·0	336·0	584·0	30	-	-	50	30	50	70	-	-	5	5
7	650·0	263·0	539·0	30	-	-	50	-	-	70	30	50	5	5
8	705·0	283·0	439·0	30	-	50	-	-	-	70	80	50	5	5
9	798·0	353·0	301·0	30	-	50	-	-	110	10	140	-	5	5
10	715·5	281·5	422·0	30	-	50	-	-	-	65	85	55	5	5
11	635·0	303·0	569·0	30	-	-	50	-	50	70	30	-	5	5
12	713·0	254·0	437·0	30	-	-	50	-	-	40	60	80	5	5
13	814·0	369·0	278·0	30	-	50	-	10	120	-	140	-	5	5
14	773·0	306·0	349·0	30	-	-	50	-	80	-	100	40	5	5
15	805·0	354·0	293·0	30	-	40	10	-	120	-	140	-	5	5

The payoff matrix as described in equation (2) can be constructed by means of the corner solutions, 6, 2, and 3:

$$\mathbf{P}' = \begin{pmatrix} 629\cdot0 & 336\cdot0 & 584\cdot0 \\ 716\cdot5 & 253\cdot5 & 433\cdot5 \\ 826\cdot5 & 395\cdot5 & 265\cdot5 \end{pmatrix}. \tag{49}$$

The measure of conflict related to this matrix, γ_1, is equal to $0\cdot517$, indicating a considerable amount of conflict among the objectives, and it is interesting to analyze further the nature of this conflict. A pairwise analysis of the conflict proves to be useful, and its results have been summarized in table 4.

When we compare the elements of table 4 horizontally, the conclusion may be drawn that the values of the five measures of conflict are rather close to one another. They all show the same picture as well as the same intensity of conflict.

Comparing the elements of table 4 vertically, we notice an intense conflict between the quality of natural environment (ω_3) on the one hand, and the quality of urban environment (ω_2) as well as the private transport costs (ω_1) on the other hand. The conflict between private transportation costs (ω_1) and the urban environmental quality (ω_2), however, is far more moderate. This can be made plausible by means of figure 3, where we find that the least-cost connections between the largest labour-demanding location (5) and the four locations with excess supply of labour (1, 2, 3, 6) all avoid the rather vulnerable location 4. Owing to this, however, the routes (3, 5) and (6, 5) will be used more intensively, giving rise to a considerable damage to the natural environment.

When the decision has to be made by a group, instead of by a single person, table 4 may shed light on the formation of coalitions. Suppose, for example, that the group consists of three persons j, advocating the minimization of objective j ($j = 1, 2, 3$). It is clear that a coalition between the persons 1 and 2 is far more probable than the two other possibilities.

Which compromise will be selected by 1 and 2? When they are equally powerful, it will very probably be a solution near ω^a, ω^c ($p = 1$), ω^c ($p = 2$), and ω^c ($p \to \infty$). Notice that these compromise concepts are

Table 4. Measures of conflict for various pairs of objectives[a].

Measure of conflict	γ_2	$\gamma_3(p=1)$	$\gamma_3(p=2)$	$\gamma_3(p\to\infty)$	γ_5
ω_1 versus ω_2	$0\cdot437$	$0\cdot355$	$0\cdot376$	$0\cdot415$	$0\cdot320$
ω_1 versus ω_3	$0\cdot952$	$0\cdot929$	$0\cdot931$	$0\cdot932$	$0\cdot909$
ω_2 versus ω_3	$0\cdot887$	$0\cdot842$	$0\cdot843$	$0\cdot843$	$0\cdot781$

[a] The measure γ_4 has been omitted, because it is completely identical to $\gamma_3(p=1)$ when only two objectives are considered.

related to the first four conflict measures mentioned in table 4. In this case, it appears that corner solution number 7 of table 3 is the best compromise for the first three compromise concepts, and ω^c ($p \to \infty$) is close to this corner. So, let us say that persons 1 and 2 agree about solution 7 as the compromise.

It is interesting to compare this solution with the compromises which would be obtained if 1 and 3, or 2 and 3, formed coalitions in spite of their strong conflicts of interests. Suppose also in these cases that ω^c ($p = 1$) is the compromise concept applied. The outcomes are shown in table 5.

Table 5 shows very clearly that persons 1 and 2 will prefer each other as coalition partners. Person 3 will prefer 2 to 1, in accordance with the fact that the conflict between 1 and 3 is even greater than between 2 and 3. The conclusion to be drawn is that, when the decision procedure is majority voting, corner solution 7 will probably be selected by the group.

Let us concentrate now on some of the concepts developed in section 2.5. The fifteen corner solutions together form fourteen faces, described in table 6.

Most of the faces consist of three corner points. There are, however, some faces with four corner points, and face 12 even has five corner points. A striking characteristic of this decision problem is that faces 1-8 correspond with a vector of weights with a nonpositive element. Hence the interior points of these faces are nonefficient. Another consequence is that the corresponding sets of side conditions, $T_1, ..., T_8$, are empty.

Faces 9-14 give rise to positive vectors of weights, however, so the conclusion here is that the interior points of the faces are in fact efficient. The sets T_9-T_{14} appear to be convex polyhedra. The simplest case, face 14,

Table 5. Coalitions and compromise solutions.

Coalition	Number of corner	ω_1	ω_2	ω_3
$(1, 2)$	7	$650 \cdot 0$	$263 \cdot 0$	$539 \cdot 0$
$(1, 3)$	10	$715 \cdot 5$	$281 \cdot 5$	$422 \cdot 0$
$(2, 3)$	4	$776 \cdot 5$	$305 \cdot 5$	$345 \cdot 5$

Table 6. Faces of the decision problem.

Number of face	1	2	3	4	5	6	7	8	9	10	11	12	13	14
Constituent corners	8	8	2	7	6	6	3	1	1	4	2	9	7	9
	9	9	7	8	8	8	6	3	5	5	4	10	8	13
	10	13	12	11	11	13	13	13	13	14	12	12	10	15
									15	15	14	14	12	
												15		

results in a tetrahedral set V_{14} with the corner points 9, 13, 15, as well as (805·0, 358·6, 293·0). So, if a side condition ω^{min} in program (35) is an element of V_{14}, the final choice of the DM will certainly be an element of face 14. The sets V_9-V_{13} have more corner points, owing to the greater number of corners of the faces.

Finally an example will be given for the interactive procedure described in section 4. The information is contained in table 7. It shows, for each step the payoff matrix $\mathbf{P}'$ and the corresponding weights vector $\boldsymbol{\mu}_j$, described in equation (40). The compromise weights have been derived by means of equation (19). The negative value of λ_2 during the first step does not cause difficulties, because the resulting compromise is still efficient. After five steps the decision problem has converged considerably —witness the fact that the ranges of the values of the payoff matrix as well as the corresponding weights have shrunk substantially.

6 Conclusion and suggestion for further research
Regional planning problems often are so complex that decisionmakers are unable (a) to comprehend the information available and (b) to provide information about their priorities with respect to the various objectives to

Table 7. Outcomes of the interactive procedure [a].

Step	Procedure	Outcomes of objectives			Weights attached to		
		ω_1	ω_2	ω_3	ω_1	ω_2	ω_3
1	minimize ω_1	629·0	336·0	584·0	1	0	0
	minimize ω_2	716·5	253·5	433·5	0	1	0
	minimize ω_3	826·5	395·5	265·5	0	0	1
	compromise	705·0	283·0	*439·0*	0·642	−0·034	0·392
2	minimize ω_1	705·0	283·0	439·0	0·645	0	0·355
	minimize ω_2	716·5	253·5	433·5	0	1	0
	minimize ω_3	826·5	395·5	265·5	0	0	1
	compromise	*798·0*	353·0	301·0	0·480	0·111	0·409
3	minimize ω_1	705·0	283·0	439·0	0·645	0	0·355
	minimize ω_2	716·5	253·5	433·5	0	1	0
	minimize ω_3	798·0	353·0	301·0	0·590	0	0·410
	compromise	715·5	*281·5*	422·0	0·491	0·118	0·391
4	minimize ω_1	705·3	281·5	439·0	0·546	0·128	0·326
	minimize ω_2	716·5	253·5	433·5	0	1	0
	minimize ω_3	748·8	281·5	386·1	0	0·629	0·371
	compromise	715·5	281·5	*422·0*	0·486	0·115	0·399
5	minimize ω_1	715·5	281·5	422·0	0·595	0	0·405
	minimize ω_2	724·3	260·3	422·0	0	0·629	0·371
	minimize ω_3	748·8	281·5	386·1	0	0·629	0·371
	compromise	723·2	262·9	422·0	0·426	0·178	0·396

[a] The values of the objectives which the DM considers as the least satisfactory elements of the compromise are shown italic. These values are side-conditions for the next steps.

be considered. The concepts and methods described in this paper look promising in the tackling of both problems.

Further research will be especially useful when it is directed to real decisions, in order to attain a clear picture of the DM's information digesting and processing capacities, and to multiobjective multiperson decision situations, in order to develop interactive decision procedures for groups.

References

Barr B, Smillie K, 1972 "Some spatial interpretations of alternative optimal and sub optimal solutions to the transportation problem" *Canadian Geographer* 16 356-364

Beckenbach E, Bellman R, 1961 *An Introduction to Inequalities* (Random House, New York)

Belenson S M, Kapur K C, 1973 "An algorithm for solving multicriterion linear programming problems with examples" *Operational Research Quarterly* 24 65-77

Benayoun R E, Larichev O I, de Montgolfier J, Tergny J, 1971 "Mathematical programming with multi-objective functions: a solution by P.O.P." *Metra* 9 279-299

Bowman V J, 1976 "On the relationship of the Tchebycheff norm and the efficient frontier of multiple-criteria objectives" in *Multiple Criteria Decision Making, Jouy-en-Josas, France* Eds H Thiriez, S Zionts (Springer, Berlin) pp 76-86

Charnes A, Cooper W W, 1961 *Management Models and Industrial Application of Linear Programming* (John Wiley, New York)

Cohon J L, Marks D H, 1973 "Multiobjective screening models and water resource investment" *Water Resource Research* 9 826-836

Dalkey N C, Rourke D L, Lewis R, Snyder D, 1972 *Studies in the Quality of Life* (Lexington Books, Lexington)

Delft A van, Nijkamp P, 1977a "The use of hierarchical optimization criteria in regional planning" *Journal of Regional Science* 17(2) 195-205

Delft A van, Nijkamp P, 1977b *Multi-Criteria Analysis and Regional Decision Making* (Martinus Nijhoff, Leiden)

Evans J P, Steuer R E, 1973 "Generating efficient extreme points in linear multiple objective programming: two algorithms and computing experience" in *Multiple Criteria Decision Making* Eds J L Cochrame, M Zeleny (University of South Carolina Press, Columbia, SC) pp 349-365

Fandel G, 1972 *Optimale Entscheidung bei Mehrfacher Zielsetzung* (Springer, Berlin)

Fandel G, Wilhelm J, 1976 "Zur Entscheidungstheorie bei Mehrfacher Zielsetzung" *Zeitschrift für Operations Research* 20 1-21

Fichefet J, 1974 "GPSTEM, an interactive multi-objective programming in water resources" *Water Resources Research* 9 837-850

Fishburn P C, 1974 "Lexicographic orders, utilities and decision rules: a survey" *Management Science* 20 1442-1471

Gal T, Nedoma J, 1972 "Multiparametric linear programming" *Management Science* 18 406-422

Geoffrion A M, 1968 "Proper efficiency and the theory of vector maximization" *Journal of Mathematical Analysis and Applications* 22 618-630

Geoffrion A M, Dyer J S, Feinberg A, 1972 "An interactive approach for multi-criteria optimization, with an application to the operation of an academic department" *Management Science* 19 357

Goicoechea A, Duckstein L, Bulfin R L, 1976 "The protrade method: a multi objective approach to decision making", paper presented to the Operations Research Society of America, Miami Beach (University of Arizona, Tucson, mimeo)

Haimes Y Y, Hall W A, 1974 "Multiobjectives in water resources systems analysis:
the surrogate worth trade off method" *Water Resources Research* **10** 615-624
Huang S C, 1972 "Note on the mean square strategy for vector valued objective
functions" *Journal of Optimization Theory and Applications* **9** 364-366
Kornbluth J S H, 1974 "Duality, indifference and sensitivity analysis in multiple
objective linear programming" *Operations Research Quarterly* **25** 599-614
Kuhn H W, Tucker A W, 1951 "Non-linear programming" in *Proceedings of the
Second Berkeley Symposium on Mathematical Statistics and Probability*
Ed. J Neyman (University of California Press, Berkeley) pp 481-493
Leibenstein H, 1976 *Beyond Economic Man* (Harvard University Press, Cambridge,
Mass)
Leinbach T R, 1976 "Transportation geography, networks and flows" *Progress in
Geography* **8** 177-207
Linstone H A, Turoff M (Eds), 1975 *The Delphi Method* (Addison-Wesley, London)
Miller D L, Byers D M, 1973 "Development and display of multiple objective project
impacts" *Water Resources Research* **9** 11-20
Miller D W, Starr M K, 1960 *Executive Decisions and Operations Research* (Prentice-
Hall, Englewood Cliffs, NJ)
Monarchi D E, Kisiel C C, Duckstein L, 1973 "Interative multiobjective programming
in water resources" *Water Resources Research* **9** 837-850
Nijkamp P, 1975 "Reflections on gravity and entropy models" *Regional Science and
Urban Economics* **5** 205-255
Nijkamp P, 1977 *Theory and Application of Environmental Economics* (North-
Holland/Elsevier, Amsterdam)
Nijkamp P, Rietveld P, 1976a "Multi-objective programming models, new ways in
regional decision making" *Regional Science and Urban Economics* **6** 253-274
Nijkamp P, Rietveld P, 1976b "Properties of multi-objective optimization models"
Research Memorandum 57 (Department of Economics, Free University, Amsterdam)
Nijkamp P, Rietveld P, 1977 "Impact analyses, spatial externalities and policy choices"
Research Memorandum 65 (Department of Economics, Free University, Amsterdam)
Philip J, 1972 "Algorithms for the vector maximization problem" *Mathematical
Programming* **2** 207-229
Roy B, 1971 "Problems and methods with multiple objective functions" *Mathematical
Programming* **1** 239-266
Roy B, 1976 "From optimization to multicriteria decision aid: three main operational
attitudes", in *Multiple Criteria Decision Making, Jouy-en-Josas, France* Eds H Thiriez,
S Zionts (Springer, Berlin) pp 1-32
Sengupta S S, Podrebarac M M, Fernando T D H, 1973 "Probabilities of optima in
multi-objective linear programmes", in *Multiple Criteria Decision Making*
Eds J L Cochrane, M Zeleny (University of South Carolina Press, Columbia, SC)
pp 217-235
Skutsch M, Schofer J L, 1973 "Goals Delphis for urban planning: concepts in their
design" *Socio-Economic Planning Sciences* **7** 305-313
Steuer R E, 1976 "A five phase procedure for implementing a vector maximum
algorithm for multiple objective linear programming problems" in *Multiple Criteria
Decision Making, Jouy-en-Josas, France* Eds H T Thiriez, S Zionts (Springer, Berlin)
pp 159-169
Wallenius J, 1975 *Interactive Multiple Criteria Decision Methods: An Investigation
and An Approach* (Acta Academiae Oeconomicae Helsingiensis, Helsinki)
Wilhelm J, 1975 *Objectives and Multi Objective Decision Making Under Uncertainty*
(Springer, Berlin)
Zeleny M, 1974 *Linear Multi-Objective Programming* (Springer, Berlin)

Zeleny M, 1976 "Multicriteria simplex method: a Fortran routine" in *Multiple Criteria Decision Making, Kyoto 1975* Ed. M Zeleny (Springer, Berlin) pp 332–345
Zionts S, 1974 *Linear and Integer Programming* (Prentice-Hall, Englewood Cliffs, NJ)
Zionts S, Wallenius J, 1976 "An interactive programming method for solving the multiple criteria problem" *Management Science* 22 652–663

The Generation and Evaluation of Structure Plans using a Decision Optimising Technique (DOT₂)

S OPENSHAW, P WHITEHEAD
University of Newcastle upon Tyne

1 Introduction

Since 1968, Local Government has probably invested somewhere in the region of £100–£150 millions in the preparation of county-wide structure plans for a large part of the United Kingdom. Yet the statutory planning process of which this is only a part has never been tested or evaluated with any degree of rigour. Indeed a number of quite fundamental questions remain unanswered, especially those concerning the efficiency of contemporary planmaking methodologies and the usefulness of the end product as a practical basis for decisionmaking. Moreover, there is growing concern about the validity of a structure-planning process which is characterised by a plethora of different planmaking methodologies and the virtual absence of any national standards.

This area of planning has attracted very little academic research, most of which has been descriptive rather than prescriptive (Drake et al, 1975), or biased towards informing research rather than practical planning; for example, Barras et al (1977). A major reason for the apparent lack of relevant research in this field is the difficulty of investigating ongoing structure-planning processes outside of Local Government. This is exacerbated by the failure of the planning teams to publish in any detail the basis for planning policies and decisions.

One solution to these problems is to attempt cooperative research with a structure-plan team in which methodological research can be run along-side the planmaking process. Unfortunately this involves a long-term commitment over a number of years. Another possible solution is to develop a realistic but hypothetical structure plan as a controlled experiment in which a number of different planning situations can be simulated and the effectiveness of various planmaking methods assessed. This paper explores a third approach. It attempts to set up an independent planmaking process, using published or otherwise available data, and then compare the results that have been obtained with those produced in the real world structure plan.

To this end the authors use a family of mathematical programming models which they call DOT₂—Decision Optimising Technique, version 2. This is used to provide independent results which can be compared with the preferred strategies of three structure plans. Thus it is possible to assess the extent to which the results of three different conventional planmaking procedures can be replicated by the use of a more explicit and formal methodology. The paper is also a test of the applicability of DOT₂ to the problems of structure-plan generation and evaluation. However, it is emphasised that these applications of DOT$_2$ are by no means the only way DOT$_2$ can be used, nor are they the most appropriate use of this technique. In fact its use in this context can only really be justified in terms of the purpose of the paper, which is to explore the validity of certain aspects of current structure-planning practice. In so doing the authors adopt a normative approach and the perspective akin to that of a mathematical programmer and make no attempt to understand the sociology of why a particular structure plan ends up looking like it does.

Section 2 contains a description of the mathematical programming models available in DOT$_2$ and which the authors use to assess the performance of three structure plans. In sections 3, 4, and 5 this approach is applied to the Durham, Cumbria, and Hartlepool structure plans, the results being compared with those produced by more conventional methods. Finally, in section 6 some implications of the results for the processes of generation, evaluation, monitoring, and review of structure plans are examined.

2 Mathematical programming models for plan decisionmaking
2.1 A mathematical programming approach to strategic choice
It is well known that many 'planning' problems can be represented within a mathematical programming framework, especially if the problem concerns the assignment of optimal values to interval scaled variables; for example, resource allocation or land-use design following Schlager (1965). Indeed these methods have the important advantage that they are more directly related to decisionmaking than most of the research orientated models which are currently used to study urban and regional systems, because the variables they manipulate represent decisions of some kind. Unfortunately not many strategic planning problems are sufficiently well defined for this kind of approach to work and statutory planning controls are generally insufficient to ensure compliance with the model's recommendations. Additionally, the nature of the problems associated with structure planning are very 'woolly' and quite different from those for which these models have previously been used.

At its most basic level forward planning involves the selection of policies, from amongst alternatives, with the explicit purpose either of achieving predetermined goals or targets, or of problemsolving. Yet for more than thirty years planmaking has followed one or other variations of the survey-then-plan paradigm, rather than adopt a more direct decision-orientated approach. There are several reasons for the popularity of this rather archaic procedure. The selection of policies is tantamount to decisionmaking, and this has long been viewed as an informal process with political overtones. Furthermore, there is the considerable technical problem of choosing any K from M alternatives by manual methods because of a combinatorial explosion in the number of solutions once M exceeds a small value.

The 'Strategic Choice' approach developed at the Institute for Operational Research (IOR) by Friend and Jessop (1969), Hickling (1974), and Sutton et al (1977) can be seen as an attempt to structure and manipulate design problems of this kind using semiautomatic but mainly manual methods. In fact it is particularly important to view the basic concepts of strategic choice as being separate from these attempts to apply them largely without the use of computer techniques. Indeed this move away from the computer causes a number of severe practical and conceptual problems. The increasing use of technical jargon should not be allowed to confer any measure of legitimacy on methods whose efficiency has not been tested; for example, the attempts to apply strategic choice to structure planning (Sutton et al, 1977).

The authors believe that the basic characteristics of the strategic choice approach are most clearly seen in the original computer method known as the Analysis of Interconnected Decision Areas (AIDA). Building upon this interpretation, the authors have developed an alternative, computer based, implementation of strategic choice, which is very different but in some ways complementary to the approach favoured by the IOR. In so doing there are two major technical problems to be overcome. First of all there is the basic combinatorial problem which involves the identification of feasible strategies, when each strategy consists of a selection of one policy alternative from each of a number of decision areas. Secondly there is the problem of evaluating these feasible solutions in terms of a number of different and possibly conflicting evaluation weights.

The IOR approach to these problems is essentially to identify a manageable number of feasible strategies by imposing a sufficiently large number of constraints on the AIDA formulation, and then to evaluate these alternatives by using various manual manipulations designed to ensure that the most robust, flexible, and rich strategy is selected. The alternative approach that the authors have implemented is to seek a set of strategies which are optimal and not merely feasible in terms of single- or multiple-criteria objective functions. It is noted that with this approach, plan generation and evaluation are carried out simultaneously and automatically. In some ways it represents a more elegant computer-based alternative to the largely manual design process the IOR prefer.

2.2 A basic zero–one integer linear programming model

Building upon the basic concepts of strategic choice, it is suggested that planmaking is essentially a decisionmaking process in the sense that a strategy or plan is based on a series of decisions concerned with the selection of policies from amongst alternatives. The major problem is how to develop an explicit representation of this decisionmaking process. Viewed from this perspective many of the models used in planning have only a very indirect relationship to this decisionmaking process. What is required is a model capable of representing the decisionmaking process implicit in planmaking, and which will thus provide a technical framework within which the very difficult planning and political factors can be related.

A basic single-objective-function model is presented first. This is basically a generalisation of AIDA made possible by reexpressing it as a 0-1 integer linear programming (ILP) problem (Openshaw and Whitehead, 1975). Let A denote the set of n alternative policies for a study region; that is $A \in \{1, 2, 3, ..., n\}$. These policies are arranged into m mutually exclusive subsets or decision areas, each of which contains two or more alternative policies or options. Thus the set A_k contains those policies associated with the kth decision area. Plan generation involves the selection of one policy from each decision area, whereas plan evaluation involves scoring these strategies in terms of one or more sets of weights.

When plan generation and evaluation are combined, the problem can be viewed as an optimisation one. In other words, select a policy from each decision area to optimise the total score on a set of evaluation weights. Thus

$$\text{maximise } F(x) = \sum_{i}^{n} c_i x_i , \tag{1}$$

subject to

$$\sum_{i \in A_k} x_i = 1 , \qquad k = 1, 2, ..., m , \tag{2}$$

where

$x_i \in \{1, 0\}$, $i = 1, 2, ..., n$, are a set of zero-one variables with a value of
    zero if the ith policy is to be rejected, and a value of one if it is to be
    accepted;

c_i, $i = 1, 2, ..., n$, is a vector of evaluation weights measuring the
    desirability, preferability, utility, or effectiveness of each policy
    alternative in terms of a single criterion.

The set of m equality constraints defined in equation (2) ensure that one, and only one, policy is chosen from each decision area. Additional equality and inequality constraints can also be defined; for example, certain combinations of policies may be regarded as logically incompatible, or the score on a set of evaluation weights may be restricted to a certain range of values.

This basic model can be used to provide an AIDA solution by setting all the evaluation weights, c_i, $i = 1, 2, ..., n$, to the same value so that maximising equation (1) will identify a list of all feasible solutions. However, there are $\prod_{i}^{m} n_i$ solutions to equations (1) and (2), where n_i is the number of alternative policies in the ith decision area. As a result, AIDA requires a large number of additional constraints to limit the number of feasible solutions to a manageable number. In many instances plan decisionmaking problems are too complex for this kind of approach, and many of the constraints necessary to reduce the number of feasible solutions are essentially arbitrary and reflect the limitations of the methodology. These difficulties are avoided if the problem is viewed as an optimisation one with unequal evaluation weights. It can then be handled in an automatic fashion with the computer doing most of the work.

2.3 A multiple criteria decisionmaking model

A major problem with the basic zero–one ILP model is the difficulty of specifying a single-objective function and of handling goal conflicts which arise when different evaluation criteria produce conflicting optimum solutions. Indeed many informal plan-evaluation procedures attempt to handle these problems. Similarly, in the IOR strategic choice approach to structure planning, fuzzy set concepts such as compromise, robustness, interaction, dominance, and satisficing occupy an important part in the conceptual framework they have developed. However, these problems may also be solved using multiple criteria decisionmaking techniques; see for example, Cochrane and Zeleny (1973).

One solution is to identify a single-objective function and then impose limits on the performance of any outcome in terms of other sets of weights. More appropriate is a form of multiple-objective-function programming based on an hierarchical optimisation method (Waltz, 1967; Eilon, 1974; van Delft and Nijkamp, 1975). This approach is appropriate to problems in which the evaluation weights designated as objective functions can be ranked in an ordinal way; for example, in terms of the 'most important', 'next most important', etc. Problems of this kind can be solved by a sequential optimisation of the objective functions arranged in rank order, so that the constrained set at each stage of the recursive process is codetermined by the optimal results obtained in the previous stages.

This approach can be modified to allow for the existence of goals or target values for some, or all, of the objective functions (Lee, 1972). The aim is then to minimise positive or negative deviations from the goals specified for each set of evaluation weights, such that the values of the deviational variables associated with the jth most important goal are minimised to the fullest possible extent before the $j+1$th goal.

Virtually all applications of these techniques have been in terms of continuous-variable linear programming problems. Here the discrete nature of the basic 0–1 ILP model makes it necessary to solve a mixed 0–1 and either integer or continuous-variable problem. Fortunately, the Land and Powell (1973) programs that the authors use are capable of solving this kind of problem as well as discrete 0–1 formulations.

Consider a three-objective-function problem based on three row vectors of evaluation weights c_j, $j = 1, 2, 3$, which are arranged according to the ordinal ranking priorities, p_j, $j = 1, 2, 3$. The corresponding goals are g_j, $j = 1, 2, 3$, and S represents the feasible area of the decision variables x, based on the constraints in equation (2) plus any additional constraints. The goal programming optimisation model would give rise to the following sequential hierarchical programming models:

Step 1

minimise $Z_1(x^{(1)}, d) = d_1^- + d_1^+$, \hfill (3)

subject to

$x^{(1)} \in S$, \hfill (4)

$\sum_{j}^{n} c_{1j} x_j^{(1)} + d_1^- - d_1^+ = g_1$, \hfill (5)

where

$d_1^- = g_1 - \sum_{j}^{n} c_{1j} x_j^{(1)}$ \hfill (6)

represents the underachievement of the strategy $x^{(1)}$ in terms of goal g_1 which is associated with the set of evaluation weights c_1 ;

$d_1^+ = \sum_{j}^{n} c_{1j} x_j^{(1)} - g_1$ \hfill (7)

represents the overachievement in terms of goal g_1 ;
$x^{(1)}$ represents a solution to the mixed programming problem defined in equations (3), (4), and (5).

Step 2

minimise $Z_2(x^{(2)}, d) = d_2^- + d_2^+$, \hfill (8)

subject to

$x^{(2)} \in S$, \hfill (9)

$\sum_{j}^{n} c_{1j} x_j^{(2)} - \sum_{j}^{n} c_{1j} x_j^{(1)} = 0$, \hfill (10)

$\sum_{j}^{n} c_{2j} x_j^{(2)} + d_2^- - d_2^+ = g_2$, \hfill (11)

where

$d_2^- = g_2 - \sum_{j}^{n} c_{2j} x_j^{(2)}$, \hfill (12)

$d_2^+ = \sum_{j}^{n} c_{2j} x_j^{(2)} - g_2$; \hfill (13)

equation (10) is necessary to preserve the performance achieved in step 1 in terms of goal one.

Step 3

minimise $Z_3(x^{(3)}, d) = d_3^- + d_3^+$, \hfill (14)

subject to

$x^{(3)} \in S$, \hfill (15)

and

$$\sum_{j}^{n} c_{1j} x_{j}^{(3)} - \sum_{j}^{n} c_{1j} x_{j}^{(1)} = 0 , \tag{16}$$

$$\sum_{j}^{n} c_{2j} x_{j}^{(3)} - \sum_{j}^{n} c_{2j} x_{j}^{(2)} = 0 , \tag{17}$$

$$\sum_{j}^{n} c_{3j} x_{j}^{(3)} + d_{3}^{-} - d_{3}^{+} = g_{3} , \tag{18}$$

where

$$d_{3}^{-} = g_{3} - \sum_{j}^{n} c_{3j} x_{j}^{(3)} , \tag{19}$$

$$d_{3}^{+} = \sum_{j}^{n} c_{3j} x_{j}^{(3)} - g_{3} , \qquad \text{and} \tag{20}$$

$x^{(3)}$ represents a solution to the entire goal program.

In this sequential process the second most important objective function, Z_2, is processed subject to a constraint specifying retention of the previous value obtained for goal one. Obviously, a tolerance could be specified to permit a partial trade-off for Z_1 with respect to Z_2. Similarly for Z_2 with respect to Z_3. In any case even if trade-offs are not allowed, the final solution is clearly a compromise between the competing goals and evaluation weights, although because of the discrete nature of the decision variables there may be a number of final solutions. Finally, it is noted that it is often possible to drop the overachievement variable, d^+, since in many strategic planning applications there is seldom any penalty for over-achievement. If overachievement does occur for any goal, then the constraints in equations (10), (16), and (17) should be modified to retain only the goal value as a constraint for any subsequent steps.

2.4 DOT$_2$

A computer program package known as DOT$_2$ has been developed to enable planners to apply various single- and multiple-function optimisation models to plan decisionmaking problems. The program is available for both ICL and IBM computers and uses a set of keyword commands to set up and execute various problem formulations easily and quickly. Appendix 1 contains an example of a set of DOT$_2$ commands. The novelty of this methodology relates both to its explicit design as a planning tool and to the formal basis it offers for plan decisionmaking. Furthermore it provides a means of implementing an alternative decision-based paradigm for plan-making (Openshaw, 1975) and allows an emphasis to be placed on continuous planmaking, monitoring, and review activities; see, for example, Openshaw and Whitehead (1977). A guide to some of the facilities available in DOT$_2$ is given in Openshaw (1976).

2.5 Application of DOT to three structure plans

The remainder of the paper is concerned with the application of DOT to three structure plans, which were chosen because they had completed their plan generation and evaluation activities and because access was possible to data and documents. However, it is emphasised that these studies are inevitably restricted by the supply of available data, and this has an effect both on the problem formulations and on the evaluation weights which are are used.

3 Case study 1: the Durham County Structure Plan
3.1 Problem formulation

The *Report of Survey* (Durham County Council, 1976a) identified fourteen major issues about which it felt that decisions needed to be reached. Accordingly, a questionnaire was distributed to all 224000 households in the County asking for people's preferences for alternative policies associated with each issue. A total of 14164 questionnaires were returned and this formed the basis for identifying a strategy. Attention is now being given to working out the policies for operating the chosen strategy.

In many ways the Durham County Structure Plan is a special case, in that the issues are resolved in favour of one strategy near the beginning rather than at the end of the planmaking process (Durham County Council, 1976c). Nevertheless, the results of the questionnaire (Durham County Council, 1976b) provide a set of evaluation weights which can be used to reassess this decisionmaking process. Appendix 2 describes the DOT problem formulation for Durham, with twelve decision areas and thirty-nine policy alternatives. Compared with the County Council's approach, some issues are ignored as being of little relevance to structure planning, and eighteen pairs of option bars are identified between pairs of policies considered by the authors to be logically incompatible.

3.2 Strategy generation and evaluation

The public's preferences for each alternative policy are available disaggregated for each of the eight District Councils as well as for the County as a whole. Each set of scores is used as weights in a series of single-objective-function DOT runs, and sets of policies are identified which have maximum public popularity. Virtually all these solutions are the same. A goal programming run is then attempted in which the stated preferences of the District Councils are given preemptive priority over the public's preferences, which, in turn, are given priority over those of a number of major organisations and institutes. The goals are defined as the optimal values obtained from the use of the same data in single-objective-function runs. Table 1 shows these results with what the authors believe is the structure-plan's preferred strategy.

Since all the results are basically similar, the question arises as to whether or not they may be sensitive to errors in the public response data.

G

Table 1. Alternative strategies for Durham.

AP	SPS [a]	SOR [b]	GPR	SE [c]	NR [c]	RDP [c]
1.1	–	–	–	–	7	–
1.2	•	100	•	100	81	100
1.3	–	–	–	–	12	–
2.4	•	11	–	12	51	25
2.5	–	89	•	88	49	75
3.6	–	–	–	–	6	–
3.7	–	–	–	–	12	–
3.8	•	100	•	100	82	100
4.9	•	100	–	100	64	95
4.10	–	–	•	–	36	5
5.11	–	–	–	–	2	–
5.12	•	100·	•	100	45	80
5.13	–	–	–	–	17	–
5.14	–	–	–	–	36	20
6.15	•	89	•	88	60	89
6.16	–	–	–	–	14	–
6.17	–	11	–	12	26	11
7.18	–	–	–	–	30	–
7.19	•	100	•	100	70	100
8.20	–	–	–	–	29	–
8.21	•	100	•	100	71	100
9.22	•	100	•	100	96	100
9.23	–	–	–	–	4	–
10.24	–	–	–	–	12	–
10.25	•	100	•	100	64	100
10.26	–	–	–	–	24	–
11.27	–	–	–	–	15	–
11.28	–	–	–	–	24	–
11.29	•	100	•	100	60	100
12.30	–	–	–	–	42	15
12.31	•	100	•	100	58	85
13.32	–	–	–	–	37	8
13.33	•	100	•	100	63	92

Key: AP, alternative policies; SPS, structure plan strategy; SOR, single-objective-function DOT runs; GPR, goal programming run; SE, sampling error; NR, nonresponse; RDP, random data perturbation.

[a] The preferred strategy is that identified from documentary evidence.
[b] Percentages relate to the number of times a particular policy is selected, using evaluation weights for the County as a whole and for each district.
[c] Percentages relate to the number of times a particular policy is selected, based on thirty replications of the data.

Indeed it is believed that before attempts are made to assess the robustness or flexibility of strategies to temporal uncertainties, an assessment must be made of the possible effects of more mundane errors in the data or uncertainties in the evaluation data. Ideally some form of stochastic programming is required (Contini, 1968); however, the discrete nature of the decision variables makes this difficult. A more pragmatic approach is randomly to perturb the evaluation weights to reflect various kinds of data uncertainty.

If we assume a random sample design, then the standard error, $\hat{o}$, of the proportion in favour of a particular policy vis-à-vis those who are otherwise inclined is given by Cochran (1963, page 51) as

$$\hat{o} = \left(\frac{N-n}{(n-1)Npq} \right)^{1/2} , \tag{21}$$

where

N is the population size,

n is the sample size

p the proportion in favour of a particular policy or issue, and

q the proportion not in favour.

If nonresponse is ignored, then the effects of sampling error can be simulated by regarding each of the evaluation weights as a normally distributed stochastic variable, with a mean equivalent to the observed data and a standard deviation given by equation (21). The single-objective-function models are then rerun thirty times using different random simulations of the evaluation weights each time. However, as table 1 shows under the heading of sampling error, the effects of these sampling error simulations is not very significant.

Another approach is to modify equation (21) to take into account the possible effects of nonresponse, given assumptions about the range of possible results (Cochran, 1963, pages 357–358). Thus the standard error can be written as

$$\hat{o} = W_1 \left(\frac{N-n}{(n-1)Npq} \right)^{1/2} + 0 \cdot 5W_2(u) - 0 \cdot 5W_2(l) , \tag{22}$$

where

W_1 is the proportion of response, that is sample size divided by population size,

W_2 is the proportion of nonresponse,

u is an upper limit on p, set at $1 \cdot 0$ in this instance, and

l is a lower limit set at 0.

Rerunning the single-objective-function models thirty times confirms the previous impression of stability despite a very large nonresponse to the survey; see table 1 under the heading of nonresponse.

A final perturbation of the data simply involves adding or subtracting uniformly distributed random numbers to, or from, the observed evaluation weights. In this instance the proportion of change was arbitrarily fixed at 12%. Unlike the nonresponse and sampling error simulations, this data perturbation is biased to a small degree. However, this also has little effect on the range of results identified in table 1; see column headed random data perturbation.

3.3 A limiting case?
The DOT formulations consistently produce results very similar to the strategy identified in the Durham County Structure Plan. This is hardly surprising because the County Council made its decision the same as the majority public preference. So stable is this particular strategy that even simulations of the massive effects of nonresponse failed to change things significantly. The reason for this stable state can be explained in terms of the way in which the alternatives were presented to the public, resulting in one policy in each decision area being overwhelmingly more popular than any other. Regardless of whether or not this is deliberate or whether or not it is a reflection of the situation prevailing in Durham, it is certainly a limiting case. With no real alternatives and widespread popular consensus, there is no doubt that the unorthodox planmaking used by Durham County Council is appropriate. Alternatively, if the problem formulation is fundamentally incorrect, the public preferences deliberately manipulated, then the resulting plan will be quite worthless.

4 Case study 2: the Cumbria Structure Plan
4.1 Problem formulation
The Cumbria Structure Plan produced a series of policy options related to seven basic decision areas. They formed the basis of a public participation exercise which resulted in 968 replies out of a theoretical maximum sample of 475 700. These evaluation data are available for the county as a whole and for six subareas. At present Cumbria are in the process of choosing a preferred strategy from four alternatives based on themes of economic potential, self-sufficiency, problem solving, and resource conservation (Cumbria County Council, 1976).

Although Cumbria have used a compatibility matrix, none of the four strategies they are evaluating can be directly related to the policy alternatives for which they have evaluation data. Thus it has been necessary for the authors to 'interpret' the four alternative strategies in terms of the original policy alternatives. This produces a problem formulation for DOT of seven decision areas and thirty-four policy alternatives; see appendix 3. In addition thirteen pairs of policies are considered to be logically incompatible.

4.2 Strategy generation and evaluation
A number of single-objective-function DOT runs are carried out to identify the best strategies for each of the six subdivisions of Cumbria and the county as a whole. A goal programming run was attempted with the goals for each subdivision being ranked by the severity of their overall problems.

Table 2. Alternative strategies for Cumbria.

AP	SPS				Combined SPS [a]	SOR	GPR	SE	NR	RDP
	A	B	C	D						
1.1	•	•	•	•	50	—	—	—	13	—
1.2	—	•	—	—	13	71	—	79	31	71
1.3	—	—	—	—	—	—	—	—	11	—
1.4	—	—	—	—	—	—	—	—	20	—
1.5	•	•	•	—	37	29	•	21	25	29
2.6	•	—	—	—	17	—	—	—	20	—
2.7	—	—	—	•	17	—	—	—	23	—
2.8	•	•	—	—	33	—	—	—	24	—
2.9	•	•	—	—	33	—	•	100	33	100
3.10	•	•	—	—	29	—	—	3	14	—
3.11	•	•	—	—	29	14	—	15	17	14
3.12	—	—	—	—	—	—	—	—	13	—
3.13	—	—	—	—	—	—	—	—	12	—
3.14	—	—	•	•	29	29	—	30	16	29
3.15	—	—	•	—	13	57	•	51	17	57
3.16	—	—	—	—	—	—	—	—	10	—
4.17	•	—	—	—	20	14	—	9	33	14
4.18	•	—	—	—	20	—	—	18	28	—
4.19	•	•	•	—	60	86	•	73	39	86
5.20	—	•	—	•	25	—	—	—	—	—
5.21	—	—	•	—	13	—	—	—	20	—
5.22	—	•	•	•	36	100	•	100	56	100
5.23	—	•	—	—	13	—	—	—	24	—
5.24	•	—	—	—	13	—	—	—	—	—
6.25	•	—	—	—	20	—	—	—	11	—
6.26	—	—	—	•	20	100	•	99	34	100
6.27	—	—	—	—	—	—	—	—	23	—
6.28	—	•	•	•	60	—	—	—	15	—
6.29	—	—	—	—	—	—	—	1	17	—
7.30	•	—	—	—	25	—	—	—	15	—
7.31	—	—	—	—	—	—	—	—	20	—
7.32	—	—	—	•	25	—	—	14	27	—
7.33	—	•	—	•	50	100	•	86	26	100
7.34	—	—	—	—	—	—	—	—	12	—

Key: as for table 1.

[a] Percentages relate to the number of times a particular policy occurs in the four preferred strategies.

As before the goals are set at the optimum results which could be obtained in single-objective-function runs. Finally, various sample, nonresponse, and data perturbation simulations are carried out. The results are summarised in table 2, together with what are believed to be the policies favoured by the four preferred strategies.

Comparative evaluation is difficult in this instance because the preferred strategies are based on more than one policy alternative within many of the decision areas. It is thought that this is a result of confusion in the Cumbria Structure Plan. The assumption that only one policy can be selected from a decision area can of course be relaxed, but in this instance this is of little help. Nevertheless, the results produced by the various DOT runs are very similar to each other, except for decision areas 1 and 3. Moreover, the effects of nonresponse are more noticeable than was the case for Durham. Furthermore, the Cumbria Structure Plan's alternative strategies generally cover the DOT results but with only a low degree of overall accuracy. None of the Cumbria strategies are very similar to the DOT results when assessed by their goodness of fit in all decision areas.

5 Case study 3: the Cleveland (Hartlepool) Structure Plan
5.1 Problem formulation
The Hartlepool Structure Plan is of particular interest because it is based on the use of the strategic choice approach, with some guidance from the Institute for Operational Research (IOR). Furthermore, it is one of the case studies quoted by Sutton et al (1977).

Three strategic issues are identified: employment, housing, and transportation (Cleveland County Council, 1976a). For each of these, two options are considered giving eight combinations. The result is an AIDA problem formulation of eighteen decision areas and forty-eight policy alternatives, see appendix 4. They also identified fifty-two pairs of incompatible policies. This AIDA formulation is part of the Hartlepool Structure Plan and can be used without modification in DOT. For the purposes of public participation a simplification of the eight strategies and three issues into four strategies and two issues is used. A sample of 700 households provides evaluation data (Cleveland County Council, 1976b).

The policy options within the four strategies and two issues are drawn up as solution streams. The advantage of this approach is summed up as a narrowing of the "... focus to a sub-set of the most promising strategies rather than to select a single preferred strategy" (Sutton et al, 1977, page 153). The eventual selection of a preferred strategy is to be based on a "... fairly crude technical evaluation, together with the results of public participation" (Sutton et al, 1977, Section A.20).

5.2 Strategy generation and evaluation

As a basis for comparison with the DOT results, the solution stream for alternative 4 is examined. This, according to Sutton et al (1977, page 175) is "... an example of a relatively complex solution stream (2,520 alternative strategies) sequenced according to choice". Yet in seven decision areas there is no choice, in another seven there is a limited or structured choice, and in the remaining four free choice.

Once again public preference data are the only evaluation weights which are available for each of the policy alternatives (Cleveland County Council, 1977). There are four sets of scores, one for each of the four strategic alternatives. A series of DOT runs are carried out to identify strategies which optimise the scores on each set of evaluation data. In this instance, the public's preference in ten decision areas does not alter whichever strategy

Table 3. Alternative strategies for Hartlepool.

AP	SS [a]	DR4	SOR	GPR	SE	NR	RDP
1.1	–	–	–	–	–	9	6
1.2	–	–	25	•	–	23	25
1.3	•	•	75	–	100	68	69
2.4	–	•	25	–	77	27	28
2.5	–	–	–	–	–	–	–
2.6	–	–	75	•	23	69	72
2.7	–	–	–	–	–	4	–
3.8	–	–	–	–	9	19	2
3.9	–	–	–	–	–	4	–
3.10	–	•	100	•	91	77	98
4.11	–	•	25	–	77	37	28
4.12	–	–	–	–	–	5	–
4.13	–	–	75	•	23	57	72
5.14	–	–	–	–	6	30	–
5.15	–	•	100	•	94	53	88
5.16	–	–	–	–	–	17	12
6.17	–	•	75	•	71	42	61
6.18	–	–	25	–	9	34	28
6.19	–	–	–	–	20	24	11
7.20	–	–	–	–	–	13	–
7.21	–	•	100	•	100	75	100
7.22	–	–	–	–	–	13	–
8.23	•	•	100	•	100	90	100
8.24	–	–	–	–	–	10	–
9.25	–	•	100	•	100	80	100
9.26	–	–	–	–	–	20	–

is chosen, whereas in other decision areas the choice polarises between those opting for strategies 1 and 3, and those preferring strategies 2 and 4.

The goal programming run is based on a ranking of the goals in accordance with the survey results, the goals themselves are set at the previous optimum value for each of the evaluation weights. Finally, the three simulations of data uncertainty have less effect than previously because, unlike the other surveys, this survey is well designed with a high response rate. Table 3 compares these DOT results with solution stream 4.

The Hartlepool Structure Plan does not have a single preferred strategy, only these four solution streams. Despite the various opportunities they offer for discussion of the alternatives within the zone of constrained choice (Friend and Sutton, 1976), they are but an early stage in the strategy generation process. A narrowing down of the wide choice contained in these solution streams is still necessary, and ultimately decisions will

Table 3 (continued)

AP	SS [a]	DR4	SOR	GPR	SE	NR	RDP
10.27	–	–	–	–	–	30	21
10.28	•	•	100	•	100	70	79
11.29	•	•	100	•	100	92	100
11.30	–	–	–	–	–	8	–
12.31	–	–	50	•	–	50	50
12.32	•	•	50	–	100	50	50
13.33	–	–	50	•	–	45	50
13.34	•	•	50	–	100	50	50
14.35	–	–	–	–	–	27	19
14.36	–	•	100	•	100	54	78
14.37	–	–	–	–	–	19	3
15.38	–	•	100	•	100	79	95
15.39	–	–	–	–	–	21	5
16.40	–	–	50	•	–	45	50
16.41	•	•	50	–	100	55	50
16.42	–	–	–	–	–	–	–
17.43	–	•	100	•	100	90	100
17.44	–	–	–	–	–	10	–
18.45	–	–	–	–	–	6	–
18.46	–	–	–	–	–	22	5
18.47	–	–	50	•	–	34	45
18.48	–	•	50	–	100	37	50

Key: SS, solution stream; DR4, DOT run using weights for strategy 4; others as for table 1.

[a] Fixed choice policies.

have to be made which will inexorably lead to a single strategy. Unless these decisions are continually kept under review and the means exist to enable the associated technical problems to be resolved, then the advantages of solution streams will be lost.

If the DOT results are compared with solution stream 4, then it will be noted that all those policies offering no choice are selected. However, ten of the policies included in this solution stream are not selected by any of the single-objective-function DOT runs. Furthermore, the DOT results show that the policies selected for strategy 2 can be defined within the solution stream for strategy 4. Moreover, as the public choice of policies does not vary greatly between strategies, it might be concluded that solution streams form an unnecessary complication to a relatively simple problem formulation. Indeed one of the problems associated with the approach used by Cleveland and admitted by the IOR is the need to "... review the probability that there may be quite a large number of alternative strategies that could be carried forward ... and this raises some question as to the capacity of the technology to deal with them" (Sutton et al, 1977, page 144).

6 Conclusions

Planning is fundamentally a decisionmaking process, so that models which can help formalise and assist this process have an immediate and obvious relevance. It is apparent that regional scientists have been rather slow to appreciate the need to relate their models explicitly to decisionmaking, with the result that many model applications have been characterised by severe problems of relevance to the planning processes they are supposed to serve. The zero—one ILP model known as DOT is an exception in that it provides a representation of the decisionmaking processes involved in planmaking.

By adopting a normative approach, it has been possible to obtain an independent assessment of the conventional planmaking methodologies used in three structure plans. This research faced a number of problems related to the generally poor quality of the available documentary evidence. Many planning reports are confusing to outsiders, contradictory, and difficult to understand without additional knowledge of what is going on in a particular structure plan. As a result it is often difficult to identify precisely why a particular strategy was chosen. In addition, it is apparent that attempts are often made to change the scope and nature of policies after the public participation stage, in order to meet criticisms of various kinds. This must present tremendous problems for monitoring and review since there is no longer a link between the plan and the evaluation data upon which it is supposed to be based.

The Durham Structure Plan avoids many methodological problems by identifying a single strategy. Yet many of the alternative issues from which the strategy was chosen are infeasible and the evaluation data merely confirm this. The Cumbria Structure Plan started off quite well, but appears to have abandoned whatever logical structure it may have originally possessed when it came to identifying alternative strategies. Hence the somewhat confusing nature of the four alternative strategies in terms of those policies used for public participation.

The Hartlepool Structure Plan seems to testify to the impracticability of the strategic choice approach. The framework used has a number of important conceptual advantages over Durham and Cumbria, but it has yet to produce a plan or strategy. Ideally it should have produced alternative policy sets which can be evaluated by "... some means of assessment by which the performance of any alternative on each criterion may be judged" (Sutton et al, 1977, page 190). Yet in practice the solution streams put forward in Hartlepool contain many thousands of possible strategies and are identified by a fairly crude technical evaluation. Furthermore, there has been no systematic exploration of alternatives by the varying of assumptions or by sensitivity testing. Yet these activities have been identified as "... critical areas for deeper exploration and consultation so as to provide a more sensitive and discerning evaluation process" (Sutton et al, 1977, page 194). Clearly this is a serious omission and an indication of the gulf that exists between the strategic choice theory of the IOR and what happens in practice.

In all fairness it is noted that the three case studies which have been examined do not properly demonstrate the full potential of DOT and are not the way DOT should be used to generate structure plans. However, it is recognised that in any case DOT has arrived too late to have much influence on the current round of structure planmaking although it may still have an impact on monitoring and review. It must also be emphasised that the authors' interpretation of the three structure plans may not represent the full story of what is happening, being based solely on the available data and documents.

Despite these caveats, there is no doubt at all that the discipline of a technique like DOT is needed to ensure consistency and repeatability simply by retaining the same ground rules. It offers a more rigorous yet practical framework which avoids the complexities and random nature of manual and less formal approaches. Furthermore it provides a basis for replication of the decisionmaking responsible for the original plan as well as for its reformulation as events in the real world move away from the assumptions embodied in the plan during its preparation. Of course DOT will not necessarily result in better or more objective plans, but it will at least ensure a degree of consistency so that the final strategy can be related to a given set of evaluation data, which may well be subjective—but at least ensure that data exist and are not simply stored in someone's head. A large part of the present problem is the plethora of planmaking methodologies, unique terminologies, and the virtual absence of any standards. Far too many structure plans seem to be buying flexibility during plan preparation by 'fast-and-fancy' footwork, the cost of which will only become apparent when it comes to implementation, monitoring, and review.

The case studies have shown that current practice, even using techniques such as AIDA, lack the explicit framework and capacity for coping with large complex decisionmaking problems, of the kind faced in structure planning. The statement by Sutton et al (1977, page 145) that "... the problem is not one of homing in on a single alternative at this stage and, at these levels, formal evaluation techniques are less useful" leads to the adoption of cumbersome and time-consuming techniques, which are in practice less efficient and do not allow a systematic approach to the comparison and review of policies in the context of a continuous planning process. Or in other words, they can result only in the maintenance of the status quo, albeit under the umbrella heading of strategic choice and a whole new dictionary of terms.

There is little doubt that structure planmaking is in a terrible state. The three case studies demonstrate the need for a logically structured, explicit framework for the decisionmaking processes responsible for the production of a structure plan. The *Development Plan Manual* (1970) does not provide such a framework, yet without one it is difficult to see how subsequent monitoring and review activities can produce any useful results.

References

Barras R, Broadbent T A, Booth D J W, Jaffe M, Palmer D J, 1977 "Operational techniques for structure planning" final report to Department of the Environment

Cleveland County Council, 1976a "Generation of alternatives" technical note 35a, Planning Department

Cleveland County Council, 1976b "Evaluation of four strategies" technical note 46, Planning Department

Cleveland County Council, 1977 "Peoples' choices for the Hartlepool Structure Plan: final report" CP 137, Research and Intelligence Team

Cochran W G, 1963 *Sampling Techniques* (John Wiley, New York)

Cochrane J L, Zeleny M, 1973 "A priori and a posteriori goals in macroeconomic policy making" in *Multiple Objective Decision Making* Eds J L Cochran, M Zeleny (University of South Carolina Press, Columbia) pp 373–391

Contini B, 1968 "A stochastic approach to goal programming" *Operations Research* 16 576–586

Cumbria County Council, 1976 *Choices for Cumbria* Planning Department

Delft A van, Nijkamp P, 1975 "The use of hierarchical optimisation criteria in regional planning" RM-41, Department of Economics, Free University, Amsterdam

Development Plan Manual 1970 (HMSO, London)

Drake M, McLoughlin J B, Thompson R, Thornley J, 1975 "Aspects of structure planning in Britain" RP-20, Centre for Environmental Studies, London

Durham County Council, 1976a *Report of Survey* Planning Department

Durham County Council, 1976b *We Need Your Views on the Future of County Durham* (booklet)

Durham County Council, 1976c *Resolving the Issues* Planning Department

Eilon S, 1974 "Goals and constraints in decision-making" in *Accounting for Social Goals* Eds J L Livingstone, S C Gunn (Harper and Row, New York) pp 218–229

Friend J, Jessop W, 1969 *Local Government and Strategic Choice* (Tavistock, London)
Friend J, Sutton A, 1976 "Structure planning as policy design" *Proceedings of PTRC Annual Summer Meeting, July 1976* (PTRC, London) pp 115-124
Hickling A, 1974 *Aids to Strategic Choice* (Tavistock, London)
Land A H, Powell S, 1973 *FORTRAN Codes for Mathematical Programming: Linear, Quadratic, and Discrete* (John Wiley, Chichester, Sussex)
Lee S M, 1972 *Goal Programming for Decision Analysis* (Auerbach, Philadelphia)
Openshaw S, 1975 "An alternative approach to structure planning: the structure plan decision making model (SPDM)" *Planning Outlook* **17** 10-26
Openshaw S, 1976 "DOT1 user manual" WP-1, Department of Town and Country Planning, University of Newcastle upon Tyne, Newcastle upon Tyne, England
Openshaw S, Whitehead P T, 1975 "A decision optimising technique for planners" *Planning Outlook* **16** 19-33
Openshaw S, Whitehead P T, 1977 "Decision-making in Local Plans: the DOT methodology and a case study" *Town Planning Review* **48** 29-41
Schlager K J, 1965 "A land use plan design model" *Journal of the American Institute of Planners* **31** 103-111
Sutton A, Hickling A, Friend J, 1977 *The Analysis of Policy Options in Structure Plan Preparation: A Strategic Choice Approach* (Tavistock, London)
Waltz F M, 1967 "An engineering approach to hierarchical optimisation criteria" *IEEE Transactions Automatic Control* **12** 179-180

APPENDIX 1

Typical DOT Input with Goal Programming Commands

```
TITLE
A Simple DOT Study Using Basic Commands
INPUT
  9  3
CLASS
  4  2  3
BARS
  7
  1  6  1  9  2  6  2  8  3  5  3  7  6  9
GENERATE
COEFLIST
    3
    20    10   5    8    0   10   100   120   105
  -200  -100   0  -10  -50    0   -80   -90   -70
     1     5   3    9    7    1     0     5     6
GETCOEF
  1
PRIMAL
GETCOEF
  2
PRIMAL
GETCOEF
  3
PRIMAL
GETCOEF
  1
GOALCOEF
  3
  1  2  3
PRIORITY
  3
  1  3  2
GOALS
  3
  125 -140  5
GOALPROG
PRIORITY
  3
  2  1  3
GOALPROG
SUMMARY
END
```

Notes: This describes a DOT formulation with 9 policies and 3 decision
areas (INPUT), with 4, 2, and 3 policies respectively in each decision area
(CLASS). Seven pairs of incompatible policies are specified (BARS).
Three sets of evaluation weights are stored (COEFLIST). Each set of
weights are used in turn in a series of single-objective-function runs
(GETCOEF, PRIMAL). This is followed by three goal-programming runs
(GOALCOEF, GOALPROG) with the goals (GOALS) being ranked in
three different ways (PRIORITY). Finally, a comparison of all the results
is requested (SUMMARY).

APPENDIX 2

Policy alternatives for Durham
1 *Population*
  1.1   Fewer people in fifteen years time
  1.2   Same as at present
  1.3   More people if sufficient jobs can be found

2 *Distribution*
  2.4   Centre of County to continue growing at the same rate as last
        twenty-five years
  2.5   Growth in centre to be restrained

3 *Appearance of the rural west*
  3.6   Preserve rural west of County
  3.7   Develop without too much regard for the appearance of the area
  3.8   Develop carefully to avoid significant damage to the appearance
        of the area with good facilities

4 *Residential development*
  4.9   Allow new residential developments only in towns/villages
  4.10 Allow new residential developments in villages without good
        facilities for public transport

5 *Public/private transport*
  5.11 Few restrictions on car use, no increase in support
  5.12 Support public transport more
  5.13 Discourage car use by restrictions on car travel
  5.14 Combination of 5.12 and 5.13

6 *Movement of goods*
  6.15 More goods carried by rail
  6.16 More goods carried by road
  6.17 About the same use of road and rail as at present

7 *Financial support for education*
   7.18 Available financial resources spread over all aspects of education
   7.19 Financial resources concentrated on certain aspects of education need

8 *Health services*
   8.20 Health services need not be improved
   8.21 Health services should be improved

9 *Shopping provision*
   9.22 Town centres maintained in full use
   9.23 New facilities provided outside current town centres

10 *Mineral extraction*
   10.24 More quarrying than at present
   10.25 About the same level of quarrying as at present
   10.26 Less quarrying than at present

11 *Wildlife protection*
   11.27 Wildlife need not be protected nor encouraged
   11.28 Action taken to protect important wildlife sites
   11.29 Action taken to protect wildlife whenever possible

12 *Appearance of County*
   12.30 Appearance of County to be improved at the same rate as at present
   12.31 Appearance of County to be improved at a faster rate

13 *Allocation of resources*
   13.32 Allocation of local authority spending to remain the same
   13.33 Some services should have a bigger share

APPENDIX 3

Policy alternatives for Cumbria
1 *Jobs*
   1.1 Attract new jobs from outside Cumbria
   1.2 Assist local industries to develop and extend
   1.3 Help people to move elsewhere
   1.4 Let the County specialise in certain industries
   1.5 Create more choice of jobs

2 *Rural economy*
   2.6 Continue present landscape conservation policies, with some change
   2.7 Conservation of resources of landscape
   2.8 Economic development of rural resources
   2.9 Regenerate rural problem areas

3 *Housing*
   3.10 Encourage more private housing
   3.11 Build more council houses
   3.12 Encourage housing societies
   3.13 Encourage exchange of accommodation
   3.14 Councils to buy up old property
   3.15 Encourage people to improve their property
   3.16 Knock down older houses and provide new ones

4 *The underprivileged*
   4.17 Allocate higher spending to local communities
   4.18 Give priority in appropriate fields
   4.19 Give priority to provision of jobs

5 *Rural transport*
   5.20 Reorganise public transport services to cut costs
   5.21 Provide better services with bigger subsidies
   5.22 Encourage alternative forms of public transport
   5.23 Reduce the need for transport
   5.24 Reduce public transport

6 *Tourist traffic*
   6.25 Allow free access by cars into the countryside
   6.26 Restrict access for cars
   6.27 Protect quiet areas from cars
   6.28 Develop new tourist areas
   6.29 Encourage tourists to use public transport

7 *Pollution*
   7.30 Accept industrial pollution
   7.31 Discourage polluting industries
   7.32 Install stronger pollution controls
   7.33 Develop methods to recycle waste
   7.34 Accept risks associated with tipping

APPENDIX 4

Hartlepool Structure Plan; Problem formulation
1 *Amount of heavy industry*
   1.1   Increase amount of land designated
   1.2   Maintain amount of land designated
   1.3   Decrease amount of land designated

2 *Redistribution of heavy industry*
   2.4   No change
   2.5   Coastal
   2.6   Inland
   2.7   Coast and inland

3 *Light/service industry*
   3.8   New sites
   3.9   Redevelopment sites
   3.10 New sites and redevelopment sites

4 *Housing locations*
   4.11 Peripheral
   4.12 Internal redevelopment
   4.13 Peripheral and internal

5 *Office*
   5.14 Out of town office park
   5.15 Town centre designated area
   5.16 Ad hoc decisions

6 *Shopping*
   6.17 Further concentration
   6.18 Neighbourhood development
   6.19 Out of centre

7 *Control of pollution*
   7.20 Increased controls
   7.21 Maintain existing controls
   7.22 Decreased controls

8 *Coastal recreation*
   8.23 High priority
   8.24 Low priority

9 *Coastal conservation*
   9.25 High priority
   9.26 Low priority

10 *Rural recreation*
   10.27 Increase
   10.28 No change

11 *Urban recreation*
   11.29 Increase
   11.30 Maintain

12 *Town centre parking*
   12.31 Restraint
   12.32 No restraint

H

13 *Industrial car parking*
    13.33   Restraint
    13.34   No restraint

14 *Rail passenger transport*
    14.35   New stations/lines
    14.36   No change
    14.37   Closures

15 *Rail freight transport*
    15.38   Support for provision
    15.39   No support

16 *Bus transport*
    16.40   Improve services
    16.41   Maintain existing situation
    16.42   Basic economic bus network

17 *Commercial traffic*
    17.43   Lorry routes
    17.44   No change

18 *Roads*
    18.45   Maintain existing network
    18.46   Rationalisation/traffic management
    18.47   Improve existing network
    18.48   Provision of new road links

Note: This is the problem formulation contained in Technical Note 35a by Cleveland County Planning Department, which formed the basis of the Strategic Choice and public participation exercises.

Information Competition and Complementation in Hierarchical Impact Assessment

PHYLLIS KANISS
Cornell University

1 Introduction

Increasingly, regional scientists are being faced with the task of evaluating the local and regional impacts of economic activities which carry with them major threats to the safety and health of populations. The risks which are associated with these new production technologies often involve long-term irreversible consequences which are extremely difficult to quantify and even more difficult to evaluate. We simply do not know the magnitude or severity of the risks to health and even survival that are posed by nuclear power plants, by nuclear fuel reprocessing facilities, or by the long-term storage of radioactive wastes. Yet today's policy decisions require that we weigh short-term economic costs and benefits of activities against these highly uncertain, longer-range impacts bearing on the commonweal.

The problem of evaluating the desirability of economic activities with uncertain yet irreversible consequences for some or all regions of a system may seem a new and unique problem facing human societies. Certainly breeder reactors and recombinant DNA pose dilemmas which have never before been confronted on earth. Yet I would like to suggest that the basic problem—that of deciding whether to undertake a new economic activity with uncertain future costs and benefits—is not a new problem at all, but one which has faced every living system since the origin of life itself. That is, every living system may be viewed as performing an economic decisionmaking problem with uncertain outcomes: it must allocate its scarce resources to activities which will maximize the probability of its survival and reproduction [1]. But it is always faced with uncertainty as to the long-term consequences of its activities, or as to changes in environmental conditions themselves.

Although there will always be unpredictable consequences of economic activities, and unforeseen exogenous environmental changes, organisms are seen to reduce the risk and uncertainty of such changes, and thus increase the probability of survival, through the intake, processing, and storage of *information*. That is, an organism collects information on its environment and on the results of its past interactions with that environment; it therefore

---

[1] Although there may be some objection to ascribing goal-seeking or choice behavior to biological organisms, the author maintains that even at the subintelligence level, there exists an effective economic optimizing process among organisms in a competitive environment, where natural selection performs the decisionmaking function. The use of such anthropomorphic terms as 'chooses' or 'seeks' will therefore represent a fiction.

chooses its economic strategy-for-survival on the basis of an evolving
information stock, translating information on 'what worked' in the past
into information on 'what will work' in the future. [For analysis of the
role of information in adaptation, see for example, Arbib (1972) and
Thayer (1972).]

In this paper, I would like to present a general model of the way any
hierarchical living system—or macro system composed of specialized micro
units—takes in information so as to evaluate the impacts of an economic
innovation on its component micro units. I will be using as an example a
specific problem facing many regions and nations today: the evaluation
of the long-term impacts of nuclear technology as a means of producing
energy. However, the general model is intended to be applicable to all
hierarchical living systems in which micro units perform different
specialized roles in an integrated macro function. It will be shown that
the task of macro information collection in such systems (the estimation
of impacts of alternative macro actions) is allocated to micro 'receptors',
each of which is responsible for the collection of information bearing on
its specialized role in the collective function. Thus, each micro unit
evaluates the impact of a macro change on one particular aspect of system
behavior, and the macro unit decides whether to accept or reject an
innovation in one specialized area, on the basis of information which is
the most relevant for the survival of the system as a whole.

If efficiently structured, a hierarchical information-processing system
will be seen to have embedded in it: (1) incentives for collection of
information on potential innovations in each specialized function;
(2) incentives for the evaluation of the costs and benefits of those
potential innovations to *other* specialized functions in the system;
(3) incentives for transmission of information among micro units leading
to the formation of 'information-agreeing' and 'information-disagreeing'
coalitions; and (4) incentives for the collection, by the macro unit, of
information which allows it to weight the importance of conflicting
information on costs and benefits supplied by different micro units. Thus,
an efficient hierarchical system will yield the information necessary to
reduce the risks of economic innovations with long-term uncertain
outcomes.

2 A theory of adaptive change
We begin by presenting a simple model of how living systems make
decisions regarding innovation in their basic pattern of economic activities.
In subsequent sections, it will be shown that these decisions are carried
out through an internal hierarchical decisionmaking process.

2.1 Information-collection activities
The decision problem of a living system is assumed to involve choosing
levels of economic activities so as to maximize the probability of survival.

In a traditional microeconomic framework, a behaving unit is assumed to possess perfect information on the alternative economic activities it may perform; that is, it is assumed to know the resource costs of any economic activity as well as the contribution that activity will make to the organism's objective function. However, in an evolutionary framework, this information is *not* a 'given': an organism must itself determine the costs and benefits of alternative economic activities and how these costs and benefits change as environmental conditions change.

Thus, the collection of information is viewed as one of the fundamental economic activities any living system must engage in to survive. The 'commodity' information is seen to have a certain productivity for the organism, through improving the efficiency of other economic activities and thus reducing survival-threatening risk. However, like any other economic activity, information collection is assumed to incur certain resource costs to the organism; for, in order to collect information, an organism uses resources and energy that could otherwise be devoted to directly productive activities.

Our theory of adaptive change requires that we make some simple assumptions about the cost and productivity functions for the activity of information collection. First, we assume that the costs of information collection will rise with the level of information collected. Second, we assume that the productivity function for the information-collection activity will vary in the following ways: (1) information must reach a certain threshold (lower) level before it yields any productivity; and (2) beyond a certain upper level of information, further increases in the level of information are assumed to lower productivity, owing to *information overload*. That is, there are assumed to be limits to the amount of information that any organism may effectively process and act upon at any one time: too much information is as harmful to the functioning of an adaptive organism as too little information.

We take the organism's objective function to be:

$$S = S(y_1, ..., y_n, y_I) \, ,$$

where
S represents the probability of survival,
y_i represents the level of economic activity i, $i = 1, ..., n$, and
y_I represents the level of the information-collection activity.
In its use of scarce resources, we assume that the organism operates each activity i under constant cost conditions, c_i being the unit cost. Accordingly, the organism confronts a linear cost function:

$$C = c_i y_i + c_I y_I \, ,$$

where C represents the total costs of activities to the organism. Further, we assume the organism has limited resources, C^0, available, which it fully uses. Accordingly, through standard optimizing procedures, we obtain, among others:

$$\frac{\partial S}{\partial y_j} \Big/ \frac{\partial S}{\partial y_I} = \frac{c_j}{c_I} , \qquad j = 1, ..., n ,$$

which represents a first-order condition for optimal levels of any economic activity y_j and the information-collection activity y_I. (In the discussion that follows, we assume that second-order conditions for a maximum value of S are met.) A change in environmental conditions will change the productivity and costs of an organism's economic activities in relation to its information-collection activity, thereby stimulating a substitution effect for the organism: the organism will substitute between the exploratory activity (collection of high-productivity information on *new* economic activities) and the performance of its existing set of directly productive activities.

Because of our assumption of negative productivity of overload information, an organism following its first-order conditions for information collection will be constrained in both the *direction* and the *extent* of its exploration of new activity patterns: it will seek the most productive information (information with high values of $\partial S/\partial y_I$) without incurring high costs of collecting the information (c_I) and will avoid negative productivities ($-\partial S/\partial y_I$) from overload. The first-order conditions will therefore place constraints on any one unit's exploration process: exploration and innovation of economic activity will be constrained by the need to economize on the collection of information, and in particular to economize by making use of old information in new ways.

2.2 Choosing a location in genotype space
We will now use this simple notion of incentives for, and constraints on, information-collection activities to show how an organism chooses whether to maintain an existing pattern of activities or to change to a new pattern. We assume that at any point in time an organism is engaged in a given set of activities or strategy-for-survival, and thus possesses a stock of information on how best to perform that strategy. This information has been acquired through a cumulative learning process on what has proven to be adaptive in the past, and thus represents 'information capital' with survival value to the organism. Thus, any change in strategy-for-survival will represent a sacrifice of part of this past accumulation of 'information capital' and the need for the collection of new information to reduce risk and uncertainty associated with an untried strategy. Thus, there are assumed to be costs (information-collection and/or risk costs) as well as potential benefits (improved adaptation) associated with any change in strategy-for-survival. [The notion of costs and benefits being associated with mutation or variation in evolved strategies-for-survival has been suggested most recently by Layzer (1975).]

We regard the organism's decision of whether or not to change strategies-for-survival as a *locational* decision in 'genotype space'—where genotype space is an n-dimensional space, any point (location) in which represents a specific strategy-for-survival. Distance in genotype space therefore indicates 'degree of newness' of one strategy from another. We assume that, as in physical space, an organism must overcome the 'friction of distance' in changing locations in genotype space—incurring *mutational transport costs* in changing strategies-for-survival. That is, in changing from a steady-state location in genotype space to a new location, an organism will incur costs either in the form of: (1) new *information* required successfully to undertake the new strategy; and/or (2) *risk and uncertainty* from changing from a strategy that was successful in the past to one which is untried. The greater the distance in genotype space that a unit moves, the more of its past stock of information it is relinquishing and the more new information will be required to reduce risk costs; hence mutational transport costs will increase with distance in genotype space. Offsetting these mutational transport costs will be the potential benefits to be derived from improved strategies-for-survival for adapting to constant or changed environmental conditions.

Thus, in deciding whether or not to change strategies-for-survival or locations in genotype space, an organism compares the expected gains of a new adaptation to the mutational transport costs of that change (new information and/or risk costs), undertaking change only when there exists a location x_i for which:

$$\tau(x_0 \rightarrow x_i) - c^{mt}(x_0 \rightarrow x_i) > 0 \,,$$

where

$\tau(x_0 \rightarrow x_i)$ represents the potential gains from moving from an existing location x_0 to a new location x_i, and

$c^{mt}(x_0 \rightarrow x_i)$ represents the mutational transport costs incurred from moving from an existing location x_0 to a new location x_i.

In accord with this condition, an organism will have an incentive to change strategies whenever it can get higher gains from allocation of resources to exploration activities than from allocation of resources to its existing directly productive activities. That is, a new opportunity or a new problem will create higher gains from relocation than from maintaining stability, and will thus stimulate the organism's exploration of new locations. However, the organism will always be constrained in this exploration by its mutational transport cost, representing the evolutionary 'friction' against change in successful past patterns. Thus, whether it is exploring a new opportunity or a solution to a new problem, it will always have an incentive to explore only those new activities which allow it to make use of its existing information stock. Relocation may in fact be stimulated by a unit's collection of information on the existence of a new strategy at which it can make better use of its existing information capital than at its present location.

2.3 Forces between units

An organism's decision of whether or not to change its past pattern of activities may be affected by the behavior of other organisms. Let us consider the impact of a discovery by one unit of a successful new mutation, or the case where some unit finds a location x_i for which

$$\tau(x_0 \rightarrow x_i) - c^{mt}(x_0 \rightarrow x_i) > 0 .$$

If this mutation proves feasible it will lower the information-collection and risk-uncertainty costs, and hence mutational transport costs, facing *other* units seeking to relocate to the location. That is, subsequent units may collect information simply on the results of the first unit's exploration process and then duplicate or even improve on that first unit's new strategy. Thus, we expect that a successful new mutation at x_i will cause $c^{mt}(x_0 \rightarrow x_i)$ to decrease for other units, and thus bring about an *agglomeration* effect: increasing numbers of micro units will have incentives to try out the same strategy-for-survival or agglomerate around the same general location in genotype space.

However, as increasing numbers of units come to exploit the same strategy or genotype-space location, the net gains deriving from the location will decrease—either because of diminishing returns to exploitation or because of increasing costs arising from competition (for example, the use of resources for securing exclusivity of exploitation). Thus, although there will be low information-collection and risk costs associated with such a strategy, the competition costs (the equivalent of a rent for a physical location) will decrease the attractiveness of these locations. Thus, as the gains at x_0 fall, the gains from changing to a *new* location, or $\tau(x_0 \rightarrow x_i)$ may rise. That is, some organisms come to find that they can get higher returns to their resources by using them for information collection (or incurring risk) to explore new, noncompetitive locations where they may avoid the 'rent' or competition costs of the colonized location. [The evolutionary advantages of changing environments or strategies as a means of avoiding competition have been cited by Waddington (1969) and Wilson (1975).] They will therefore substitute mutational transport activities for directly productive activities (including the payment of 'rent') to explore a new strategy. Thus, increasing exploitation and competition at a successful strategy will stimulate some organisms to deviate from that strategy to explore something new—leading to *deglomeration* in genotype space.

When all feasible strategies-for-survival are exhausted by these agglomerative and deglomerative mutations, it can be shown (Kaniss, 1977) that units will have incentives to explore *cooperative* strategies-for-survival—that is, strategies in which micro units cooperate to jointly produce the outputs contributing to each unit's survival. Such cooperation leads to the performance of a new, more complex function which takes advantage of decentralized independent information processing and decisionmaking of units performing specialized activites. [The notion of complex forms building up from the combination of simpler already-evolved components has been developed by Bronowski (1970) and by Simon (1973).] However, in order for a reliable, integrated collective function to be performed, the independent decisionmaking of micro units must be constrained or coordinated through *hierarchical control*. That is, the decisionmaking process of each specialized unit in the collective function is constrained by a macro unit, which performs its own information-collection process to assure the reliability of the collective function. [For a description and model of the functioning of hierarchical control systems, see Pattee (1973) and Mesarovic et al (1970).]

3 The approach to change of a hierarchical control system
We will now consider the way such a hierarchical control system is structured so that the decision of whether to maintain a past pattern of economic activities or undergo mutation (innovation) in these activities is allocated to its component units.

3.1 Constraints on decisionmaking
In a hierarchical control system, a macro unit is assumed to place constraints on the activities of its interdependent micro units in order that a reliable collective function be performed over time. [For the role of coordinative constraints in hierarchical systems, see Whyte (1965).] Micro units continue to perform their specialized activities through an independent decisionmaking process—taking in information on whether or not to adjust their strategies-for-survival, so as to maximize the probability of survival. However, under hierarchical control, they are constrained in the range of strategies they may undertake. For, in an interdependent system of units, one unit may find the net gains of relocation positive, while other micro units, and hence the macro function, may be adversely affected by such a change in a micro strategy.

Thus, the hierarchical control unit, in order to maximize the probability of the survival of the collective function, will prohibit micro units from occupying those new genotype-space locations which may be beneficial to the unit but which are potentially disruptive to the macro system *as a whole*. In other words, the hierarchical control unit will impose infinite costs of relocation for certain disruptive locations, or:

$$c^{mt}(x_0 \rightarrow x_{d(i)}) = \infty \qquad \text{for } x_d = x_{d(1)}, ..., x_{d(n)} \text{ ,}$$

where $x_{d(i)}$ represent a micro location which is disruptive to the macro function. Thus, in considering whether to accept or reject a micro strategy change (leading to macro strategy change), the macro unit evaluates the costs and benefits of that change (its impacts) to each of its constituent units, weighting these costs and benefits by the importance of each unit to the collective function. Or:

$$\sum_i w_j [\tau_j (X_0 \rightarrow X_i) - c_j^{mt}(X_0 \rightarrow X_i)] \gtrless 0 \text{ ,}$$

where

$\tau_j(X_0 \to X_i)$ represents the gains to micro unit j of a *macro* locational change from X_0 to X_i,

$c_j^{mt}(X_0 \to X_i)$ represents the mutational transport costs to unit j incurred by the macro locational move,

w_j represents the importance of the micro unit j in the macro function,

X_0, X_i represent two macro locations, each of which represents a vector of micro locations.

The macro unit will prohibit those micro locational changes which lead to macro locational changes for which the costs to the system as a whole exceed the benefits.

The macro unit is assumed to obtain its information on micro costs and benefits from the micro units themselves, since each micro unit will be able to evaluate the impact of a macro change on its specialized function at minimum additional information-collection costs. Therefore, each micro unit will evaluate $\tau_j(X_0 \to X_i) - c_j^{mt}(X_0 \to X_i)$, or the benefits and costs to itself of its own locational changes as well as from other units' locational changes, and pass this information on to the macro unit. The macro unit may therefore receive *conflicting information* from its micro units on the desirability of different changes, since each specialized function will be impacted differently by a change in the macro activity pattern. It is the task of the macro unit to compare and reconcile the conflicting information of its micro units so as to determine whether a change will benefit or harm the system *as a whole*. Thus, the macro unit will place weights (w_js) on the information of different micro units, to indicate the importance of that micro function to the macro activity, and will decide whether to accept or reject a micro locational change on the basis of an 'information-agreeing' majority coalition of micro units.

3.2 Incentives for micro locational changes

Micro units will continue to have incentives to explore new strategies as long as their exploration does not violate the existing pattern of coordinative constraint. Thus, at any point in time, each micro unit will be 'testing' its environment in order to determine whether higher benefits or lower costs of activities may be obtained at a new location through innovation. Whenever

$$\tau(x_0 \to x_i) - c^{mt}(x_0 \to x_i) > 0 \quad \text{and} \quad x_i \neq x_d$$

the unit will change locations from x_0 to x_i.

Within a hierarchical control system, there will be a tendency for micro units to cluster around the different strategies which have been proven in the past to represent high returns over costs (strategies needed by the macro function). Thus, there is *specialization of function* among micro units, but there is *redundancy* in this specialization, since more than one unit will tend to agglomerate around a specialized strategy needed by the system. Micro units in each specialized agglomeration will be collecting information specifically on the adaptiveness of that particular systemic function to environmental conditions—that is, information indicating whether the existing strategy for performing the specialized function should be modified or replaced by a new one. Each unit within the agglomeration will have an incentive to increase its share of the gains from the system and decrease the share received by other units in the agglomeration by finding the most efficient strategy for performing the function.

Thus, there is a kind of *information competition* between micro units in an agglomeration: those micro units which have an advantage in the performance of the existing strategy will have an incentive to collect information that indicates continued efficacy of this strategy in performing the systemic function. However, those units which are disadvantaged in the performance of the existing strategy will always have an incentive to collect new information which indicates the obsolescence of that strategy and the existence of an improved alternative. Thus, within each specialized agglomeration, there are incentives for both the conservation of existing strategies (old information) and the exploration of innovative strategies (new information).

3.3 Micro mutation
Let us suppose that one unit, in 'testing' for new environmental opportunities, discovers an alternative strategy for performing its specialized function. That is, it finds a new strategy where it can make more productive use of its existing stock of information and resources, or a genotype-space location x_i for which

$$\tau(x_0 \rightarrow x_i) - c^{mt}(x_0 \rightarrow x_i) > 0 \,,$$

and therefore chooses to relocate.

If the new mutation does not violate the existing pattern of constraint, it will be allowed to develop; the unit will continue to explore the new strategy in accord with its own decisionmaking process. If a developing innovation is found desirable by some units, and is unopposed by other units, it will be accepted by the macro system. However, some new mutations, while benefitting certain micro functions, may at the same time create adverse changes in the conditions facing other micro units. In these cases, conflicting information on the desirability of the innovation will be picked up by micro units and passed on to the macro unit.

3.4 Response of other micro units to a mutation
Agglomeration and information complementation. If the initial micro unit is able to survive at its new location, it effectively produces new information for other units—on the existence of a new strategy offering increased gains over costs. Therefore, a successful mutation will lower the

information-collection and/or risk costs (and hence mutational transport costs) facing other units seeking to relocate—units which are more risk-averse or informationally deficient in comparison with the 'scout'. Thus, an agglomeration of micro units will form around the new strategy as other micro units find that the benefits of the new strategy exceed the mutational transport costs that must be incurred to reach it. Importantly, each micro unit attracted to the agglomeration will use its own information stock—which may be unique from the scout's—to develop the new strategy further. That is, the scout 'opens up' the new region of genotype space to exploration; subsequent units may take the results of the first unit's exploration as a given and add new information to it. Thus, with each agglomerating unit, the new strategy gains information (information formerly applied to the old strategy) which helps to make it competitive. Micro units in effect engage in *information complementation*: each unit adds its somewhat unique information to the common development of the new strategy. This information complementation will extend beyond the specialized agglomeration; that is, micro units performing *other* specialized functions in the collective activity may derive gains from the new strategy and will thus have an incentive to add their unique information to the development of the new strategy. Therefore, an 'information-agreeing' coalition of micro units will be forming among units performing different specialized functions in the macro activity: with each unit 'agreeing' on the benefits (over costs) of the new strategy, and passing this information on to the macro unit in order to influence it to accept the new strategy.

Opposition to the new mutation: information competition. Units which are making high gains from the existing strategy and whose capital (both resources and information) invested in the existing strategy would be made obsolete by the new strategy will also have an incentive for exploration: an incentive to collect information on the *defects* of the innovation, or why its acceptance would be undesirable for the system. In other words, they have an incentive to engage in 'information competition' with the innovator. Thus, at the center of the opposition to a new strategy will be members of the same specialized agglomeration as the innovator, units whose specialized information stocks allow them to detect the weaknesses of the new strategy at minimum additional information-collection cost. These units may be joined by 'latecomers' to the agglomeration around the new strategy: that is, with increasing migration to the new strategy, there will result decreasing returns to subsequent units seeking to relocate—owing to diminishing returns or rising competition costs. Thus, some of these units will choose to use the same information they could have used to pursue the innovation, to criticize it. This nucleus of opposition to a new strategy will also have an incentive to gain support or information agreement from other micro units outside the specialized agglomeration—units performing other ·
specialized activities which would be adversely affected by the acceptance

of the new strategy. Thus the opposition will also engage in information complementation, seeking to attract other micro units—whose unique information stocks would add informational strength to the opposition—to an 'information-agreeing' coalition.

Thus, the appearance of a new mutation will stimulate two different kinds of 'research incentives' in the system: the proponents of the innovation will collect information on the potential benefits to the system of the innovation, while the opponents of the innovation will collect information on the potential costs to the system of accepting the new mutation. Thus, there is information competition in *evaluation* as well as in exploration. Each group seeking to maximize its own gains from the system will collect that new informaton that will make the information of the other group either obsolete or wrong—information which is transmitted to the macro system. At the same time, each group seeks to attract other micro units to join it in supporting its evaluation of the desirability of the new innovation—units whose information is 'complementary' to their position: that is, each unit will transmit information to other units on the potential benefits (or costs) those other units would receive from acceptance or rejection of the mutation. Thus, each group tries to gain an 'information-agreeing' majority coalition which will influence the macro unit's decision.

These processes of information competition and information complementation lead to an efficient method of collection of information on the costs and benefits of an innovation for a macro system as a whole. That is, the costs of collecting information of both an exploratory and evaluative nature are minimized, since both these processes are allocated to the units whose existing specialized information stocks allow them to collect, at minimal additional costs, information concerning a new strategy. Thus, the system not only contains incentives for innovation but also incentives for some units to use their specialized information stocks to criticize each new innovation.

Moreover, in order to influence the decision of the macro system, micro units have an incentive to transmit information to other units—micro units performing other specialized functions in the system—and to gain access to these other units' information on the desirability of incorporating or rejecting the new strategy. Thus, the evaluation of the costs and benefits of the new strategy will extend beyond the specialized sector of the system from which the innovation—and its opposition—originated.

Thus, the macro unit receives information from its different, specialized 'receptors', indicating how the acceptance or rejection of the new strategy will affect different aspects of the system's performance. The macro unit receives only the *results* of each specialized unit's information-collection process, stripped of irrelevant detail. It is assured of the reliability of this information by the information-competition process through which micro units themselves test each other's information and information-collection processes. Thus, the macro unit obtains its information on the impacts of a new strategy for its components efficiently (through decentralization of information collection, with each unit specializing in collecting different kinds of information) and reliably (micro units test each other to see if the information is correct).

The informational task of the macro unit, then, is to apply weights to the information of its specialized receptors, so as to determine the importance to the system as a whole of the beneficial or adverse effects of a new strategy to its different components. Once it estimates these weights, it will choose to accept or reject the new strategy on the basis of the survival interests and information of a majority coalition. That is, it evaluates how the innovation will affect the survival of the system as a whole. Thus, the macro system will allow an innovation to develop if only a small number of micro units (with low decision weights) oppose it, and will reject a strategy which is opposed by a majority coalition of micro units and favored by a small minority.

4 The example: the innovation of nuclear power production
Let us now apply the theory of hierarchical impact assessment to a particular technological innovation or 'mutation': namely, the use of nuclear technology to produce electric power. [My information on the history of nuclear power development comes primarily from Glasstone (1967) and Lapp (1956).] The development of nuclear reactor technology may be viewed as a decentralized decision by members of one specialized agglomeration in the system (nuclear scientists) to increase their gains from the system by applying a stock of information accumulated over past periods to new strategic uses. This stock of information pertained to the discovery of nuclear fission and the means for controlling the nuclear chain reaction so as to generate energy. After the initial theoretical breakthroughs of the 1920s and 1930s, nuclear scientists sought governmental support for further research by applying their discoveries to what was at that time a crucial national demand—military armaments. That is, the first use to which the new information stock was put was the development of a new, competitive strategy for waging war, and this use led to the 'mutation' of the atomic bomb. After the war, however, when the United States initiated a program to support 'peacetime' uses for nuclear technology, a new systemic demand was created; scientists now faced incentives to use their evolved stocks of information on nuclear fission to explore a new, competitive strategy for the production of electric power. That is, they found that the costs of information collection (or the risk costs of searching for a new strategy) were less than the potential gains to be derived from the innovation. Thus the nuclear scientists, in effect, engaged in 'information competition' with the existing producers of electric power, challenging conventional strategies with innovative strategies.

The response of certain other micro actors in the national system to the new mutation, was support and 'information complementation'. That is, the new mutation found a demand for its research outputs from other units in the system: the national government, as well as public utilities and equipment manufacturers, who together funded the research. As a result of the availability of funding, the strategy began to attract an 'agglomeration' of scientists, each seeking gains through the use of his or her own unique information to develop the best configuration of the new mutation: that is, the most efficient, least costly, and least risky technology for the production of power through nuclear fission.

Thus, a coalition of scientists, government administrators, and manufacturers formed to spur the development and refinement of the reactor—a coalition which represented an influential force for acceptance by the system as a whole of the innovation. The opposition to the development of nuclear power—at its inception—was restricted to a limited number of micro units with small weights in the macro system's decision calculus. Thus, the macro system did not simply allow the development of nuclear power to proceed, it encouraged it with its own research funding. It ignored the information passed on to it by a small number of critics, viewing these critics as 'alarmists' with insufficient technical expertise to evaluate the safety of reactors and incompetence to view the long-term potential benefits for the system as a whole. Indeed, this research was stepped up in response to increasing energy demands by the system, and the limitations on the supply of fossil fuels to meet these growing energy needs.

However, with the further development of nuclear technology and the construction of actual nuclear power plants, some micro units in the national system began to pick up information indicating the adverse effects of these plants. That is, the early critics of nuclear power, whose objections had been dismissed or ignored by the macro system, were joined by increasing numbers of micro units with greater influence in the macro system. Scientists who were members of the nuclear profession itself, and thus who possessed the *specialized information* on nuclear technology needed to point up (with credibility) a significant danger of these plants, began to join the opposition. For instance, in Britain, a report made on behalf of the Royal Commission on Environmental Pollution (1976) was highly critical of the use of plutonium and fast-breeder reactor technology. This report on the dangers of nuclear power, made by Sir Brian Flowers, a prominent and respected nuclear physicist, succeeded in attracting the attention of the national press and public at large. As one reporter commented, "Suddenly, nuclear energy problems—for years the province of a handful of people usually considered to be teetering on the lunatic fringe—became headline news" (Patterson, 1977).

In effect, Flowers, and scientists like him from within the nuclear physics profession, had the information necessary to convince members of the macro system (the society at large) that there are weaknesses in the 'nuclear strategy' and particularly to the high-risk breeder reactor. These critical scientists are members of a specialized agglomeration (nuclear physicists) who find higher gains to putting their information capital to use in opposing the innovation (presenting information to the macro system encouraging it to invoke a constraint against such macro activities) than to using the same information to support the innovation. Thus, they become the initial mutation opposing the nuclear strategy, and form the nucleus for an agglomeration of other groups—with *different* stocks of information—opposing governmental approval of such plants.

For example, environmental groups such as the Friends of the Earth and the Oxford Political Ecology Research Group joined antinuclear groups such as Half-life, as well as local community groups in the vicinity of the planned sites of the plants; legal and civil rights groups also became 'attracted' to the issue of nuclear power, and added their information to the opposition. Importantly, each of these groups, through its independent information-collection processes, has developed a somewhat unique stock of information with which to evaluate the impacts of nuclear power plants. No one group alone possessed the information that was necessary to influence the macro system to prohibit the innovation. But when they came together, they complemented each other's information: technical–scientific information was combined with legal expertise, information geared to public protest and gaining media attention, as well as information on the objections of local residents to plant construction and operation. A coalition of micro units is thus formed representing *different kinds of information*, all indicating the dangers of proceeding further with the innovation. Thus the macro unit receives, through decentralized information-collection processes, the information it needs to assess the impacts of the new activity.

And, indeed, in Britain the environmental secretary Peter Shore responded to just this sort of coalition in his decision to delay approval of British Nuclear Fuel Limited's proposal for expanding its spent nuclear fuel reprocessing plant in Cumbria. The coalition of opposition sparked Shore to set up a public inquiry into the desirability of the breeder reactor in general. These public hearings will create an incentive for the opposition to collect information which will indicate the undesirability of breeder reactors—and in particular to increase the size and influence of their coalition by gaining access to other micro units' information which also says 'no'. However, this same research incentive faces the proponents of the breeder reactors: the scientists and utilities (British Nuclear Fuels Limited) will have an incentive to collect new information to refute the claims of their opponents—and in the process to develop new modifications of the initial mutation that will solve the weaknesses pointed up by other micro units, with different information stocks. That is, they will also try to form coalitions with other segments of the population—for instance, with powerful unions whose interest may be the jobs to be supplied by the construction of the new plants, or with citizen groups seeking low-cost energy. In other words, they also seek to stack up information to transmit on the desirability of the strategy as viewed by a coalition of units with different evaluative criteria. Thus, both the proponents and the opponents of the breeder reactor try to collect and transmit information to segments of the population as a whole, in an effort to obtain the majority coalition of information-agreeing units.

The final decision of whether to limit the use of nuclear technology in Britain, as well as in the United States, West Germany, France, and other countries, is uncertain at this time; it will depend on the information that emerges in the next few years, in the coalitions that are formed between different segments of the population, and of course the political weights that these segments of the population hold in each national government.

5 Summary and conclusions

This paper represents an attempt to show how a hierarchical system should be structured so as to create incentives for innovation to its micro units, as well as incentives for the evaluation of these innovations by other micro units in the system, so as to ward against threats to long-term system survival. We were particularly interested in the efficient collection of information, both as to the benefits of possible innovations in systemic strategies, and as to the costs that they might incur. That is, in the model presented, micro units represent 'specialized receptors' of information—with different information stocks (as well as different self-interests) with which they evaluate the costs and benefits to themselves of an innovation in systemic strategy. Moreover, they are stimulated to engage in both information competition and information complementation with other units, in order to influence the macro system to act in their own interest. The macro unit's decision on whether to incorporate or reject an innovation is then based on the results of these decentralized information processes: it takes action on the basis of an 'information-agreeing' majority coalition of its micro units and therefore achieves a balance between overly radical and overly conservative approaches to systemic change.

References
Arbib M, 1972 *The Metaphorical Brain* (Wiley Interscience, New York)
Bronowski J, 1970 "New concepts in the evolution of stratified stability and unbounded plans" plans" *Zygon* 5(1) 18-40
Glasstone S, 1967 *Sourcebook on Atomic Energy* 3rd edition (Van Nostrand Reinhold, New York)
Kaniss P, 1977 *Dynamical Processes in Hierarchical Systems* Ph D thesis, Cornell University, Ithaca, NY
Lapp R, 1956 *Atoms and People* (Harper Brothers, New York)

Layzer D, 1975 "Genetic variability and biological innovation" unpublished manuscript,
Harvard University, Cambridge, Mass
Mesarovic M D, Macko D, Takahara Y, 1970 *Theory of Hierarchical, Multi-level Systems*
(Academic Press, New York)
Pattee H, 1973 "The physical basis and origin of hierarchical control" in *Hierarchy
Theory* Ed. H H Pattee (George Braziller, New York) pp 71–108
Patterson W C, 1977 "Setback for plutonium: British Nuclear Fuels Limited"
Environment **19** (March) 41–43
Royal Commission on Environmental Pollution, 1976 *Air Pollution Control. An
Integrated Approach* Cmnd 6371 (HMSO, London)
Simon H, 1973 "The organization of complex systems" in *Hierarchy Theory*
Ed. H H Pattee (George Braziller, New York) pp 1–28
Thayer L, 1972 "Communication systems" in *The Relevance of General Systems
Theory* Ed. E Laszlo (George Braziller, New York) pp 93–122
Waddington C H, 1969 *Towards a Theoretical Biology* volume II (Aldine, Chicago, Ill.)
Whyte L L, 1965 *Internal Factors in Evolution* (George Braziller, New York)
Wilson E O, 1975 *Sociobiology: The New Synthesis* (Harvard University Press,
Cambridge, Mass.)

British Colliery Closure Programmes in the North East: from Paradox to Contradiction

J KRIEGER
Harvard University

There is something very dramatic about the closure of a colliery. Perhaps this is because the act is so final. A unique complex of human relations is transformed overnight into, simply, a hole brimming with flooded, misshapen, and decimated capital, the surrounding village blighted once and for all time. The closing of whole sets of collieries, a phenomenon which has overrun the North East in successive waves since early in the nineteenth century, and which has in the last two decades signalled a cruel transformation in the economic and social fate of the entire region, displays effects which are multiplied well beyond the sum of the effects of the individual colliery closures. What is more to the point here, *ad hoc* explanations of 'geological exhaustion' and vague economic justifications cannot explain the quick succession and statistical clustering of closures in the North East during three distinct periods: on Tyneside in the 1830s, in South West Durham in the interwar period, and throughout the Durham and Northumberland Division of the National Coal Board, in particular, between 1958 and 1968.

The first two periods have been convincingly explained as a function of interregional uneven development manifested in the particular characteristics of capital formation and the investment practices of the capitalist coal combines. These largely determined the pace and character of development in the North East in coal and related industries up to the period of nationalization. The explanation of closures as representing a comprehensive strategy by the capitalist combines to maintain their profit structure under conditions of (a) overproduction, and (b) failing export markets, seems unassailable:

"If the pace of capital accumulation in the combines was linked to resource definition and exploitation, conversely, restrictions in output and hence restrictions on the realisation of surplus value and on new investment in fixed capital in activities winning coal or ironstone, for example, often created situations where resources were defined out of existence. It became 'cheaper' for combines to write off collieries and allow flooding and consequent destruction of reserves rather than to reinvest a portion of realised surplus value in the surface and below-ground fixed capital necessary to turn the reserves into use values. In the North East the case of South West Durham in the interwar period repeated the experience of the Tyneside collieries in the 1830s, the pits were allowed to flood and reserves were destroyed in this manner on a mass scale" (Carney et al, 1977, page 55).

This argument is as convincing for the 1830s and particularly the inter-war period as it would be inappropriate if applied to the period since nationalization, notably 1958–1968. The basis for this assertion involves a consideration of the structures of demand for coal in the two periods and the very different patterns of response in the privately owned as compared to the nationalized industry.

1 The structure of demand

The 1958–1968 period reflects a serious downturn in demand for coal, in all markets (foreign and domestic) except the electricity supply industry. This decline was due most directly to an increasing substitution of oil for coal with the availability of new oil resources after Suez. As a result the state intervened to stabilize coal demand with a series of protectionist measures, including the banning of coal imports between 1959 and 1970, a placing of a duty on fuel oil, and the statutory instruction beginning in 1967 that the Central Electricity Generating Board (CEGB) purchase coal in excess of 'commercial' requirements (for which it would be compensated up to six million tons per annum). Nevertheless, the period does not reflect a general condition of *overproduction* (as we saw in the interwar period). Rather, the industry faced a changing structure of demand—with a decline in demand for coking coal and domestic use but an increase in total and relative consumption by the CEGB—which had a differential impact on particular collieries and regions.

In response the NCB increased the tempo of technological innovation and colliery reconstruction to improve productivity, and introduced more comprehensive manpower strategies to cut labour costs through planned and induced 'voluntary wastage'. Thus an understanding of failing demand—although not a generalized situation of overproduction comparable to that of the interwar years—must condition an explanation of colliery closures in the 1958–1968 period. But precisely because the responses of capitalist coal owners and the NCB were fundamentally different in the face of 'objective market factors' one must look beyond the bare facts of demand structures to explain the colliery closure programme of the 1960s. In particular one must consider the immediate context which conditioned the impulse to nationalize the industry and which influenced the operational imperatives which have governed the 'new' industry ever since.

2 The impulse to nationalize

By the close of World War II, nationalization of the coal industry had become a matter of broad concensus, unifying Labour Party socialists, forward-looking capitalists, and their Tory representatives around a moderate 'social-democratic' proposal for meeting the problems of postwar planning. The industry was technically obsolete, and in the absence of massive investment in machinery, the reconstruction of inefficient but geologically sound pits, and the sinking of new, modern, and potentially more profitable collieries, the general demands of reconstruction—and the needs of capitalists for realization of surplus value throughout private industry—could not effectively be met. Clearly the capitalists in the North East and elsewhere were unwilling to pursue this strategy. Thus a series of moderate nationalizations of basic and moribund industries with compensation "beyond the wildest dreams of avarice" were initiated by the new Labour Government. These interventions by the state to facilitate reconstruction of the economy, provide for a modicum of 'central' planning, and yet preserve the general organizational principles of a capitalist Britain, were taken at the urging of the working class to be sure—but also with the definite acceptance by contemporary business interests and the grudging endorsement of their parliamentary representatives. In 1946 Winston Churchill for example endorsed the Coal Industry Nationalization Bill, noting that major state intervention provided the only hope for reorganizing the industry and providing the massive injection of capital for the needed technological innovation. Simply put, nationalization of coal was intended to rationalize capital. Nonetheless an explanation of the operating imperatives of nationalized industries must take into account the essentially 'extracapitalist' character of the 'public owned' enterprise.

The nationalized industry is not bound by the immediate exigencies of capital accumulation, even less is each colliery expected to achieve profitable results by the logic of capitalist management techniques, for example, rapid technical innovation and investment in fixed capital to achieve short-run competitive advantage over sectoral competition. As an element within the general sphere of state activities, nationalized industries are meant to facilitate capital accumulation *by capitalists* through the stable and cheap provision of basic commodities, but not to *be capitalist* in themselves. The original nationalization statutes require simply that the industry break even on the balance of good and bad years (although revisions in the 1960s, officially enunciated in the 1967 *Review of the Finances of the Nationalised Industries*, included stricter accounting procedures and imperatives to operate in the black). But a 'cross-subsidization' of good and bad collieries and differentially productive regions is considered normal operating procedure, as is the continued operation of losing ventures to ensure the supply of particular types of coal (for example, coking coal from Sacriston, a pit with eighteen-inch seams in central Durham). Thus closures under the NCB are not reasonably viewed as the direct effect of pressures on valorisation or avaricious capitalist unconcern which effects a 'snatch and grab' mentality toward the rescuing of fixed capital by the destruction of unprofitable collieries.

Consequently a different mode of inquiry seems necessary to explain closures under nationalization, a logic of explanation which reflects the changing logic of capitalist development in the postwar period. This task, in turn, requires an examination of coal closure policy in the North East which is grounded in an understanding of the mode of operation of a nationalized industry—part of the administrative apparatus of the contemporary capitalist state. As background to this understanding I will offer (1) a broad account of the general features of the contemporary capitalist state which underlie the impulse to nationalization and its general character in Britain (linked to the changing logic of capitalist development to which I referred above), and (2) a sketch of the modes of operation of the administrative apparatus of the capitalist state and the contradictory *political* imperatives which govern decisionmaking within this sphere. My explanation of the coal closure programme of the NCB in the North East in the decade from 1958 to 1968 will follow from these arguments. In particular, I will suggest that the coal closure programme reflects contradictions of capitalist development which are located in, and expressed through, the administrative agencies of the state. These lead to a paradoxical set of decisions which follow a political logic (however inconsistent), and which can be illuminated only dimly by reference to economic criteria and regional policy alone.

It seems useful therefore to begin with a brief discussion which locates coal nationalization within the historical evolution of the contemporary capitalist state.

3 The changing logic of the capitalist state
The liberal state was constituted within a 'political sphere' and operated, insofar as it intervened upon the 'economic sphere', through an *allocative* mode to provide general conditions for economic development/capital accumulation and to rectify market imbalances. But the state did not directly replace market mechanisms as such or engage in production. 'Market rationality' remained the organizing principle for economic relations, its normative acceptance framed and delimited state activities, and the representation of these activities, in bourgeois democracies. This implies, *imperatively*, an ideology that encourages a depoliticization of the class relationship and of the public realm[1]: economic exchange is fair exchange, economic processes are governed by an 'invisible hand' nudged as necessary by a state which is presented as being class-neutral and neutral as among intraclass interests. The economic and political spheres remain, by and large, separate. The class basis of the state remains hidden, at least putatively, behind the veil of parliamentary 'democracy'.

[1] The notion of the public realm—'public sphere' or 'public body'—has come into recent usage through its application by Jurgen Habermas as a sphere of nongovernmental opinion-making. "Citizens behave as a public body when they confer in an unrestricted fashion ... about matters of general interest." Although more historically grounded by Habermas within the development of capitalism, the notion (and the processes involved) bear a remarkable kinship to the sphere of general will formation in Rousseau. See Habermas' *Strukturwandel der Öffentlichkeit* (*Structural Transformation of the Public Sphere*) (Luchterhand, Neuwied and Berlin, 1962).

Thus opposition grounded in the relation of wage labour to capital came to light as economic crises at the systemic level, as the interruption of the process of accumulation; it came to light as the level of action, that is, of observed conflict directly in class conflict located within productive relations, that is, as industrial conflict (with political consequences, of course).

The interventionist state, born in the requirements of accumulation and legitimation in the late nineteenth and twentieth centuries, and particularly at the close of World War II, is defined by the inclusion of *productive mode* (to supplement the *allocative mode*) of state activities. This definitely breaks the putative insulation or separation between the economic and political sphere, pushing sharply out the boundary of state activities. The state becomes engaged in economic planning and increased public ownership, by definition, acting imperatively to counter economic crisis. According to this model of the interventionist state in advanced capitalism, the state cannot fully compensate for the economic crisis, but can only mediate it, that is, resolve the crisis by political means.

The political and economic spheres are recoupled, which repoliticizes the relations of production. The state intervenes in production and planning and acts through its agencies in a mode that can neither be explained adequately with reference to the prerequisites for the continued existence of capitalist production, nor wholly derived from the imminent movement of capital. This movement is no longer simply realized through a market mechanism that can be justified by a principle of fair exchange embedded in formally democratic processes. The movement is now the result of economic forces in conjunction with political countercontrol, with the result that class opposition tends to find new expression. The fundamental economic crisis tendency asserts itself in political and cultural crises in which class opposition is manifest in three tendencies:

(1) *Rationality crisis.* The administrative system, functioning by criteria of Weberian purposive rationality, does not succeed, by its sovereignly executed administrative decisions, in reconciling and fulfilling the imperatives received from the economic system (bound as it is, at the same time, by political imperatives).

(2) *Legitimation crisis.* The legitimizing system, that is, the system of social will formation in the public realm, does not succeed in maintaining the requisite level of mass loyalty, while the imperatives taken over from the economic system are carried through. The crisis derives from the problem that the fulfillment of governmental planning tasks tends to repoliticize the public realm and thereby place in question the formally democratic securing and disposal of the means of production. That is, the formal fairness of the market is seen to be replaced by the perfectly visible hand of the state, thus placing in doubt the class fairness of the state constituted as formally democratic.

(3) *Motivation crisis.* The sociocultural system changes in such a way that
it becomes dysfunctional for the state and the prevailing system of social
labour. Two motivational patterns which are essential to the continued
existence of the economic and political systems erode: civic and familial-
vocational privatism. Conditions of motivation appropriate to limited civic
participation in a depoliticized public realm, on the one hand, and a family
and career/work orientation suitable to the consumption, socialization, and
labour requisites of capitalism, on the other hand, are systematically
undermined. The crisis may be perceived in changing attitudes toward
education and work, for example, absenteeism, the absence of status-
oriented career and work orientation, etc (Habermas, 1976).

The moderate nationalizations of major but moribund industries with
massive compensation which took place in Britain directly after the War—
coal nationalization first and foremost among them—are preeminent
examples of the intervention of the capitalist state according to this
modern allocative/productive mode. Of the crisis tendencies briefly
identified above, the tendency toward rationality crisis most directly
suggests the dimensions of capitalist contradiction which are located
within the administrative apparatus of state agencies. These tendencies,
I suggest, have set the conditions that govern coal closure policy. It is
important, therefore, to look a bit further into the dynamics of this
rationality crisis.

4 Rationality and rationality crisis
The thesis of rationality crisis is based upon a set of fundamental theorems
concerning the operation of the capitalist mode of production: first, that
capitalism generates contradictions and, second, that the activities of the
state proceed by an operational logic which remains distinct from the
rationality of private business organizations.

4.1 Contradictions
The first theorem suggests that the process of the development of a
particular mode of production is, at once, the process of destruction of
the very preconditions for the reproduction of society by this mode.
Claus Offe (1975) expresses this well, when he writes,

"Contradictions become manifest in situations where ... a collision
occurs between the constituent preconditions and the results of a
specific mode of production, or where *the necessary becomes impossible
and the impossible becomes necessary*" (emphasis added).

Without speaking to their validity, Offe proceeds to cite classical examples
of Marxist theorems of contradiction, expressed through this formulation.
For example:

"The 'law' of the falling rate of profit maintains that what is necessary
for the accumulation process of capital (namely, the introduction of

labour-saving technical change) turns out to make further accumulation impossible (due to the decreased share of variable capital out of which surplus value and hence profit can solely be extracted)" (Offe, 1975).

The point is that contradictions are not 'dilemmas' in the sense of conflicting demands upon a particular institution; nor indeed are they located at the level of individual decision, nor specific institutional setting. 'Contradiction' as an analytical category always refers to fundamental processes through which a society reproduces itself.

4.2 Rationality

The second theorem suggests that state activities operate by an extra-capitalist logic. Efficiency criteria or the clear Weberian purposive rationality which govern business operations—and which are attributed by Weber to bureaucracies—cannot adequately be applied to state activities. This is both a problem of measurement and, more important, one of conception. Whereas, for example, a private rail service might be evaluated on simple grounds of cost, reliability in meeting schedules, return on investment, and the like, the determination of British Rail's success (!) requires a more complex and elusive calculus. What is the impact on regional patterns of investment, settlement patterns, tourism, and commerce of the closing down of a particular service which has operated at a 'loss'? What is the effect on employment or opportunities for the enjoyment of leisure time and family life? The influence upon specifically capitalist relations which can be evaluated according to straightforward efficiency criteria must be weighed alongside the more ephemeral 'social costs' which cannot be measured. But measurement is not the key issue. The more significant point is that the evaluation according to social and political dimensions must proceed by a set of criteria which are divorced from British Rail's profit and loss sheets. In fact, for this determination the criteria of private exchange and accumulation are fundamentally replaced by political and social criteria which cannot be specified readily. Whether British Rail functions in the red or in the black is only one among many considerations, and a decidedly contingent concern, which, in itself, becomes a political as much as an economic matter.

Thus the operational rationality of state agencies is quite different from business rationality, and not nearly so easily specified. The tendency toward rationality crisis reflects the combined impact upon the state administration of the two processes suggested by these theorems. Capitalist contradictions are displaced onto the mechanisms of the state such that the state agencies are unable to reconcile through their administrative decisions the political/social demands with the demands for continued capitalist accumulation. *Necessary policy decisions become impossible, and impossible decisions necessary.* This contradiction in the logic of governance comes to light in the articulation of policies which appear as the 'natural' outcome of the tug-of-war between political demands and the

imperatives of 'efficient' management of resources directly under state
control (so as to successfully promote accumulation by capitalists).

The nationalized industries, viewed as productive enterprises which at
the same time represent most vividly the political face of the contemporary
capitalist state, present a ground where this tug-of-war seems particularly
fierce. Decisions within the coal industry, and the pit closure programme
in particular, exemplify this contradiction in the logic (and hence, practice)
of governmental action in a most dramatic and direct way.

5 The coal closure programme
It is necessary now to move from the conceptual to the more empirical
side of this explanation of the colliery closure programme of the 1960s in
the North East region.

5.1 What happened
The interwar period marks the worst incidence of closures in the history
of the North East. In Durham, for example, in eleven months from
1925–1926 some forty-two pits were closed by the private coal owners.
By contrast, the immediate postwar period saw relatively few closures, the
first decade of nationalization being a period of high investment and
modernization in an effort to produce 'coal at any price'. Expansion of
output and stable manpower in the North East indicated a situation under
which closure in nearly all cases followed only from genuine exhaustion of
reserves. In Durham the entire decade 1947–1957 witnessed only fifteen
closures and a loss in manpower of 9000 (from 109721 to 100881).
Later, as many collieries and nearly as many men would be lost in a
single year (1968).

The first postwar slump in 1957 indicated a major change in the fortunes
of the industry, and led in 1958 to the beginning of a pit closure programme
which was principally market oriented. It was also drastic. Between
January 4, 1958 and February 2, 1968 120 collieries were closed in the
North East Area. Manpower in Durham fell from 97924 in 1958 to
44160 a decade later. A series of concentrated coastal pits replaced the
age-old pattern of village collieries scattered throughout the county.

5.2 The explanation
At this level the facts of the matter are in little doubt. The hardship and
dislocation of miners and their families; problems of redundancy and the
'forced march' south to more stable coalfields; changing settlement and
employment patterns; and the general deindustrialization of a region—all
this lies outside the concerns here. The problem is to explain the closure
policy, by and large a labour policy with disastrous effects on an important
sector of its support, a policy which is full of paradoxical elements, a
policy which at once seems 'logical' and 'bungled'.

Was the impossible necessary? Was the necessary truly impossible?
Empirical investigation through primary research into Coal Board

documents, interviews of NCB and Union officials, and the consideration
of secondary accounts suggest, on first view, a confusing web of divergent
perceptions, contrary directives, and *ad hoc* decisions initiated within a
very weak and uncertain set of government parameters. This is no
explanation. This is simply the recognition of a paradox—a dead end.
I suggest, on the contrary, that the policy can be explained coherently, as
a reflection of contradictions in the logic of governance faced by a
government agency which (a) cannot reconcile political/social with economic
demands for efficient management of resources, and (b) has no criteria for
measuring 'social cost' comparable to efficiency criteria operable in private
industry—and no statutory obligation to consider the calculations.

This operational logic can best be explored, and its essentially
contradictory character explicated, by briefly tracing the explanations and
perceptions of the decisionmaking process which are offered at different
levels of the administrative hierarchy:
1 the Government (the Cabinet and relevant Ministries),
2 Regional Policy Formulators (those who develop North East coal
closure policy),
3 Regional Policy Articulators (those who are actually responsible for
carrying out the decisions)[2].

5.2.1 *The Government*
The inner workings of government on controversial policy matters do not
often reveal themselves unambiguously—even less often is there clarity and
anything like completeness. Richard Crossman's diaries present the unusual
case of a generally reliable account of Government attitudes, perceptions,
and perspectives on closure policy. (I am indebted to John Carney both
for acquainting me with the Crossman diaries in this connection and for
the selection of quotations included here. Indeed, his counsel has been
invaluable throughout.) The account is particularly clear on the policies at
the height of the closure programme, in the winter of 1967 and the early
months of 1968.

On the 15th of July, 1967 Prime Minister Wilson and the Chancellor,
Mr Callaghan, spoke to the Durham Miners Gala, and met afterwards with
representatives from the Union and the Coal Board. They were told the
"real facts" about the "disaster which the Government's closure policy was
precipitating". Crossman reports, "James Callaghan got cold feet when he
was told that the closures this winter would create 15 000 unemployed

[2] The discussion of levels (ii) and (iii) of the administrative hierarchy is based on
interviews with regional NCB and NUM officials in the North East during the winter of
1976-1977, and on the review of selected papers maintained in the archival collections
of the National Coal Board, North East Area Headquarters. See, for example, "Notes
of a Special Manpower Meeting (Durham Area)" held in the Conference Room, Board
Annexe, Divisional Offices, Team Valley Trading Estate, November, 1965; "Manpower
Plan", Northumberland and Durham Division, December quarter, 1965.

men at a time when unemployment is due to rise to 750000" (Crossman, 1976, page 437). Three days later, on the 18th of July, there took place an all-night sitting on the Coal Industry Order which had been arranged in response to pressure from the Miners' Group of MPs. Richard Marsh, Minister of Power, read a long statement on pit closures; the miners' MPs protested hollowly, feeling bound at the end of the day to support the Government. On the 31st of July, the Cabinet Committee on pit closures had its most crucial meeting, a meeting which leaves little doubt as to the dimensions—the contradictory imperatives of economic efficiency and political/social demands resolved through haphazard tug-of-war—which underlie the construction of governmental policy. It is worth quoting Crossman at some length on this meeting.

"I went up early this morning because I specially wanted to attend the Cabinet Committee on pit closures ... Jim Callaghan and Harold came back from the Durham Miners' Gala so shaken that they proposed—first in S.E.P. [Steering Committee on Economic Policy] and then in Cabinet—that we should postpone the pit closures this winter in order to cut the number of unemployed by about 15,000. There were two papers. First an analysis of the situation and then a summary of the proposals. The analysis made it clear that we already have 30 million tons of surplus coal for this winter and it will grow to 50 million tons if we postpone the closures and start the closure campaign next year. *It's in view of this surplus that Cabinet took its decision on fuel policy* which cut back a long way further the amount of coal to be produced, marketed and sold in the years immediately ahead. The total cutback is therefore fixed. On the other hand, exactly which pits will be closed and how many of them is not nearly so clear and the Minister couldn't even give us the list for this winter. Eirene White, who sat next to him, remarked that the latest list showed five collieries in South Wales which had always been reckoned as the most modern and on which vast sums had been spent which were now due for closure. Dick Marsh replied that once we agreed to the new total cutback we agreed to these South Wales closures. I said this was absurd. Cabinet could agree with an economic analysis but before it agreed the closures it would have to consider the social impact. *I then turned to Marsh and said, 'Where is your paper on the social impact of the closures?' There isn't one of course.* What he ha tried to do is a deal with the Treasury under which he makes the closure and then placates the miners by obtaining £140 million for redundancy pay if they retire after the age of fifty-five. No doubt this was thought sufficient when it was assumed that there would be a fully employed economy. But now we're going to have 750,000 unemployed this winter and next and the closures come in an atmosphere not of full employment but of unemployment. No-one in the Ministry seems to have taken this into consideration. We then ask him whether it would be possible to car out the Callaghan–Wilson idea and either postpone this winter's closures or revise the list downwards. Marsh replied that of the 15,000 men thrown out this winter only 3,500 would be redundant and he asserted roundly that it would be impossible to hold up any of the closures without losing millions of pounds on surplus coal. He then showed us the letter he'd written to Callaghan, which is about the most snubbing negative I've seen. The fact that he can send it indicates the weakness of central control in this Government. Indeed, the lesson of this meeting was the apalling fact that after three years the Labour Government had evolved neither an instrument for assessing the social impacts of its actions nor an instrument for ameliorating that impact upon the community. The only concrete result of this long meeting was that Marsh was instructed to report to S.E.P. at our first meeting after we come back from our holiday on September 6th" (Crossman, 1976, pages 451–452; emphasis added).

Further reports by Crossman on Cabinet and Cabinet Committee meetings affirm both the characteristics of Government policymaking on the closure programme and the substantive considerations brought to light in the July 18th meeting. Even allowing for editorial elaboration by Crossman to elevate his own position and purify his attitudes, an exchange with Callaghan concerning the 1967 White Paper on financial obligations of the nationalized industries (on October 18th) is extremely instructive.

"The paper on the nationalized industries was [very] disconcerting. This is a paper which the Chancellor has been struggling to produce, really revising the 1961 decision that the nationalized industries should be run strictly commercially, and defining where prices were to be fixed by purely financial targets and where they were to be socially costed. We had exactly twenty minutes to consider it. Having rung Harold beforehand and prepared a number of amendments with Tommy I insisted on tabling them, much to the annoyance of my colleagues. As I got up from the table I said to Callaghan, 'This is a very poor paper'. 'What does it matter?' he said, 'It's only read by a few dons and experts'. 'Well I'm one don', I said, and he replied, 'You're a don who knows nothing about the subject. Personally as Chancellor, I couldn't care less and I took no part in composing it'. Here was a key issue of socialist strategy and the Chancellor of the Exchequer washes his hands of it" (page 527).

This key issue of governmental strategy—the reconciliation between social and economic imperatives by which to govern the nationalized industries— and its confused and inadequate consideration reflect what I have called the rationality crisis. This contradiction in the logic of governance was manifested in the case of the closure policy, as I have suggested, in decisions which are haphazard and appear to be the 'natural' outcome of the tug-of-war between fundamentally irreconcilable imperatives.

On 21 November, in Cabinet the Prime Minister and the Minister of Power split, each as it were representing one moment in the contradiction. Wilson, arguing on social grounds, urged that the closure programme planned for the coming eighteen-month period be rephased and slowed down. Marsh, responding from the economic or 'efficiency' perspective, replied, "You can't rephase it because you can't sell any more coal and we've already got some 30 million tons of stocks piled up and there's no more room to pile coal". The outcome: the Cabinet agrees only to postpone the debate in Parliament and have Wilson speak to the miners' representatives.

5.2.2 *Regional policy formulators*
A regional Coal Board official responsible for formulation of coal closure policy refers to closure decisions as a "circular process". He suggests, simply, that questions concerning the specifics of how it was decided that a particular pit or set of pits be closed, have "no precise answer ... every case is an individual case within certain broad rules which have varied from time to time". Throughout the decade under consideration, closures were in the broad sense related to the situation in particular markets and problems of immediate surplus capacity. The particular choice of pits was dictated by questions of economic viability. The determination of economic viability, however, "tends to be circular. It is a case of striking a balance. At the moment, our immediate concern is to maximize output. In former years we had been cutting back to meet the market. Now we will have pits working which are very heavy losers, [in order to] meet the market". He suggests that there is "political interference" at the level of the 1967 determination of White Paper on Fuel Policy, which "wrote down the role of coal". A different kind of direct political intervention would come later: "About 1970 we had a list of pits for closure, the government applied overall control on the rate of closure—where they requested to defer [closure] on social grounds, *they* were willing to take up the cost".

A similar vacillation between social and economic imperatives is reflected in the contemporary explanation of regional Coal Board officials to representatives of the Durham Area Unions at a special manpower meeting held in November 1965. A high-ranking official reports that the Government had agreed to write off £400 million capital, which would give relief to the Board of £30 million in interest payments in the coming fiscal year. The Government agreed also to give an additional £25 million to stabilize prices. But there was a specific *quid pro quo* for this largesse— the Government demanded in return over a two-to-three-year period the closure of persistently losing collieries. The regional official conceded that the Government *insisted* on the closure of these collieries as part of the bargain for capital reconstruction, and had required of the NCB at short notice a list of pits to be closed. This list had been prepared without consultation at the regional level. When challenged by a representative of the Union to indicate why pits to be closed on economic grounds could not be saved by price increases, the official responded that price increases were a "political matter". This characterization of pricing policy in its relationship to the colliery closure programme directly contradicts the explanation of his colleague, above, that the colliery closures had been instituted "to meet the market". If prices for particular grades of coal are set politically, then what has become of the notion of the market as fundamental regulator of policy? Economic efficiency criteria for planning and investment are *in the actual operation of the industry* taken to be inadequate.

Thus, the contradictory economic efficiency and political/social imperatives which, I have suggested, constitute the operational rationality of governmental policymaking are reflected in the perceptions of the regional policy formulators of the closure programme.

5.2.3 *Regional policy articulators*
The story is rather different at the level of policy articulators. A regional NCB official, responsible for the actual administration of the closure policy argues that all decisions were made on the basis of "exhaustion of reasonable reserves". Are there economic considerations? "Profitability", he responds, "is very low on the set of reasons. Although a colliery is taking a loss, it contributes to the overhead ... if you take that away, other collieries have to bear [the cost]". A colleague confirms, "95% of the closures are due to exhaustion of realistic reserves". Were there pressures from the Board? The official responds that cheap oil was a factor, but that there was no articulated policy from the Board. "Lord Robens [Chairman of the NCB] wanted to break eggs with a stick." Robens was a great advocate of rapid mechanization in the 1960s, and "mechanization was the death knell of a lot of these small pits". But are there specific guidelines for determining which pits must close? The official argues that there are not (a fact unanimously confirmed by regional officials in the North East and elsewhere). "The Director gets figures, they stick out like a sore thumb." At this level, the administration is viewed as technical and precise. There is no room, it seems, for consideration of the more ephemeral social costs.

6 Concluding remarks
This is by no means an exhaustive study of the North East coal closure programme of the 1960s. The regional effects of the policy have remained entirely unexplored. At best, a plausible speculative framework has been offered for viewing a complex and apparently inexplicable policy, understood only partially and in contradictory ways by the Government, and by NCB regional formulators and articulators of the programme. I have argued that what appears as paradoxical and haphazard reflects fundamental contradictions of capitalism which have been displaced from the economic to the administrative sphere, and now come to light in policies which cannot

fulfill the irreconcilable imperatives of accumulation and legitimation. When 'efficient' management is necessary, then consideration of social costs becomes impossible. In this way, the closure programme reflects new crisis tendencies in the modern capitalist state.

Acknowledgements. Thanks are due to J Carney, R Hudson, J Lewis, and R Taylor for their advice and criticism in the preparation of this paper, and to the Regional Policy Research Unit at Durham University for providing me with invaluable assistance throughout the period of my research in the North East.

References

Carney J G, Lewis J, Hudson R, 1977 "Coal combines and interregional uneven development in the UK" in *London Papers in Regional Science 7. Alternative Frameworks for Analysis* Eds D B Massey, P W J Batey (Pion, London)

Crossman R, 1976 *The Diaries of a Cabinet Minister. Volume 2: Lord President of the Council and Leader of the House of Commons, 1966-1968* (Hamilton, London)

Habermas J, 1976 *Legitimation Crisis* translated by T McCarthy (Beacon Books, Boston)

Offe C, 1975 "Introduction to Part II" in *Stress and Contradiction in Modern Capitalism* Ed. L N Lindberg (D C Heath, Boston)